Ginger Baker

The Illustrated History of
Rock Music

Dave Hill of Slade

The Illustrated History of
Rock Music
Jeremy Pascall

Pink Floyd

HAMLYN
London · New York · Sydney · Toronto

This book is dedicated to Lloyds Bank,
the Nationwide Building Society,
the Inland Revenue and HM Customs & Excise (VAT)
without whom it would not be necessary.

Published by
The Hamlyn Publishing Group Limited
London · New York · Sydney · Toronto
Astronaut House, Feltham, Middlesex, England
Copyright © The Hamlyn Publishing Group Limited 1978

ISBN 0 600 37605 2

Dave Vanian of the Damned

Contents

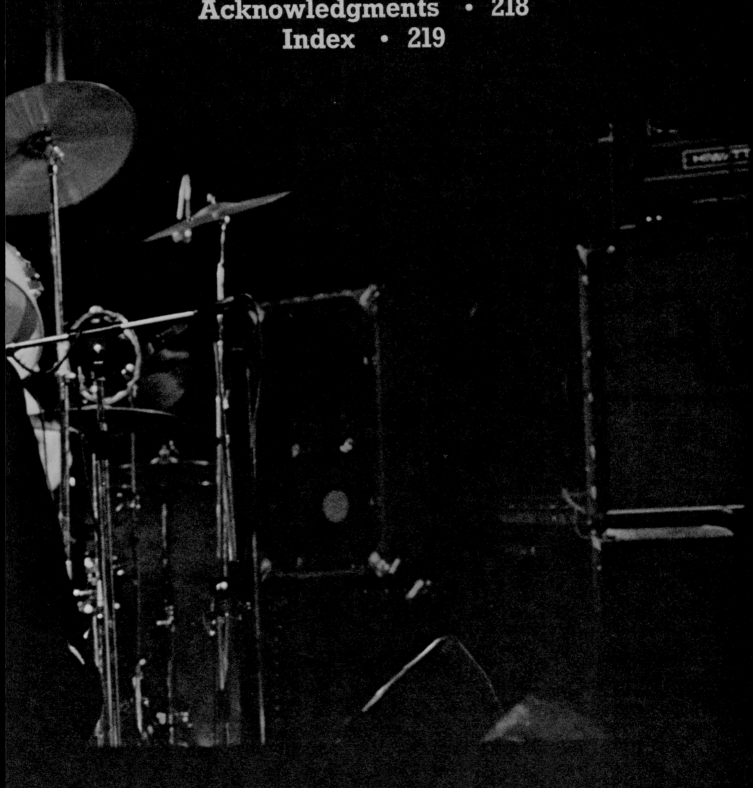

Rock & Roll: 1954-1958 • 12

The Pop Years 1958-1962 • 34

The Beat Boom: 1962-1967 • 58

The Age of Rock: 1967-1970 • 100

The Splintered Seventies • 154

Bibliography • 218

Acknowledgments • 218

Index • 219

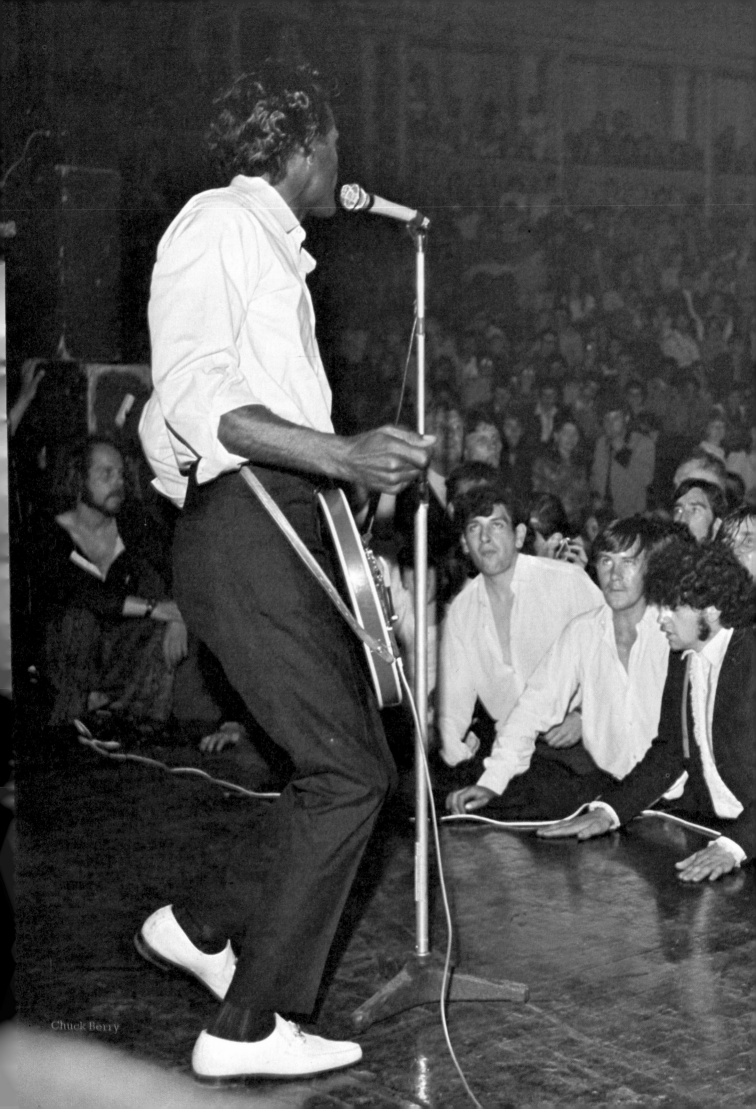

Chuck Berry

ROCK & ROLL

ROCK & ROLL

1954-1958

It was a revolution. It changed the lives of a generation. By extension, it changed the lives of their children. It spread across the world. It altered the course of history. It scared authority rigid: forced the adult world to reassess itself.

Most remarkable of all, for something so profound, it was a revolution without blood.

Rock & roll changed *everything*, if you were a teen in the Fifties. The way you looked, the way you talked, the way you dressed, the way you walked, the way you danced. It changed the way you looked at the world, at authority, at your parents. But, most of all, it changed the way you looked at yourself.

Before rock & roll, youth between the ages of 12 and 20 had been either overgrown kids or cut-down adults. Either way, they had conformed to their parents' view of themselves. They had dressed in imitation of their parents, and, generally, shared their tastes in miniature or dilution.

Rock & roll wiped that out. Rock & roll created a separate tribe, with its own rituals, its own uniform, its own mysteries, its own language, its own music. Rock & roll created teenagers.

Music has done all this. An extraordinary, raucous, crude, shouted music. It was charged with energy and driven by a manic, crashing pulse. But you cannot describe it. You can hear it, you can feel it. Oh yes, you can *feel* it. But you cannot break it down and analyse it.

Popular music has never existed to be analysed. It has existed purely to give pleasure. Rock & roll, more than any other popular music, defies intellectual examination.

So, we will not say what it is. But we *can* find out where it came from. At the crudest, rock & roll is black man's music interpreted by white performers.

In America after the Second World War, the blacks were still oppressed. They were segregated, down-trodden and tucked neatly away in their ghettos. They lived a life apart from the dominant whites. They, like the teenagers who were about to assert their individuality, had their own music, their own dances, their own slang. They even had their own radio stations. And these stations played their own 'race' records.

The records favoured by young American blacks featured rhythm & blues. This, crudely, found its roots in the rural blues but, with the mass migrations from the Southern farms to the cities, had picked up a new urgency. The traditional blues sound had taken on the echoes of life in the teeming streets. The pace, vibration, jangle, clatter and roar of the cities was reflected in the electric drive of urban blues.

This music was exclusive to the blacks. Few whites ever heard it and of those who did, fewer still appreciated it. It certainly never made any impact on the music that entered the national pop charts. In fact, few black performers ever reached those charts. And those who did had deserted their own musical roots to a very great extent and adopted those of the 'Italian' crooner school as exemplified most successfully by Frank Sinatra. People like Nat 'King' Cole were supreme stylists, great artists but they owed very little to their own black tradition.

Among young whites there was an increasing feeling that the national pop charts did not reflect their taste. They probably did not know *what* they wanted to hear. They just knew that what they were offered was not it. But back in the early Fifties what option did they have? If it wasn't on the main radio networks, it didn't exist.

The option was there but it took some finding. If some of the young urban whites twiddled with their radio dials in a restless attempt to escape from Rosemary Clooney, Frankie Laine, Doris Day and their ilk, they might just pick up a station that was beaming to a different world. And they might luckily strike a programme that featured . . . well, how *do* you describe it? It didn't have a name because, officially, it didn't exist.

But it was there. And young whites started hearing what young blacks had long known about. A music that was all their own. And it was mostly their own because no white parent would tolerate those 'jungle rhythms' in the house.

You cannot pin a date to the emergence of rock & roll. But you can nominate a year, a man and an incident. Put these elements together and you have a significant step on the road to rock.

The year was 1952. (Some sources claim it was the previous year, but most agree on '52.) The man was a disc jockey, 30 years old and feeling that every ambition had been frustrated, called Alan Freed. He'd always believed that he could be a topline radio personality; he'd tried for the top by auditioning in New York and been turned down. Instead, he'd settled for fronting a

Bobby-soxers queuing for a Johnny Ray concert in the days before rock & roll.

musically safe evening show on WJW in Cleveland, Ohio.

By one of those extravagant ironies, Freed's hearing was impaired but there was nothing wrong with his 'ear', that instinct that knows a sound is utterly right for its time. Sometime during '52, Freed found himself in a record store owned by Leo Mintz and marvelling at the spectacle of white teens buying up 'race' records. He saw them jiggling to the strident sounds of tenor saxes and the pumping piano styles favoured in R & B. He registered all

Bill Haley and the Comets.

this and he took a step that seems simple and obvious in retrospect but which was, for its time, quite extraordinary. He somehow persuaded his station manager to schedule a programme each week that featured this 'tabu' music.

When fronting this new programme Freed adopted the name 'Moondog'. Whether this was because he felt it was more in character with the music or to protect his true identity should the show fail is not known but it certainly worked. He called his weekly rampage *Moondog's Rock And Roll Party*.

Rock & roll? Why rock & roll? Surely it was just one of those meaningless phrases that somehow

slides into the language? Well, it was certainly black argot and both words had recurred in records for some years. It is doubtful whether Freed actually put 'rock' and 'roll' together for the first time. But he undeniably introduced the phrase into common parlance.

From the start, horrified parents had objected to rock & roll because, they insisted, it was 'dirty' and 'obscene'. In one respect they weren't far from the truth. Rock & roll *was* euphemistic. Rocking & rolling was dancing. And since dancing is simply a vertical expression of a horizontal passion it took no great imagination to guess what the euphemism stood for!

As Charlie Gillett has pointed out (in *The Sound Of The City*) 'rocking' and 'rolling' had long been used as sexual substitutions in R & B. And were soon identified as such when the music came 'overground'. As soon as white or 'approved' black artists started covering 'race' songs the record companies stepped in with a blue pencil and cleaned them up. Thus a song that originally implored 'roll with me Henry' was diluted to 'dance with me Henry'!

So Freed settled for rock & roll, whether he knew what it meant or not. And rock & roll the music became. It was low, and it was dirty, and it did start teens flaunting themselves in a most provocative

13

The first white stars of rock & roll: Bill Haley and the Comets.

manner and, no doubt, many a maidenhead was lost to its rhythms on the back seat of Dad's borrowed auto. And for all these reasons, Alan Freed's show became required listening for the teens, both white and black, in the Cleveland area.

Freed sold his musical ideal to his listeners. He yowled at them, he shrieked along with the records, he crashed his fist on the console in time to the beat. He and they were joined in a strange communion of sound. A sound that was 'illicit', that was exclusive, that was hated by 'adults' and authority, that was *theirs*. Soon Freed tried to extend this rock camaradie to a physical event, and the next year – March, 1953 – organized a *Moondog Ball* to be held in the Cleveland Arena. He expected success; he got an inundation. The venue could hold about 10,000 people. Many times that number turned up. (Estimates vary between 30,000 and 80,000.) It was quite unmanageable and what was worse, about a third of those present were black! In deeply-divided

Cleveland the thought of black kids and white mingling was abhorrent.

The significance of this in hindsight was not, as the city fathers thought, that so many blacks should be in the same place as whites at the same time, but that two white kids to every one black teen should turn up for a show featuring exclusively Negro performers.

Freed had tapped a flood and it carried him upwards with its momentum. Seeing his success in Cleveland, a New York Station, WINS, signed him in 1954. He dropped the Moondog persona and quickly became celebrated in his own right. Indeed, for a time in the mid-Fifties Freed and rock & roll were synonymous; Ian Whitcomb (in *After The Ball*) asserts that for a while record companies paid him to use the term!

His WINS show topped the New York ratings and the vibrations started spreading outwards. He was the midwife of rock & roll and was soon reaping the reward of his acuity. He involved himself in every aspect of the phenomenon. His name on a record, movie hoarding, radio show, promotion or commercial exploitation was an endorsement of

the product's validity. If it said 'Freed' it was genuine rock & roll.

One of his most celebrated endeavours was his package shows featuring the top R & B and rock & roll stars and held at the Brooklyn Paramount in New York. These were more than just rock & roll concerts, they were tribal gatherings to which youth flocked to celebrate its oneness, to be together, to feel the strength of numbers and be reassured by a crowd of like-looking, like-thinking, like-loving thousands. On top of which, Freed put on the greatest line-ups of talent imaginable. Freed and his shows made a deep impression on those members of a generation who could get to see him. Linda McCartney (then, of course, Eastman) remembers cutting school in wealthy, secure, up-state Scarsdale and slumming down to Brooklyn. 'They'd have 20 acts on 24 hours a day. Alan Freed was the MC but sometimes they'd get Fabian or Bobby Darin to MC. I remember seeing Chuck Berry sing *School Days* for the first time.'

In those early, crazy, riotous years Alan Freed was Mr Rock & Roll. He cast a huge, benevolent, avuncular presence over his unruly protegé music and its growing thousands of adherents. As one young girl who queued in freezing weather to catch his show at the Paramount said: 'I really dig Alan because he's not like most older people. He makes me feel wanted – not like my own father who when he gets home every night just flops into a chair with the paper, switches on the TV and grabs for a beer'. (Quoted in *After The Ball*.)

Freed was enormous. He smashed Frank Sinatra's box office record at the Paramount. He was, undoubtedly, rock & roll's first star. He was a leader, an influencer, a trailblazer. But he was not a performer. He didn't stand up on stage and make the music. Rock & roll still needed its first singing star and to really make strides that star should be white.

When he arrived he was a most improbable figure, the man least likely to succeed in rock & roll. William John Clifton Haley was born in Michigan in 1927, so that by the time he was a huge international star he was nearer 30 than 20 and looked decidedly unhip. He tended towards corpulence, had execrable taste in suitings (with strident plaids and string-thin ties much in evidence) and teased his forelock into a quite extraordinary style he was pleased to call a 'kiss curl'. He looked, and often acted, like a small-time hick who got lucky and couldn't quite believe it.

But there was more to Bill Haley than that. Haley, like Freed, had the 'ear'. He had flogged around the country playing flea-bite gigs with a variety of bands in a number of styles. His most recent outfit (before the Comets) were the Saddlemen who had started out playing Country and Western in a style which seems to have been related to the Western Swing style of Bob Wills and his Texas Playboys.

As he schlepped his weary way from date to date he noticed that the college kids, in particular, were adopting the street-talk and the swaggering dance styles of young blacks. Now Haley, like many brought up on country music, was well aware of black musical idioms and liked their beat. He took the two styles and made a fusion, bringing the black R & B emphasis to country music. Then he extracted a pinch of slang and mixed the whole heady brew together. He has claimed that the resultant sound was rock & roll and that he invented it. Freed, he has conceded, gave it a name and took it to the people but the *sound*, the *style*, that fusion of black forms to white were his.

What Haley did was to recognise a void, define what was missing and tailor a sound to satisfy the unarticulated yearnings of youth. As he has said: 'Around the early Fifties the musical world was striving for something new, the days of the solo vocalist and big bands had gone. About the only thing that was making any noise was progressive jazz but this just went above the heads of the average listener. I felt that if I could take a beat the listeners could clap to as well as dance to, this would be what they were after. From that the rest was easy . . .'

It is said with characteristic diffidence, but one wonders just how easy it was at the start. One suspects that this odd synthesis of two seemingly exclusive styles would rather startle the listener at first. He has admitted that, initially, rather than delight a whole new audience he actually alienated two well-established ones: 'We got where we weren't accepted as country-western or rhythm & blues. It was hard to get bookings for a while'.

Slowly the new form came together and started acquiring its own identity. 'We were something different, something new', Haley has said. 'We didn't call it that at the time, but we were playing rock & roll. We were lucky. We came along at a time in which nothing new was happening in the music field . . . We had an open market. It was easy to hit a home run.'

Haley's first record of any note was *Crazy Man Crazy* made on the small Essex label. It did rather well (being the first rock & roll disc in the charts) and started bringing attention to the group and its sound. Decca took a chance and signed him but must have been disappointed with the performance of his first release for them, *Rock Around The Clock*. Mind you, this had a strange parentage having been written as a 'novelty foxtrot' by a venerable pair of Tin Pan Alley songsmiths, the lyricist of which was 63 years old! Those, surely, are not bloodlines from which rock & roll hits are sired?

For his next effort, Haley looked to a safer bet and did what so many of his white colleagues were to find profitable, covered a song already recorded–probably with local or 'race' success–by a black artist. In this case it was Joe Turner's lusty *Shake, Rattle And Roll* which was, in the habit of the day, dry-cleaned somewhat before release in 1955. This did the trick. *Shake, Rattle And Roll* was a big hit in the States and rock & roll was just starting to break through.

As rock & roll gained in prominence in the States, parents became increasingly alarmed by the changes wrought on their children. Not only did they click their fingers and move their gum-filled jaws in time to this abysmal noise that emanated from the family phonogram, they took to dressing and speaking in a most singular manner. In addition, the papers were full of the hooliganism, violence and criminality of the young and the epithet 'juvenile delinquents' was to be heard everywhere. In fact, the young posed a terrible threat to adults. You only had to look to the cinema to see that. Look at the young hoodlums who were becoming stars–Marlon Brando looked like a punk and could hardly even speak! And there he was, leading a bunch of motorcycle thugs in *The Wild One*, a movie so shocking that it had been banned in Britain. In addition, there was that young wretch James Dean who walked with a slouch, never had a good word for anyone, and in *Rebel Without A Cause* kicked against his perfectly decent home and went to the bad.

The next thing you knew there was a movie being made about a young teacher who was doing his best to win over the tough ruffians in his class. He tried hard. He even took his treasured collection of jazz records in to play to them. And what did they do? Smashed them! Why? Because all they wanted to hear was the crashing cacophany that had played over the opening credits.

The film was *Blackboard Jungle* and if you'd looked hard at the credits you'd have seen that the technical adviser to the movie was one James Myers. Now James Myers had an alter ego called Jimmy McKnight who wrote songs. One of the songs he wrote was *Rock Around The Clock* and *that* was the song playing over the credits.

The film caused a stir and did well. The song positively exploded into the consciousness of a generation. It became an anthem. Indeed, in Lillian Roxon's memorable phrase 'it was the *Marseillaise* of the teenage generation'. It was a true and, for the time, astonishing phenomenon. In 1955 it went to number 1 in the States and was in the charts for 22 weeks. In Britain it reached number 17 early that same year and then re-entered the charts in October and went to number 1.

Almost exactly one year later it reappeared in the Top 10 and rose to 5.

Bill Haley was a very, very big star and became a bigger one with a quickie, low budget, cynically exploitative movie named after his huge hit. To our sophisticated eyes *Rock Around The Clock* is a pretty shoddy film, a thin, impoverished thing, a curiosity. But to the teens of the Fifties who craved anything about their new, and unlikely, hero, it was perfect. It was a film just for them, about their group and their music. (It even had Alan Freed!) And they embraced it. Enthusiastically.

If you believe the press accounts of the time, every cinema in every town in which the movie played had every seat ripped from its mounting and its upholstery slashed to shreds.

Riots broke out and chain-wielding thugs ran riot through the streets terrorising innocent citizens. On the other hand, there *may* have been some jiving in the aisles, some good-humoured high spirits and the odd, accidental breakage due to over-exuberance. It didn't matter what the truth was, it scared adults witless and the film was banned entirely in many countries.

For a while, Haley was one of the biggest stars in the world. He followed up this amazing popularity with records like *Mambo Rock*, *Razzle Dazzle*, *See You Later Alligator*, *Rockin' Through The Rye* and *Don't Knock The Rock*. This last came from a follow-up film from the same stable as the first and was in many respects similar (it also featured Freed) but had the added advantage of Little Richard singing

Tutti Frutti and *Long Tall Sally*.

It was, however, still extremely gauche and its threadbare plot sadly set the pattern for so many rock films over the coming years. The publicity material of the time offers a synopsis that is to become wearisomely familiar: 'Rock & roll singing idol Alan Dale finds his home town torn between teenagers who worship the sensational rhythm and indignant adults who think they're sinners. At an out-of-town rock jamboree featuring Bill Haley and his Comets, a riot breaks out. But Dale and Alan Freed, agent (sic), determined to show rock & roll is not unhealthy for teenagers, stage another show and manage to convince their adult audience that rock

Teddy boys and their girls in the typical fashions of the time.

& roll is no wilder than the Charleston and the Black Bottom of a past generation.'

There's no denying that there is a basis of truth in that creaking screenplay. The generations *were* split and many parents thought their children were 'sinners' or worse. But they were not to be persuaded that rock & roll was no more outrageous and harmful than the dances of their youth. At least not yet.

Perhaps if Bill Haley had continued at the same meteoric rate he would have bridged the gap between teens and their elders. He was, after all, an essentially modest and charming man. He *looked* so evidently benign. He was obviously bewildered by the monster he had bred and, when asked by the press what he thought of it all, would scratch his head and declare, 'I'm just a country boy'.

The trouble was, he couldn't last. He was always more popular in Britain than America, and when he made the trip across the Atlantic, was met at the dockside by countless thousands. But once even these rabid fans had seen him in the flesh, there could be no gainsaying the truth. Bill Haley was not the stuff of which mean, moody, sexually-aggressive rock & roll superstars are made.

Perhaps he was the Father of Rock & Roll but the trouble was that he played that paternal role too well. He was in age and spirit closer to the parents than the kids. He faded as fast as the comet that christened his band and, like the same celestial body, duly reappeared every so often for a brief flash of light–older, portlier, less hirsute; an object of nostalgia. He was jostled aside by a younger, sexier man. A magnificent example of raunchy youth.

Elvis Aron Presley was rock's first superstar and one of the very few the music has ever created who can be compared to the demi-gods of Hollywood in its great era. Elvis was to rock what Clark Gable was to the movies. They were both universally popular, they both towered over their contemporaries. They both

A 21-year-old Elvis Presley on stage in Tupelo, Mississippi.

shared a title–granted by their colleagues–and wore it as if by divine right. They were both simply, 'The King'.

Presley, again like Gable, was a sex symbol–rock's first sex symbol. The true sex symbol achieves his or her status by appealing equally, but differently, to both sexes. Presley did this by causing acute sexual stimulation in young women without alienating their boyfriends/lovers/husbands. Indeed, he was so triumphantly masculine that those men imitated and sought to emulate him. While the girls writhed and squealed, their males hunched a shoulder, cocked a lip, twitched a knee, trained a lick of hair and cultivated a Southern drawl. Both sexes recognised–and revelled in–greatness.

Elvis Presley was born on

8 January 1935 in Tupelo, Mississippi. Economically, it was the wrong time and the wrong place. Years later he said: 'I could say we lived on the wrong side of the tracks. But in those days in Tupelo, there wasn't really a right side of the tracks. No one was eating too good. We never starved but we were close to it at times'.

The family moved to Memphis, Tennessee, hoping to find a better life. The improvement, if such it could be called, was minimal and the threat of hunger, unemployment and bad health dogged the Presley family during those years.

But, in one respect at least, Elvis *was* now in the right place at the right time. If we go back to that crude definition of rock & roll being black R & B adapted for whites, then Memphis was geographically a

17

Above: *Elvis Presley began recording for RCA Victor early in 1955.*

Below: *Presley and parents outside the home he bought for them in Memphis.*

point at which these two ingredients met. Right there a young man with an ear for music could hear just about anything from the dirtiest blues to the most mawkish country death ballad. And Elvis Presley *had* an ear.

Presley listened intently to everything and he took it all in. The trouble was that by the time he came to make his first records he could sing in so many styles there was a danger he was going to be written off as a brilliant musical mimic. It took some time for his producer, Sam Phillips, to discover that Presley had a style all his own.

Presley, it seems, had been a curiously solitary youth. This may have resulted from the fact that he was a twin whose brother, Jesse, had died during birth and Elvis may have felt an unidentified loneliness as a result. Certainly, his mother doted on her surviving son and he on her. In his teens he developed his own, highly individual, mode of dress. His colour sense was dramatic–favouring blacks and violent pinks–and he grew his hair unfashionably long, greased it and slicked it back into a pronounced 'duck's ass'. Down his finely-planed cheeks he sported a legendary pair of sideburns.

Carl Perkins, his contemporary, fellow Sun Records artist and writer of *Blue Suede Shoes*, remembered that this individuality brought Elvis in for a degree of mockery. 'People would laugh . . . and call him sissy,' he told *Rolling Stone*. 'He had a pretty hard road to go.' But even then he was, innately, creating a look that would sweep the world's youth.

He'd begun singing in church, belting out a form of white gospel. He'd been particularly impressed by the holy-rolling, bible-thumping preachers who shouted and leapt and threatened Hell's fire, working their congregation into a lather of remorse, and an ecstasy of divine fervour. He was learning his trade through his pores, taking it in by osmosis.

At 18 Elvis Presley–a truck driver–was almost ready. The story of his introduction to the man who was to be the catalyst seems a pure invention of a publicity machine. Except that it happens to be true. Elvis wanted to record two songs on a disc he could give his mother for her birthday. He went down to a tiny studio in Memphis and, after hesitating and trying to quell his nerves, pushed through the door and talked to secretary/receptionist Marion Keisker. She checked with the boss. Within a few minutes Elvis Presley and Sam Phillips were in a studio together for the first time.

Elvis sang the Ink Spots' *My Happiness* and *That's When Your Heartaches Begin* and Phillips seems to have caught an echo in his voice. Not a blinding revelation. Just a snatch of something different. A hint of blackness.

Nothing very much happened. Elvis was still around and Sam Phillips had a sound in his head that he couldn't quite capture on disc. He tried Presley with a few songs in different styles and the eager youth matched the styles to the songs like the good mimic he was.

The discovery of the unique Presley sound also reads like something out of one of the many abysmal movies he made in his later years. Reason tells one not to believe it but so many people involved have testified to its veracity over the years that we are forced to accept it. Phillips persevered with Presley and finally decided to try him on some blues. They went into the studio with an Arthur 'Big Boy' Crudup song called *That's All Right (Mama)*. They had worked hard, trying for this sound that Phillips had in his head and making little progress. A break was called, the mikes switched off and Presley and his musicians, Scotty Moore and Bill Black took a breather.

But Presley was full of spirits, reached for his guitar and started hammering out *That's All Right*. His voice punched the words and his body, freed from inhibition, started to move as he felt the song. Moore and Black picked up the refrain and soon the three were, as they say, cooking.

At which point Phillips returned and heard the impromptu session. One can only apologise for the resultant dialogue but assure that, to

the best of one's researches, it is what transpired. Phillips: 'What the hell are you doing?' Moore: 'We don't know.' Phillips: 'Better find out fast—and don't lose that sound. Take it from the start again and we'll tape it'.

At last Phillips had caught the sound he wanted. But why, the inquisitive observer has to ask, did it take him and Presley so long to come around to blues material, especially when he knew of Elvis's love for artists like Crudup? Perhaps Elvis answered that a few years later when he revealed to an interviewer that 'they would scold me at home for listening to (people like Crudup and Big Bill Broonzy). "Sinful music," the townsfolk in Memphis said it was. Which never bothered me, I guess'.

In the deeply segregated South it just was not *done* for a white boy to sing the blues. With this in mind, Phillips played safe that evening and also had his boy sing a totally acceptable number, *Blue Moon Of Kentucky*.

Phillips pressed the songs and started toting them around the local radio stations. And he started eliciting the oddest responses. When he took the blues song to a black station, they asked who that country boy was. When he took *Blue Moon Of Kentucky* to a country music station they couldn't understand why a black kid should be singing *their* songs!

The gates of Gracelands, Presley's home in Memphis, Tennessee.

But *That's All Right* started getting some airplay. This helped it to sell and soon Phillips' Sun Records had a good-sized local hit. Presley started to build up a reputation around the South. He auditioned for the most prestigious of all country radio shows, *Grand Ole Opry*, but was turned down. Perhaps he sounded too black. But *Louisiana Hayride*, next most influential showcase, did take him and he did well enough to be signed for a year. At the same time he was crashing all around the South, playing gigs and rejoicing under the sobriquet of 'The Hillbilly Cat'.

Already he was gaining intense audience response. His first major concert was in August, 1954, at the Overton Park Shell Auditorium in Memphis. 'I was doing a fast-type tune that was on my first record,' he later recalled. 'Everyone was hollering . . . everyone was screaming . . . Then I came off stage and someone told me everybody was hollering because I was wiggling.'

It didn't take him long to realise that the decibel level of the screams was in direct ratio to the amount of wiggle he put into the act. More wiggle, more screams. He wiggled a lot.

All this was happening in the sticks. And it was going to stay in the sticks unless Presley could find

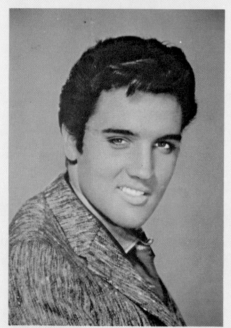

Elvis Presley, the king of rock & roll, was the first and arguably the greatest star rock music ever produced. His innovative mixture of rhythm & blues and country music plus his unique phrasing of a song have influenced all who followed him.

Colonel Tom Parker (left) and Presley meet the mayor of Memphis, Tennessee.

himself a manager who thought big and could follow up the thoughts with actions. Sam Phillips and his Sun label just didn't have the resources to break Presley nationally. And, strangely, Phillips didn't seem to have the inclination.

A word ought to be said at this point about Sam Phillips. He is a most remarkable man, who, in the Fifties, seemed to have an uncanny knack of finding talent. He, like Freed, is one of rock & roll's midwives. He found Presley and liberated the unique talent within him. At various times during this period he also recorded such rock & roll notables as Jerry Lee Lewis, Johnny Cash, Carl Perkins and Roy Orbison. Not one of them stayed with him although every one went on to success. Phillips never seemed to mind. He'd happily sell the contract

of his potential stars to people who would build them up and then sit back in Memphis taking care of his own business. He never wanted, it seems, to be in the big league.

Before he broke Presley, he'd concentrated on recording his beloved black artists and was responsible for some of the earliest work on disc from Howlin' Wolf, B. B. King, Ike Turner and Junior Parker. He'd lease these recordings to bigger companies around the States, content to let them take the big risks and reap the rewards. Many a time he could have made a multiple fortune out of the talent that passed through his studio. He never bothered. Jerry Lee Lewis once said of him: 'Sam's crazy. He's as nutty as a fox squirrel . . . he ain't got no sense'.

Presley now needed to be hustled out of the South and into the big time. He needed a drum-beating dynamo. He got Colonel Tom Parker who, in a

matter of months, parlayed his boy from regional popularity to national superstardom. Parker had an undoubted genius for selling and a quite astounding dedication to his client. He did marvels but, as he would be the first to admit, he was selling a remarkable product.

Sam Goldwyn, that most extrovert and colourful of Hollywood producers, once said: 'Producers don't make stars. God makes stars and the public recognises His handiwork'. In Presley's case that was certainly true. By the time Parker came on the scene as fulltime manager in 1955, Elvis had created his look and had found his style, then all the Colonel had to do was get the right contracts and put his boy in front of as many young audiences as possible. Sexual chemistry would do the rest.

News of Presley's astonishing presence was filtering through to the major companies in New York. With Haley and the new music making a stir, any talent scout worth his salary was keeping his antennae finely tuned. Haley might only have been the first shots in the battle, you couldn't tell where the big bombardment might be coming from.

At RCA Steve Sholes had heard *That's All Right (Mama)*, noted Presley's name and watched for developments. One development was that certain companies were showing interest in Presley's Sun contract but nobody knew how much he was worth. Parker orchestrated the bidding but Sam Phillips was looking for the biggest sum he could get. In the end RCA offered $35,000 for the Sun contract (which had about a year before expiry) and all Presley tapes recorded by the company. There was a further $5000 paid to Presley to cover any royalties Sun might owe him. Today $40,000 looks like a piffling amount. Then it was virtually unprecedented. No kid who had never had a national hit had ever been valued so highly. And Steve Sholes was in fear of his job in case he had made a mistake.

He hadn't. As one perceptive commentator noted: 'Elvis's drape jackets, pegged pants, and mop of brilliantined hair . . . His sideburns, boudoir eyes and his bumps and grinds . . . All these have an explosive effect on bobbysoxers'. *Nobody* had *ever* had the effect that Presley did on stage. Sinatra had earned screams and swoons; Johnny Ray had grabbed his share of noisy adulation. But Presley just simply caused riots.

Pat Boone, who was a pretty big star at the time singing a lot of cleaned-up, washed-down rock & roll, 'borrowed' from black artists, played a date with Elvis quite early in the latter's career. Over 20 years later he remembered Presley's impact vividly. He told *Rolling Stone*: 'The first time we met was at a record hop in Cleveland where Elvis was my supporting act. Which was the only time that happened. I never again wanted to follow Elvis. I was very glad I had this big hit record going for me so that when I came on stage it wasn't totally anti-climactic'.

As early as 1954, in Jacksonville,

Florida, Presley had been on the receiving end of violent adulation. There, the girls had almost pulled him into the audience, stolen his shoes, dismembered his jacket and ripped the right leg off his trousers.

By early 1956 Elvis Presley was at number 1 in the American charts with *Heartbreak Hotel* and launched upon the most spectacular, successful and profitable solo career in modern popular music. And with him the age of rock was born.

There was no holding him after that. Even though the parents and the preachers and the authorities and the critics and the old-established stars and the media moguls *hated* him. Or, maybe it was *because* all those straight *Thems* hated him.

It didn't matter how much they ranted and raved and editorialised and condemned and burnt his records and his effigy, Elvis Presley was unstoppable and so was rock & roll.

Presley was the greatest commercial exponent of rock & roll but he was not the only one, nor was his the only rock & roll style. Rock & roll defies description but it was broad enough to cover the diverse styles and talents of such as Little Richard, Fats Domino and Chuck Berry. In fact, Charlie Gillett has in *The Sound Of The City* identified five types of rock & roll.

He defined them as the Northern style of Bill Haley; the 'New Orleans dance blues' style of Fats Domino and Little Richard; the rockabilly school from which Presley sprang to be followed by Jerry Lee Lewis, Roy Orbison and other fellow Sun stars; the Chicago urban blues of Chuck Berry; the black group sound most easily recognised in the work of the Platters.

All of these contributed to the richness of rock & roll and deserve attention.

At the time Bill Haley started making waves, a few giant recording companies held a virtual oligopoly. They were so well established that they very nearly controlled what was released and what the public heard. Haley slipped past them. True, a big company, Decca,

signed him but it's doubtful if they really knew what they were dealing with. The greatest shock of all was the way that young white kids were connecting with the rough, unschooled and, to the major companies, completely unacceptable music of the blacks.

But there was obviously a demand for this sort of thing and the majors decided to supply it. But in a controlled way. Racial prejudice was so deeply-ingrained into corporate thinking that it was just inconceivable a black group of artists that *sounded* black should make the charts. It just couldn't happen. (Well, of course Nat 'King' Cole got into the charts. But he didn't *sound* black, did he?) So, they thought, *if* the kids *must* have these songs we'll get a white guy to record them. A real clean-cut white guy.

Charles Eugene Pat Boone was so clean-cut that he was hardly believable. He wouldn't kiss his female co-star in *April Love* because when he'd consulted his wife about it she asked him how he'd feel if she spent all day kissing Rock Hudson. And he turned down two TV series because the sponsors were a tobacco and beer company. He also wrote a book called *Twixt Twelve And Twenty* which counselled this newly-discovered creature, the teenager, to step in line and wash regularly and listen to his/her parents' advice.

Pat Boone.

A very comforting sort of chap, Pat Boone. Very different from that nasty, dirty Elvis Presley who, rumour had it, stuffed lead pipe down the front of his underpants before he went on stage.

It is difficult to realise now that the Pat Boone of *Speedy Gonzales*, *April Love* and *Love Letters In The Sand* is also the Pat Boone of *Tutti Frutti*, *Long Tall Sally* and *Ain't That A Shame*. And that in terms of sales and popularity Boone was second only to Presley in the years between 1955 and 1959 in the States.

Now that rock has a well-chronicled and much-plundered history, laurels for the three great rock & roll songs above go to those who deserve them—Little Richard for *Tutti Frutti* and *Long Tall Sally* and Fats Domino for *Ain't That A Shame*.

Both fit into Charlie Gillett's 'New Orleans dance blues' category of rock & roll. They share certain characteristics in common; both are black, both feature piano strongly and both were recorded in that musical melting-pot of New Orleans. Otherwise, it is difficult to think of two more dissimilar men!

Fats Domino's style is quietly humorous, rollingly relaxed with the odd burst of vibrant boogie-woogie piano work. Even when rocking he seems to be easy and unforced. He was making hits long before rock & roll—indeed he had a million seller with his first ever single, *The Fat Man*, way back in 1949—and seems to have been rocking long, long before anyone else. He continued his hit-making without interruption and the coming of rock only seems to have con-firmed the rightness of his music. He swung into the Fifties without a noticeable change of style or direc-tion. *I'm Walkin'*, *Ain't That A Shame* and *Blueberry Hill* all racked up huge sales along with many other hits.

In contrast, Little Richard (real name Richard Penniman) was a lunatic, frenetic, hyperactive rocker. He was flash, fast and full of cocky self-esteem. His songs were mostly gibberish, accompanied by a crashing, storming piano style. No wonder adults always complained

Early and late pictures of Fats Domino, a major creator of rock music.

that you couldn't understand the words of rock & roll songs. But what they didn't realise was that the words were meaningless. It was the total sound that mattered. To shout 'A-bop-bop-a-loom-op A-lop bop boom!' made no sense at all. Nor did the next five lines which simply repeated 'Tutti frutti au rutti' (pro-nounced tooty-frooty o rooty). That was not the point. A Little Richard record was 2½ minutes of pure enjoyment. Sex compressed on wax.

Tutti Frutti was as meaningless in

Tokyo, Paris, Berlin or London as it was in New York. Or, rather, it was as meaningful if you were the right age and your ear was tuned to, and your body twitched with, the sheer nonsensical exuberance of it. Little Richard's 'oohs' and 'bops' and 'woos' were international rock call-signs, a sort of instant Esperanto that could be understood and reacted to in any part of the world. And that is

one of the reasons why rock spread with such amazing rapidity.

Pat Boone took the work of these two great rock pioneers and made them bland. He sold millions of records and for years his name was reviled in rock circles because he had found God (something he shared with Little Richard, incidentally) and was clinically clean. But Pat Boone also brought rock & roll, in an acceptable form, to millions who were not ready for it in its rawest state. He accustomed their ears to its cadences and gear shifts, its swoops and its peaks. Perhaps the musical swoops and peaks were shallower and less steep than those of Little Richard and Fats Domino but they were still there. And, what is more, there was still room for the original artists to do very well out of their own songs. In the same year that Boone sold a million with *Ain't That A Shame* (1955), the song was also registered as Domino's own – and, astonishingly, tenth – million selling disc. (In the same year he also sold gold with four others – *Thinking Of You*, *All By Myself*, *I Can't Go On* and *Poor Me*! Fats co-wrote four of them with Dave Bartholomew.) And Little Richard sold a million of *Tutti Frutti* despite Boone's cover version.

These figures show that, despite the major record companies' direst prognostication, black artists *were*

Little Richard, the self-proclaimed king of rock & roll, in frenetic action.

acceptable to white ears and *were* selling in vast numbers. It is true that they weren't selling in the same quantities as Presley and Boone but, by the same token, neither of those stars wrote their own material (apart from maybe contributing a line – particularly in Presley's case – and receiving a composer's credit, and share of royalties, in return).

In Chicago was a man who did write his own material. He wrote songs that were so accurate, so brilliantly evocative of youth and its life and love and aspirations in the Fifties that he's frequently been called 'The First Poet Of Rock'.

His work is in sharp contrast to the gobbledegook of Little Richard. Chuck Berry had something to say. He said it clearly and wittily. He articulated the fact that rock & roll was here to stay. Rock & roll had superseded every other form so 'roll over Beethoven' and 'dig these rhythm and blues'.

In *Rock & Roll Music* Berry says it all. He gets right to the heart of the matter in a very few words. He's 'got no kick against modern jazz/Unless they try to play it too darn fast' because that tends to 'change the beauty of the melody' and makes it sound 'like a symphony'. He rejects the Latin rhythms so beloved of

adults at the time, he 'don't care to hear 'em play a tango . . . a mambo . . . a congo' so just 'keep a-rockin' that piano'. All he wants to do is dance. That is what rock & roll is all about.

Although Berry was already some years older than his teen audience when he broke through in 1955 with *Maybellene* – he was either 24 or nearly 30 depending on whether you believe he was born in 1931, the most commonly-quoted date, or 1926 – he somehow intuitively knew what they were all about. He understood perfectly how they felt about things. And he put it all to music.

He knew they hated school and in *School Days* he enunciated its boredom, the day ticking through tedious routine until the bell sounds and 'you finally lay your burden down' to rush out, round the corner to the 'juke joint'. There for the drop of a coin you can have the music you love, pumping life back into you. Because: 'All day long you've been wanting to dance/Feeling the music from head to toe/Round and round and round you go'.

In *Almost Grown* he crystallised the agonies of being, in Pat Boone's deathless phrase, 'twixt twelve and twenty'. You're just an ordinary kid, you string along at school doing your best, toeing the line. You don't mix with bad company or get into trouble. All you want to do is find a

lyrics, or subject matters in cold black and white on a page like this is nearly to destroy Berry. Those words weren't meant as poetry, they were meant as lyrics to a really rocking song. If you want to know just how good Berry was, play his music.

Apart from Elvis, Chuck Berry was the single most influential artist in rock & roll. Indeed, he is one of the most influential artists in all rock. His presence will be felt down the years. Whenever rock seems to be getting stale, someone will go back to basics and rediscover the energy, wit and originality of Berry and be inspired by it.

Perhaps one of the reasons why Berry felt such kinship with the kids, and why he became their musical spokesman, is because he'd been something of a badass in his own youth. He'd come from a reasonably comfortable background but had broken out in his teens, bungled a robbery and ended up in reform school for three years.

Music had been central to his life since adolescence and he continued to play after reform school and while he was working for General Motors and later as a hairdresser. He played mostly blues but was catholic in his taste and perfected most of the current guitar styles. Over the years he turned himself into a really first-rate guitarist–as can be heard on any of his records; he pioneered a chiming riff that opens *Sweet Little Sixteen*, was 'borrowed' note for note by the Beach Boys on *Surfin' USA* and has become one of the great guitar clichés.

Music became increasingly important and he started earning extra money at nights playing with combos around St Louis. He had also begun to write, mostly in an R & B style, and realised that if he was to achieve anything he would have to go to the centre of urban blues, Chicago.

Early '55 found Berry in the 'Windy City', doing the rounds of the clubs and studying at the feet of the maestros. One night he asked Muddy Waters if he could sit in and

job and save up for an auto and go riding with your girl. You don't make waves and you don't ask much. All you want is that they 'Don't bother me, leave me alone/ Anyway I'm almost grown'. As a synopsis of adolescent feelings it cannot be bettered.

This was Berry's genius. In a phrase he zeroed straight in on the heart of teen life. His heroines– *Carol, Little Queenie*–were the teen goddesses the boys lusted after but they were also deeply-rooted in reality. *Sweet Little Sixteen* lived for rock & roll and its stars (she's 'just gotta have about half-a-million signed autographs'). At night she dresses the part–'tight dresses and lipstick' and 'high heel shoes'–but deep down she's got 'the grown-up

blues' because in the morning it's back to school.

You can learn all you need to know about being a teenager in the Fifties from Chuck Berry's songs. Indeed, you can learn all you need to know about being a teenager at any time from them. Only the detail– the fashions, the auto types, some slang–has changed; the truth exists still in the feelings, the emotions, the violent swings between joy and frustration.

There's a touch of genius about Berry's work. Perhaps he was the first rock writer to really try to *say* something. The reason he stands out is that he spoke entirely in idiom. He talked about being a rock & roller in the language of rock & roll, in the music of rock & roll. Looking at his

The original Platters, a Doo-wop group whose first hit was Only You *in 1955.*

then astounded the guitarist with his dexterity. Waters got him an introduction to Leonard Chess at Chess Records who liked what he heard enough to take two songs, *Wee Wee Hours* and *Maybellene*.

Exactly what happened next is in some doubt. What is known is that Alan Freed and another disc jockey, Russ Fratto, sat in on the session and both their names appear on the writers' credits of the record. What, if anything, they contributed is impossible to ascertain. It's possible that Freed advised Berry and Chess about getting a rock & roll sound to the song, but it also seems impossible that Berry should need any help. Anyway, Freed certainly plugged the disc enthusiastically in New York and it sold a million.

Berry was set and, to take a phrase from *Maybellene*, was 'motorvatin' over the hill'. He shouted 'Hail, hail rock & roll/ Deliver me from the days of old'. And, in a thoughtful interview with Ralph Gleason years later, summed up his idea of what rock & roll really is. 'Names of it can vary, but music that is inspiring to the head and heart, to dance by and cause you to tap your feet, it's there. Call it rock, call it jazz, call it what you may. If it makes you move, or moves you, or grooves you, it'll be here.'

Apart from the giants–the Berrys, Presleys, Haleys, Dominos–the first wave of rock & roll was made up of other, lesser-known, artists. And of some truly great, one-off records.

The fifth style of rock & roll, as identified by Charlie Gillett, was what he described as 'vocal group rock & roll'. Or what is more colourfully called 'Doo-wop'. This is just as it implies; the music of a group of black singers who chant 'doo-wop, doo-wop, doo-wop', behind a lead voice. (And occasionally throw in the odd 'shang-shang' or 'dap-dap'.) Doo-wop was a stage in a tradition of black vocal harmony groups starting, perhaps, with the Ink Spots back in the Thirties and continuing in a hundred variations through groups like the Drifters, the Four Tops and onto the really extremely sophisticated and smooth sound

of the Stylistics in the Seventies.

The Doo-wop groups of the Fifties were rawer than either their predecessors or successors. They had started as bunches of friends singing for fun on the tenement stoops. Lack of money kept instruments to a minimum and so unaccompanied vocal harmony was what marked the style most. (This style has come to be called acappella from the Italian *a cappella* for 'in the early church style' or 'choral music to be sung unaccompanied'.)

In the early Fifties a number of Doo-wop groups, mainly named after birds, got into the studios and recorded a series of songs that found favour first among blacks but then started spreading outwards and charting. Most of these were

one-hit wonders, but remembered with great affection. Most notable were the Penguins' *Earth Angel*, the Chords' *Sh-Boom* and the Crows' *Gee*. (The latter is frequently cited as being the first ever true rock & roll single.) Such groups led the way for the much longer-lasting, much more successful and much smoother sound of the Platters who had big hits with *Only You* and *The Great Pretender* in 1955 and continued with discs like *My Prayer* and *Smoke Gets In Your Eyes* until the early Sixties.

As can be seen, the diversity of rock & roll–from Elvis to the Platters, Berry to Little Richard, Haley to Domino–was great. And this was just the music in its infancy, the first wave of the assault.

Things happened very fast between the entry of the first rock record ever into the chart–*Crazy Man Crazy* in 1953–and the emergence of Elvis Presley as a major superstar in '55. The face of music had been changed. But, already there was a second wave of, generally, younger stars who were hustling to get their own piece of this very lucrative action. And these young stars were to hone down the rawness of early rock & roll and help it develop.

Coming out of the same Presley rockabilly tradition were several other artists who had, at one time or another, passed through Sun records. The two most truly founded in rock–at least at that time–were Jerry Lee Lewis and Carl Perkins.

Lewis was a white equivalent to Little Richard in that he was a wild man on stage (he calls himself 'The Killer') who assaulted, rather than played, his piano. His style was absolutely manic (and, indeed, hardly seems to have calmed as the years have progressed); one leg atop the instrument, his hands flailed down onto the keys as he screamed his songs, interspersing the words with wild whoops. In fact, he was much more a visual than a chart star. He could pack auditoria and get the kids raving but he registered in the top selling list only rarely. Two of his that did make it, however, were solid gold, unalloyed classics–*Whole Lotta Shakin' Goin' On* and *Great Balls Of Fire.*

Lewis was, self-avowedly, 'crazy' and, years before such things became common knowledge, lived what has become known as a 'rock life-style'. He was always hard-drinking, fast-living–a roistering hellion. This was reflected in his on-stage persona. Sadly, though, it was his personal life that destroyed him. While on a tour of Britain in 1958 the Press learned that his newly-wed, second wife was only 13 years old. The baying headlines drove him out of the country and virtually wrecked his career for several years. He returned to his first love in music, country, and earned a good living

Two views of Jerry Lee Lewis whose shows were packed with energetic assaults on the piano.

through the late Sixties and Seventies, still rolling along in his own uninhibited way.

Another country boy was Carl Perkins, who contributed one great rock & roll hymn in *Blue Suede*

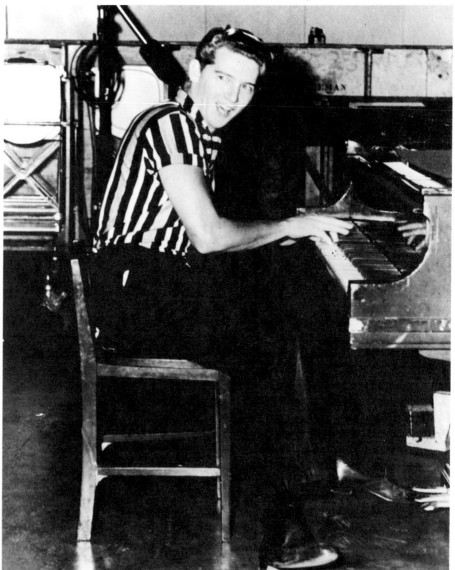

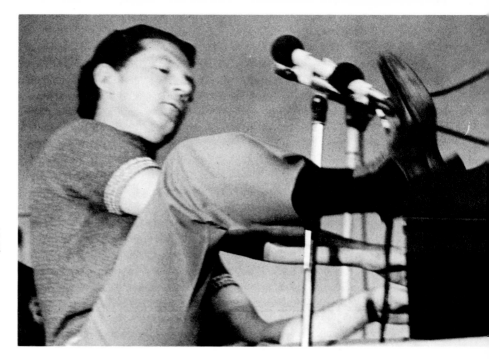

Shoes. This chronicled the narcissism of the age; it didn't matter what you did to the man or his possessions as long as you didn't tread on his shoes! It sold a million for him and did the same for Elvis. That was really the sum of Perkins's contribution; he, like Lewis and a one-time Sun stablemate, Johnny Cash, returned to country roots.

Two other country boys made an impression on rock & roll that was out of all proportion to their time involved with it. One contributed two definitive teen anthems– *Summertime Blues* and *C'mon Everybody*–and was a very big star in Britain but, according to Irwin Stambler (in his *Encyclopedia Of Pop, Rock And Soul*), 'in the US hardly anyone knows his name. Even people who pushed three of his singles [the third was *Sittin' In The Balcony*] high on the hit charts in their teens . . . have to refresh their memories by rehearsing some of those old recordings before the name Cochran registers'.

If this is true, it's a mystery. *Summertime Blues*, which Eddie Cochran co-wrote with Jerry Capehart, has a touch of Chuck Berry's witty incisiveness about it. A kid trying to have a good time during the vacation is also plagued by the need to earn some money. Both his boss and his family séem to conspire against his love life and he decides to take his problem to the United Nations! As a final resort he called his congressman and:

'He said (quote)/"I'd like to help you, Son, but you're too young to vote".'

Sadly, the two songs show little more than a promise of what Eddie Cochran might have produced. He was extremely popular in Britain and toured there in 1960. In the course of it, the car in which he was travelling ran off the road and into a cruelly unyielding lamp-post. Cochran was killed and passed into the necrology of rock.

As if still conforming to some worthless script for an exploitative B-movie, the Cochran story throws up an outrageous coincidence. Almost exactly a year before his death, he had recorded a maudlin song called *Three Stars*, which had

been written by a disc jockey called Tommy Dee, as a 'memorial' to three rock stars who had died in a plane crash.

One of these was a close friend of Cochran and he apparently recorded this shoddy piece of pinchbeck emotion in order to raise money for the men's families. In the event it was not released until after Cochran's own death but that does not detract from the listener's embarrassment at hearing: 'Well, you're singing for God now'/In his chorus in the sky./Buddy Holly–I'll always remember you,/With tears in my eyes'.

A lot of people felt like that in 1959 even if they didn't express it quite so sickeningly. Buddy Holly stands at the crossroads. He's a rock & roller who smoothed the music down but stopped it becoming bland. His voice was way out in front of the record, leaving the backing where its name implies it should be–behind him. His diction was crystal clear, more comprehensible and less raunchy than Elvis's. He expressed adolescent longings in a more restrained way than Chuck Berry. He was almost pure pop but there was always that drive behind him that owed more to the rock & roll feeling than the dictates of commercialism.

Buddy Holly (né Charles Hardin Holley) was born in Lubbock, Texas on 7 September 1936, and like so many of his contemporaries was strongly influenced by country music. But unlike many of those contemporaries, the twin influence of black music is far less evident in his work. It was as a country singer that he gained his first, small, successes. He was signed to Decca in 1956 but his releases for them did nothing. It's likely that they were already being swamped by the all-pervasive rock & roll.

Holly, seeing the straws in the wind, decided that Decca were not going to re-sign an unsuccessful country singer, and so started looking for a new outlet. He picked up with some old friends and

Top: *Carl Perkins in 1960.*
Middle: *Johnny Cash.*
Bottom: *Eddie Cochran.*

started experimenting at a studio in Clovis, New Mexico. This was run by Norman Petty whose background in music was rather more conventional than that experienced by most rock producers.

Petty, seeing that Holly was not a naturally aggressive rocker in the Elvis mold (in fact when Holly had tried to sing like Elvis the results were said to be dire!) started tailoring his production to suit his protegé. Where Elvis, for example, snarled, Holly hiccoughed! It was a most distinctive feature of his voice and betrayed a rather endearing lack of self-confidence that, when allied to mock-defiant lyrics–like *That'll Be The Day*–gave Holly a 'little boy lost' appeal! (This was further emphasized by Holly's appearance. His hornrim specs lent a shy, bookish air, while the rather sober suits contrasted sharply to the silks, spangles and lamés of his rivals.)

Petty realised that there were two sides to Buddy Holly. One was what might be dubbed the 'Superman' attitude in which he's manly, capable and secure in his dealings with the opposite sex. The other is his 'Clark Kent' persona, the hesitant, unsure side. (He even looked a bit like Clark Kent!) Petty saw a way of turning this to commercial advantage. He put Holly records out on two different labels under two different names.

The 'Superman' records were issued on Brunswick under the Crickets' name and featured Buddy fronting his group of that name. (The Crickets had a shifting population but Sonny Curtis and Jerry Allison were the nucleus.) Songs by the Crickets included *Oh Boy*, *Not Fade Away*, *Maybe Baby*, *That'll Be The Day* (the first hit and million seller) and *Think It Over*.

The 'Clark Kent' discs included *Peggy Sue*, *Listen To Me*, *Rave On* (an exception to the general rule, it sounds like it should be a 'Superman' recording), *Everyday*, *Words Of Love* and *Heartbeat*. They were issued on Coral.

Both did well. In 1957 the Crickets' *That'll Be The Day* and Buddy Holly's *Peggy Sue* both won gold discs. In addition, *Oh Boy* charted.

By 1958 he and the Crickets in one guise or other were racking up hits in the States–*Maybe Baby*, *Rave On*, *Think It Over*, *Early In The Morning* and *Heartbeat* all made *Billboard*'s Top 20. But by now the Superman/Clark Kent schizophrenia was becoming acute.

Holly and Norman Petty both saw a long and established future for the singer. Buddy seemed content to be groomed into a sort of rock balladeer and Petty had started adding pizzicato strings to his songs, most notably on *It Doesn't Matter Anymore* and *Raining In My Heart*. This was completely contrary to the spirit of rock & roll. The raw edges were being chipped off and the music polished into a streamlined commercial production.

At around the time that Holly was veering towards the 'ballads with a beat', he started recording and living in New York. The Crickets wanted to stay in Texas and a rift opened between them. In early 1959, Holly undertook a tour without the Crickets (that is the *original* group including Curtis and Allison, instead he had assembled another band under that name which included Tommy Allsup and Waylon Jennings) and set off on a punishing schedule.

By the time the roadshow reached Clear Lake, Iowa on 2 February 1959, everyone was exhausted. Holly decided to abandon the tour bus and hire a plane to take him to Moorhead, Minnesota so that he could get there ahead of the main party, make some arrangements, get some cleaning done and grab a sleep.

The plane never arrived at its destination. It crashed into a field about eight miles from the airport. Buddy Holly was dead. As were The Big Bopper (J. P. Richardson) and Ritchie Valens, the other two of the *Three Stars* on the song title. (The Bopper had had a recent big hit with *Chantilly Lace* and Valens with *Donna/La Bamba*.) Buddy Holly was 22 years old. He immediately went into the rock pantheon of fame. His fame grew after his death, the remembrance flames fuelled by judicious releases of unheard (and often completely remixed and

redubbed) tracks that Petty 'discovered' at fairly regular intervals.

It's impossible to say what he *might* have done. He might have 'gone showbiz' in the way that Elvis did. He might have become one of the great writers. His contribution in the short time before his death suggests he had the ability.

To Don McLean in *American Pie*, and to many of that Fifties generation, Buddy's crash marked the day the music died. You can pin it down to the very early hours of 3 February 1959 if you must, but by 1960 rock & roll *was* dead. And for a number of reasons. Buddy was dead, a year later so was Cochran. In 1959 Elvis went into the army and was, to all intents and purposes, dead for two years. (He returned a very changed man.) Jerry Lee Lewis was banished in disgrace for his marriage to a child bride. Soon Little Richard would find religion and drop out of music. And Chuck Berry was fighting for his liberty.

In 1959 Berry was charged with offences under the Mann Act–accused of transporting a minor, a female employee at his St Louis club–across a State line with an immoral intent. The details are confused, the proceedings dragged on for two years and Berry ended up with a jail sentence for another two. His brilliant career was temporarily wiped out. It was to be some time before he resumed.

In effect, by 1960 almost the whole front rank of rock & roll had stopped performing (at the very least temporarily) for one reason or another.

The day of his death, Buddy Holly was due to appear in Moorhead, Minnesota. The bill was obviously depleted but, in the best tradition of the very worst backstage movie, the survivors decided that the show must go on. Instead of staging two performances, they put on just one and filled the gap by drafting in local talent. A spot was given to a band from Fargo High School called the Shadows. The lead singer was Bobby Velline. He became far better known as Bobby Vee.

Rock & roll was dead. The age of pop dawned.

Buddy Holly (centre) and the Crickets took rock & roll and smoothed it down.

GO BO Diddley

ELVIS PRESLEY

THE VERY BEST OF FATS DOMINO

ELVIS PRESLEY / LOVING YOU

CHERISHED MEMORIES

EDDIE COCHRAN

Elvis Presley No.

MONO

THAT'LL BE THE DAY   Buddy Holly

THAT'LL BE THE DAY BUDDY HOLLY

Gene Vincent

THE POP YEARS
1958-1962

Above: *GI Presley at Gracelands.*
Opposite: *The softer image of Elvis.*

Pop took over. But what *is* pop? Generally, it's the name given by adults and newspapers and other uninformed sections of the community to teenage or popular or chart music in general.

For our purposes, it is the music that dominated the charts between the death of rock & roll and the coming of the Beatles. That, of course, is broad enough. So let us further define it by saying how pop was, and is, different from rock & roll.

Rock & roll was a *spontaneous* music. It erupted, almost unbidden, into the consciousness of youth. It was uninhibited in form, content and performance. It was, very nearly, a force of nature. And it shook the Tin Pan Alley popular music establishment to its very core. The moguls in record companies, publishing houses and other offices that manipulated public taste had not decreed rock & roll would happen. Nowhere was it scheduled for this rude, crude, unmannered music to appear. They did not take kindly to it and, for a while, were so surprised (not to say shocked) that they could not summon the energy to counterblast. But slowly they sought to reaffirm their power.

As we have seen, they attempted to blanch the beat by giving black songs to goody-goody white artists. That was only partially successful because these uppity black folk still managed to sell millions of records. They could control neither the record buyers nor the charts. But they could control other things.

They controlled the media. They dictated who could and could not appear on television. They could influence the playlists on some of the radio stations. They controlled movies. Slowly, inexorably, the establishment clawed its way back to dominance. A good example is the way that Presley fared on TV and in films.

On television they framed him in camera from the waist up only. Anything beneath his navel was considered far too lascivious for family viewing. They took him out of his pink drape jacket and black pegged pants and put him into a tuxedo!

On film he started promisingly. He had a potent presence that, harnessed right, could have turned him into a considerable screen performer, if not actor (there is a difference). His first four movies were the best he ever made, mostly because they took elements of his character. In *Love Me Tender* ('56) he's a confused kid caught up in the American Civil War; in *Loving You* ('57) he's a confused kid who is puppeteered into stardom; in *Jailhouse Rock* ('57) he's a confused kid who accidentally kills a man; and in *King Creole* ('58) he's a confused kid who gets mixed up in the underworld of New Orleans. (The last, incidentally, was his favourite. 'For the first time,' he said, 'I'm playing someone other than Elvis Presley.')

The army changed all that, of course. By now there was far too much money at stake and as soon as a successful, proven formula could be found, Presley was slotted into it and walked a celluloid treadmill.

This is almost exactly what happened in the record business at large. By the end of the Fifties, there was just too much cash to be made out of teenagers to allow the business to be run by a bunch of amateurs or hicks. They just couldn't take the chance that a record by an unknown kid from a one-street town in Texas, recorded at a one-horse studio *might* take off. If it did could they be sure of maximising profits by having the kid follow up with a second or even third hit?

No, no. That was far too risky. What was needed was a formula. A look, a sound, a style. Get those right and package them. Sell them via radio and TV shows and you can be sure (well as sure as you can ever be in this cockamamie business) that you've got a long-running hit on your hands.

And in essence, *that* was pop. It was teen music cynically packaged. It was music made for commercial purposes only. It was, by and large, music without a spirit. It was the antithesis of rock & roll. Pop was the deodorant to the sweat of rock & roll.

This is not to say that all pop between rock & roll and the Beatles was lousy. There was some ex-

Frankie Avalon (above left), Ed Byrnes (above right) and Bobby Rydell (left).

cellent material but the majority was simply peddled to the masses as ear-fodder and, because there was little or no alternative, the masses–us–accepted it.

Now, here's an extraordinary exchange that somehow sums up the twin adult attitudes of the period. It comes from the House of Representatives Special Subcommittee on Legislative Oversight (whatever that means). These worthy gentlemen were investigating alleged payola (the offering of bribes and inducements to disc jockeys) in pop.

A Representative named Derounian was questioning Dick Clark, then the most influential DJ in America and host of the incredibly popular TV show *American Bandstand*. Mr Derounian quoted Mitch Miller–before rock & roll he was America's most successful popular music producer with artists like Guy Mitchell, Rosemary Clooney, Frankie Laine, Johnny Ray–at Clark.

Miller had said of *American Bandstand* and the artists it regularly promoted: 'You would not invite

those unwashed kids into your living room to meet your family, why thrust them into the living rooms of your audience?'

That was one attitude to the pop stars of the time. And it was quite extraordinary, because the people Miller was talking about were the cleanest, smiling-est, nicest, most acceptable boys-next-door you could ever hope your daughter would bring home! But the truth was, as far as Mitch Miller was concerned, they weren't Guy Mitchell, Frankie Laine, Johnny Ray . . .

Derounian followed-up by suggesting to Clark that his programme ran to 'your format, you get a big hunk of young man who has got a lot of cheesecake to him and the kids are thrilled by this on the television program–and then you play his records, but you don't have him sing too often. That is the way you sell records and that is a pretty cute way to do it'.

Dick Clark denied this charge vehemently but he must have known that Representative Steven Derounian had come very close to the truth. No-one, least of all the

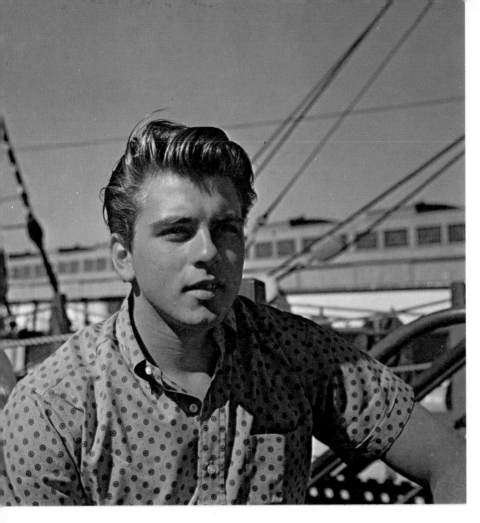

Fabian.

artists themselves, could ever claim that Frankie Avalon, Fabian and Bobby Rydell were great singers. Or even particularly arresting personalities. But they shared certain qualities in common: they all lived around Philadelphia, the city from which *American Bandstand* was beamed to a breathless teen nation, five days a week; they all boasted Italian antecedents – Avalon né Francis Avallone, Fabian né Fabiano Forte Bonaparte, Rydell né Robert Ridarelli; they all conformed to a stereotype of male beauty. In effect, they were cut-down crooners; the new generation of the very people and style that rock & roll had reacted against. Were not these young men simply newer models of Sinatra, Como, Dean Martin (né Dino Crocetti), Frankie Laine (né Francis Lo Vecchio) and others? Without, of course, the vocal ability.

If proof be needed of the cynicism with which pop was produced in this period, take the story of Fabian. Our narrative now shifts from being a lousy movie script to a Stan Freburg

parody. The sad thing is that you can't parody this truth.

Chancellor Records in Philadelphia were looking for a new star so Frankie Avalon, knowing what was required from his pop contemporaries, mentioned a good-looking kid of his acquaintance. This kid had everything; that is to say he looked like a cross between Elvis Presley and Ricky Nelson. Consequently one of the Chancellor executives went to look at this potential goldmine.

He found, according to Chancellor's co-boss Peter DeAngelis (and quoted in Tony Cummings's *The Sound Of Philadelphia*), that Fabian 'was so pretty we just knew he had to be a commercial proposition so we signed him up. We taught him a few things vocally but he never did go much on singing . . . Anyway, in '58 we did a thing on him called *Lillie Lou* which sold a few around Philadelphia. We were spending quite a lot of money on publicity, getting him known, you know'.

'His next thing was *I'm A Man* and when he did that on *Bandstand* the girls went wild. Then came *Turn Me*

Loose and *Tiger* – that sold a million – and we had a monster . . .'

Some monster! To be as kind as possible, Fabian lacked conviction. The three songs mentioned above are all written in the Elvis Presley mould. They are all diluted versions of *Trouble*. They require a snarl, a sneer and a guttural roar to convince. Fabian was a nice, open-faced chap with a lovely smile. He was to snarling, sneering and guttural roaring what Adolf Hitler was to embroidery!

That anecdote just about sums up the attitude of the moguls towards their market. At the worst they treated their audience with utter contempt. At the best they said 'we're giving the kids what they want. Or, rather, what we think they want'. The top and the bottom of pop was making money.

The best way to do that was to virtually control all the processes of hit-making. In those investigative hearings, Dick Clark was cleared of the payola charges but was forced to divest himself of some of his business connections. Surely there must have been a clash of interests when the man who was running the most powerful TV plug show in America (and if *Bandstand* put enough behind a disc it stood a damned good chance of making the charts) was regularly featuring artists who recorded for companies he wholly- or partly-owned, as was the case with the Hunt and Swan labels respectively?

(The tragedy of the payola hearings was not Dick Clark – who went back to *American Bandstand* and increased success – but Alan Freed, the man who had started it all. He was found guilty, never worked in media again and died in 1965.)

Pop equated with money. It was a business. Pop was the period between the crashing exuberance and naturalness of rock & roll and the first realisation in the Sixties that there was art to rock. So the pop moguls gave the kids what they seemed to want, or what the moguls thought they wanted, or what the moguls thought they should have. The Pop period included the Philadelphia Sound, the dance crazes, the Skiffle Boom, the Trad Boom (both

the latter being largely British phenomena) and rock & roll.

Rock & roll? Yes, non-American rock & roll. British and European R & R have not been included in the first chapter because it is the author's contention that they do not constitute real rock & roll. They were, from the start, ersatz. The British never threw up a *true* rocker for the simple reason that rock & roll was an indigenous American music. There was no tradition of black music in Britain, and although much American country music found its earliest roots in English folk tunes, it had been so transformed as to be unrecognisable to British ears.

The kids in Britain loved rock & roll. American rock & roll. They embraced some Americans to them in a way that America never did. Cochran, as already mentioned, was one prime example. The other was Gene Vincent, who was in the car with Cochran on the day he was killed. Vincent gave one great rock song to the world – *Be-Bop-A-Lula* – and had two further million sellers in the States with *Bluejean Bop* and *Wear My Ring* but his popularity soon waned in his native land. The explanations for this differ. Some say he was too low down and dirty for his time. Limping Gene (his leg was permanently stiff from an injury sustained during service in the navy) was too fundamental for a market dominated by squeaky-clean Ricky Nelson and his chums. Jack Good, however, tells a very different tale.

Jack Good invented rock television in Britain with the weekly show *6.5 Special*. He had heard *Be-Bop-A-Lula*, reckoned that such a sound could only come from a tearaway and invited him to cross the Atlantic and appear on the show. When he met Vincent in person he got a terrible shock. He was faced with the most bashful, courteous Southern gentleman imaginable, a sort of young, singing Colonel Sanders!

Good had a strong theatrical streak (later fully-exploited as director of *Catch My Soul* and *Elvis*) and decided to tailor Vincent to the

Tommy Steele.

40

mental image his music had conjured. He dressed him entirely in
black leather, schooled him in
scowling, forced him to limp more
heavily than necessary and created
a generally diabolic image.

It worked, brilliantly, and Vincent
was always a welcome and lauded
visitor to Britain long after his
popularity had waned elsewhere.
But one of the reasons for his success in Britain was because he was,
demonstrably, the real thing and
made British rockers look tame.

And that is why British rockers
come, for the purposes of this book,
under the heading Pop. It was
obvious to London's Tin Pan Alley
that the kids wanted rock and that
few *real*, i.e. American, rockers
were coming over with any regularity. (Presley, of course, never did
at all, even though Britain was, for
his last ten years, the most loyal and
enthusiastic market.) So home-
grown rock stars had to be created,
and as quickly as possible.

The first was Tommy Steele (né
Hicks) who had his first hit, *Rock
With The Cave Man*, in 1956. As a
song it had one advantage in that it
was, at least, written by Britons. This
was decidedly unusual as most 'rock
& roll' records by British artists
were simply tepid copies of the
American originals. Steele co-wrote
it but to show the veracity of the
song as rock & roll, Lionel Bart also
had a hand in it. A considerable
composer Bart (of *Oliver!*) might be,
rock & roll he was not.

And nor, at heart, was Steele. He
was full of Cockney cheek, charm
and a warm personality. He was,
essentially, an entertainer. His first
disc passed for rock, his second hit
was a cover of Guy Mitchell's
Singing The Blues and within a year
or so he was churning out happy
hummables, making family entertainment films and thinking about
being a 'proper' actor.

One of the great clichés among
the pop performers in Britain at this
time was the line, in answer to a
question about future ambition: 'I
wanna be an all-round entertainer
and buy me muvver a 'ouse'. And
virtually every one of the top

The UK Elvis? A young Cliff Richard.

The Shadows had many hits, both on their own and with Cliff Richard.

performers did just that. Cliff Richard (né Harry Webb)–pop's Peter Pan–DID make a good-ish rock record–*Move It*, again, surprisingly, by a British writer–before settling into an astonishing pop career that started in 1958, included an astonishing 50 Top 20 hits by 1975, shows no signs of flagging and actually cracked the US market for the first time in the mid-Seventies!

Adam Faith (né Terry Nelhams) never had a hit with a rock & roll song. His was pure, smooth, Italian-suited pop from the start. He was blond, had an amazingly strong, well-chiselled face, few inches, a quick, intelligent mind and a strange way of pronouncing certain words. 'Baby' seems to gain a syllable and emerge as 'bye-e-bee'! He was fantastically successful, extremely shrewd and possessed a genuine and burning desire to be a 'proper' actor. He made it. He also became a

highly-successful producer and manager in the Seventies and guided Leo Sayer to spectacular popularity.

Steele, Richard and Faith were the big three but there were scores of others. There was even a British equivalent of the Philadelphia scheme–except that instead of taking good-looking kids of Italian extraction and giving them solid WASP names, Larry Parnes took good-looking working class lads and gave them aggressively virile names.

In this manner Parnes–known in the pre-decimal business as 'Mr Parnes, Shillings and Pence'–built up his stable and Clive Powell became Georgie Fame, Reginald Smith was transformed into Marty Wilde and Ron Wycherly into Billy Fury. In addition his string included such unlikely creations as Dickie Pride, Johnny Gentle, Vince Eager and Duffy Power.

Of them all, Billy Fury was probably the closest a Briton ever came

to the spirit of rock & roll. He was incredibly handsome, his face strongly reminiscent of Presley's. He came from Liverpool, that great musical melting pot, perhaps the only town in Britain where black music and country *had* mixed, thanks to the constantly mobile population of seamen. He was from a tough background. He wrote his own songs. On top of it all, he moved well and could rock a bit.

He started promisingly with some decent singles–*Maybe Tomorrow*, *Colette* and *That's Love* all of which made the charts–and even caused a stir because of his suggestive movements. He also produced an album–*The Sound Of Fury*–which has been, retrospectively, described as 'one of the classic rock & roll albums . . . almost authentic rockabilly throughout'. After that, however, he went the way of them all, squeezed into sharp suits and took to beat balladeering. Though, in fairness, he did that a damn sight better than most. It was surely only

Left: *Adam Faith discovers the perils of crooning.*
Below left: *Marty Wilde had hits to 1962 before fading away.*

ill-health that stopped him surviving, like Richard, Steele and Faith, through the decades as an enduring entertainer.

In the absence of real ethnic music, the British teens adopted some very curious styles, two of which sprang directly out of the jazz tradition. The first was skiffle and it became interlinked and rather confused with rock & roll in those early heady days following 1956. For example *6.5 Special* would feature a British 'rock & roller' followed by a skiffle star and both would receive about equal adulation and screams.

Skiffle was music made on improvised instruments. Or, to take a definition from the knowledgeable, George Melly in *Owning Up* describes it as: 'A kind of sub-jazz in which kazoos, tea-chest and broom-handle basses, seven-gallon jugs, and empty suitcases replaced the more conventional musical instruments. Presumably in the first place these improvised instruments were the invention of poor Negroes unable to afford the proper thing, but during the Twenties skiffle music caught on as a novelty, and in particular a white group called The Mound City Blue Blowers achieved considerable vogue. By 1953 the public had naturally enough forgotten about skiffle, and only the serious jazz-record collector knew what the word meant'.

As Melly, who was a jazz shouter of some renown – not to say notoriety – at the time with the Mick Mulligan Band, recalls, the first person to revive skiffle was Ken Colyer. Colyer ran a band that adhered strictly to the New Orleans style of jazz but he leavened his evenings by holding sessions in which he, Lonnie Donegan and Chris Barber foresook their usual instruments (trumpet, banjo and trombone respectively), took up guitars and upright bass and launched into spirited attacks on black blues and folk numbers.

Colyer's band dispersed and when Barber reformed it, again with

Donegan, he kept the popular skiffle interludes and even included one item from them on a live LP. This track was Lonnie Donegan singing *Rock Island Line*. It became so frequently requested on the few radio shows that featured pop music that it was decided to put it out as a single.

The record was very simple, very direct. It struck a chord and quickly entered the British Top 10. And, astonishingly, it did exactly the same in the States. 'Astonishingly', because hitherto all the traffic had been one-way. But there, in a year of Presley's dominance, 1956, Lonnie Donegan from Glasgow, Scotland was re-exporting an American tune in a bastardised American idiom back to its country of origin!

Suddenly Donegan was a star and skiffle the rage. It threw up few stars and few good discs; the most notable were *Last Train To San Fernando* by Johnny Duncan and the Bluegrass Boys, *Freight Train* by Chas McDevitt and Nancy Whiskey and the *Cumberland Gap*, a hit for both Donegan and the Vipers.

Its attraction lay in the fact that it was truly accessible music. *Anybody* could play skiffle, and cheaply. You didn't need to spend much money. Cut a hole in the top of an upturned tea chest, poke a broom handle through it, tie a string between the top of the broom and the tea chest (which acts as a sound box), pluck the string and lo! a crude, very crude, bass. Rhythm came from a washboard and the

main musical thrust from a very basic acoustic guitar and mastery of about three chords thereon.

Its importance was not as a music trend (it was shortlived and Donegan soon deserted it for the music hall knockabouts of songs like *My Old Man's A Dustman* and *Does Your Chewing Gum Lose Its Flavour On The Bedpost Overnight?*) but because it introduced a whole generation to the possibility of making music. Everyone formed skiffle groups. Most gave up. But some stuck with it, trading their cheap guitars up and eventually buying amplified electric axes. One such was John Winston Lennon who formed a skiffle band called the Quarrymen in Liverpool.

The other jazz-inspired cult that swept Britain was Trad. It had enjoyed a mini-boom shortly after the war and a number of bands had played on a reasonably full-time basis through the years of rock & roll which threatened, at one time, to do for it completely. George Melly recalls, in *Owning Up*, meeting Tommy Steele at a TV studio where they were both plugging their latest discs. Neither knew the other or his work but they soon fell into conversation. Master Steele, young, rich, very, very confident, offered Mr Melly some sartorial advice, suggesting that if he took more care about his personal appearance he would go further, faster in show business. He then inquired what make of car Melly ran. On learning that the jazz singer did not possess one, 'he looked at me with the sort of pity usually reserved for the badly deformed'.

But the day of the Trad jazzman was yet to come. (Or, at least, some Trad jazzmen. Melly and Mulligan seemed content to earn a steady, unspectacular living in Trad's second division.) Perhaps because of the interest aroused by skiffle, certainly as a result of increasing 'Bohemianism' – this was, after all, the days of Kerouac and the beatniks – and undeniably as a result of increasing political awareness, there was a renewed interest in jazz. Particularly Traditional, Dixieland and New Orleans jazz.

Jazz went with the Campaign for

Nuclear Disarmament, beat poetry and *The Outsider* and *Look Back In Anger*. Young men were angry, young women looked like Juliette Greco, or tried to, and they would congregate in cellars to spout the sort of crap that earnest young people will always consider profound.

Trad, like so many movements – musical or otherwise – started in the basement (literally underground) and spread out, blinking into the light. The young marched to its rhythm from Aldermaston to central London every Easter on the great Ban The Bomb demonstrations, fornicated enthusiastically to it in sleeping bags strewn across the aristocratic grounds of Lord Montagu's 'pad' at Beaulieu and danced to it on riverboats down the Thames.

And suddenly, world-weary musicians with beer guts, retreating hair-lines and wracking smokers' coughs, found themselves in neat uniforms, air-conditioned buses, huge auditoria and belting out show tunes to a roughly jazz beat.

The first Trad hit can be identified as *Petite Fleur* by Chris Barber's band, which reached the British Top 10 in 1959. In 1960 Mr Acker Bilk and his Paramount Jazz Band – sporting Edwardian bowlers, striped waistcoats and a whimsically-ornate style of publicity – were charting regularly, and then came Kenny Ball who took numbers from *High Society (Samantha)*, *The King And I (March Of The Siamese Children)* and even *The Alamo (The Green Leaves Of Summer)* and turned them into hits. Within a remarkably short period of time, these – and others – became very popular and owed less and less to the jazz rootstock from which they had originally sprung.

Winter and spring, 1961/62, saw the peak. In that period Kenny Ball and Acker Bilk had monster hits with *Midnight In Moscow* and *Stranger On The Shore* respectively. Both were Top 10 hits in Britain (Bilk's, his own composition for a children's

The Tom Collins Jazzmen play to the Bishop of Colchester and friends.

TV serial, reached number 1 and remained in the charts for 39 weeks) and both crossed the Atlantic where *Moscow* did better than at home by getting to 2 and *Stranger* repeated its chart-topping. Significantly, neither Ball nor Bilk followed up this success in the States.

In Britain, too, the bubble was bursting. The Trad boom was being replaced by a more insistent beat. A beat that would not be heard in America for several more years. In America, teen pop still held sway and there seemed to be a production line that churned out bijou star-ettes and dance crazes to fill the insatiable demand.

It is easy to give the impression that everything that came out of the pop era was without merit. This is false. Some of it was excellent. Much remains in the memory with affection, more with amusement.

Two good things emerged from that period. Rock & roll chart stars had been predominantly white and almost exclusively male. Pop drove a spike through this double chauvinism.

For the first time in the age of rock, girl singers found success and the two top girls, who were far and away more successful than any other females of the time, were Connie Francis and Brenda Lee.

Connie Francis (née Constance Franconero) was the female equivalent of Frankie Avalon and the rest.

But with the one important proviso that she could hold a tune far better than her male contemporaries. She was the blueprint of the teen dream goddess. Pert, smiling face, bouncy energy, full, flaring skirt, she exuded healthy good-humour that was offset by the occasional knowing wink. She broke first with an updated standard–*Who's Sorry Now?*–that took her into the charts in 1958. Her next was much better-aimed at the market–a ridiculous, bubbling piece of aural comic strip called *Stupid Cupid*. Thereafter she swerved between this style of teen-trouble bopper and a sort of souped-up torch song (though, in truth, the flame was guttering) like *I'll Get By* and *Among My Souvenirs*. Her best was surely *Lipstick On Your Collar*, a tragic tale sung with unrelenting cheerfulness that sprang direct from the pages of *Marty*, *Roxy*, *Mirabelle* or any of the love/romance comics of the day.

Brenda Lee was something else again. She was the nearest to rock & roll that any woman–and most men–of the period came. And she didn't arrive on the scene until 1960. She was tiny and yet her whole body seemed to be a sound-box for her extraordinary voice. A voice that someone described as 'part whiskey, part negroid and all woman'. If it occurs to you that the same description could be, and in as many words was, applied to Janis Joplin nearly a decade later, you'll get some idea of how Brenda Lee was performing outside her time. If she'd been a few years older she'd have been the only female rock & roller; a few years younger and she'd have been one of the great ladies of rock.

She had a country background and was knocking the ears off folk at the age of 12 when, apparently, she cut her first record, the country standard *Jambalaya*. Her potential was spotted and she was given a fairly routine pop song called *Sweet Nothin's*. Connie Francis would have dealt with it adequately but Brenda Lee's voice just picked it up and hared off with it. It was enough to establish her as *the* top female singer of the time, even eclipsing Connie Francis who had a two-year head start on her with hits from 1958.

From now on she alternated slow, smouldering numbers with out-and-out belters. The very best of the latter was the amazing *Let's Jump The Broomstick* which was made in 1961 but sounds like it came from five years earlier. The trouble is that, like so many others, Brenda Lee could not keep up the momentum or, more likely, her record company couldn't find the right material for that voice. She soon started putting out rock-a-ballads (in the phrase of platter spinners of the day) like *Speak To Me Pretty* and *Here Comes That Feeling*, which she handled, typically, with far more assertion than any rival. Some indication of her pre-eminence may be found in the fact that Brenda Lee was still notching up considerable hits as late as 1966, long after most of her contemporaries had been made redundant by the Beatles and the Mersey Sound. But both she and Connie Francis had trailblazed for their sisters, who were to play an increasingly important and creative part in the rock music of the next decade-and-a-half.

While Lee and Francis opened it up for the ladies, an even more significant breakthrough was being made by black artists. In *The Sound Of The City* Charlie Gillett gives some figures that indicate the progress made by black artists in the white charts. In 1955 only 9 of the 51 records to enter the Top 10 were by blacks. By 1963 37 of the 106 Top 10 entries were from black performers. In nine years the number of records in the Top 10 had doubled but the proportion of black artists to white had quadrupled.

One of the reasons for this was the increasing sophistication of black music. It had been virtually suppressed by white radio stations because of its raucousness (the very attribute that appealed to the teens); it was dubbed 'jungle music' and considered far too primitive for nice white folks.

By the late Fifties things had changed. There were still the almost impromptu 'Doo-wop-ers' but some white producers and writers had

begun to see the potential in harmony groups and started refining their sound. This sort of black music moved out of the ghettos and into the plush offices of the recording companies. This move across the tracks was not just geographic, it was also reflected in the smoother, less edgy sound. Gillett dubbed the result 'uptown rhythm & blues'.

The most successful and influential writing/production team to wreak this change was Leiber and Stoller. They had written Presley's hit *Hound Dog* and followed up for him with *Love Me, Jailhouse Rock* (for which film they wrote most of the score) and *King Creole*. But their first love had been the blues and they were most interested in working with black harmony groups.

In the first Doo-wop wave at the end of the true rock & roll era, it had been noticed that most of the groups were one-hit wonders. The reason for this is that they were scooped from the street, recorded and dumped back in the ghetto. The business was pretty irregular in those days. Contracts were virtually non-existent, royalties barely admitted and a successful record might bring a group–who, after all, could hardly believe what was happening and were pleased just to see their names on a record–an expensive present.

This attitude was repugnant to Leiber and Stoller. Not only were they interested in fostering and improving acts, they were craftsmen writers and producers and expected their artists to give as much in rehearsal and preparation as they did. They didn't pull anyone off the streets to sing a song. They found their group, discovered what its vocal strengths were and then wrote material to suit those strengths. They rehearsed the bands, making sure they were note perfect before recording them.

Occasionally, Leiber and Stoller would 'cheat' a little. One of the first groups they worked with were the Robins. For them, Leiber and Stoller wrote a number that has subsequently been lauded as a classic– *Riot In Cell Block Number Nine*. It was a musical version of one of the Warner Brothers' 'prison dramas'

The Coasters.

popular in the Thirties. In it the lead singer, a con, tells of a revolt by inmates and the actions of the guards to stop it. (It's interesting to note that about the time the song was written and recorded a reasonably successful movie telling much the same story was released. It was titled *Riot In Cell Block 11*!)

The narrator's role is crucial to the success of the record but Leiber and Stoller discovered that none of the existing Robins could sing it in just the way they had envisaged. So they drafted in another singer, Richard Berry, to handle the part and put the record out without any indication that the Robins had received help!

Leiber and Stoller's next project was with the Coasters, and here they

hit a great streak. There was a touch of Chuck Berry about their work– the ability to humorously convey a teenage dilemma and wed it to a rock beat. Their first big success was a double-header *Young Blood/ Searchin'* which reached positions 8 and 5 respectively in the *Billboard* Hot 100. This was followed by a smaller hit, *Idol With The Golden Head*, but they came straight back to form with an absolutely inspired number– *Yakety Yak*.

This is stream-of-consciousness nagging! A catalogue of parental hectoring to the teen who only lives for the important things in life. For four verses the unfortunate adolescent is harangued and threatened by his mother: 'Take out the papers an' the trash/Or you don't get no spending cash/If you don't scrub that kitchen floor/You ain't gonna

An early version of the Drifters.

rock and roll no more/Yakety yak, don't talk back'.

The words seem to bore through the brain like a buzzsaw and even years later it evokes the unwelcome sound of parental authority pouring scorn and disapproval upon the head stuck in a magazine or cocked to hear the strains of a record player. It evidently struck a response in teens who suffered under just such a repressive regime; they bought the record into the number 1 spot.

They also took to the humour of the next three Coasters/Leiber and Stoller outings–*Charlie Brown* ('Who walks in the classroom cool and slow/Who calls the English teacher "Daddy-o"' Poor Charlie, always in trouble! All he can answer is with the lament–haven't we all

howled it?–'Why's everybody always picking on me?'), *Along Came Jones* (a gloriously witty send-up of the banality of Western series on TV) and *Poison Ivy*, This is a lovely song that compares a girl with her namesake plant that causes fearful irritation: 'She's pretty as a daisy but look out man she's crazy/ She'll really do you in, if you let her get under your skin'. If you are foolish enough to tangle with her, 'you're gonna need an ocean of calamine lotion' to get over the results!

This was pop writing of a very high standard indeed. It's true that the group was used as a vehicle to get the song over to its best advantage but the Coasters weren't just puppets in the sense that they were being manipulated and abused. Everyone benefitted from

Leiber and Stoller's work. (For example, each of those four songs reached the Top 10.)

After success with the Coasters, Leiber and Stoller moved on to yet another black group, one whose career–in a variety of incarnations (between 1955 and the present at least 12 men have sung lead for them on recordings; Johnny Moore has contributed most with sterling and well-known work coming from two men who made good solo careers, Clyde McPhatter and Ben E. King)–has survived violent fluctuations.

The Drifters started in about 1955, mostly as a back-up group to Clyde McPhatter. Then they were a pretty raucous rhythm and blues outfit and doing well enough to gain a twice-yearly engagement for ten years at Harlem's premier venue, the

49

Apollo. But by 1957 the group had more or less disintegrated.

The name still had commercial potential even if the original members had taken their name literally and drifted off. Jerry Wexler at Atlantic—and one of the most respected men in the recording business—saw there was mileage left in a harmony group under that name and soon put together another set of singers, led by Ben E. King, out of what had been the Crowns. The new band was handed over to Leiber and Stoller who started exercising their production skills. They did not, however, write very much for the reconstituted Drifters. This was because the group—under their direction—evolved a romantic, rather sophisticated sound and frankly Jerry Leiber's brilliantly witty, and sometimes rather acerbic, lyrics were not suited to this style.

Leiber and Stoller's work with the Robins and Coasters had been based on simple instrumental back-ups. But the first single for the Drifters took them—and black music—into a new direction. *There Goes My Baby* has been called 'one of the greatest records of all time'. (That was, admittedly, by a self-avowed fanatic—Bill Millar—on the sleeve of a compilation album.) It was, certainly, remarkable. For a start, it used strings—something almost unheard of in black group recording at the time—and a most unusual beat.

Mike Stoller explained this to Charlie Gillett (in his book *Making Tracks, The History Of Atlantic Records*) thus: 'Jerry and I both liked the baion, a Brazilian rhythm . . . The rhythm should have been played by a tympani player, but there wasn't one, so the drummer played . . . It was the first rhythm & blues record I know of that had strings on it—it had a sound that we could hear in the arrangement, a pretentious Rimsky-Korsakov/Borodin pseudo line'. (In fact, while the strings are lush, there's one figure that sounds like it owes more to Tchaikovsky and, in particular, *The 1812 Overture*. It is very similar to a riff—transposed to

Brook Benton had 15 hits in the three years before the Beatles arrived.

50

guitar – used by the Move a decade later on their first single *Night Of Fear*.)

The mingling of quasi-classical, Latin and R & B styles on record could have sounded preposterously overblown. In the event, the production was conceived with such restraint and care that it was entirely successful.

This set the mark on the Drifters' recordings for the next few years. Recordings that included such hits as *Save The Last Dance For Me, Some Kind Of Wonderful, Sweets For My Sweet, When My Little Girl Is Smiling, Up On The Roof, On Broadway, Under The Boardwalk, Saturday Night At The Movies, At The Club, Come On Over To My Place.* Of these, Leiber and Stoller took writing credits on only one, *On Broadway* (and even these were shared with Barry Mann and Cynthia Weill). They didn't produce them all, either. Somewhere between *On Broadway* and *Under The Boardwalk*, Bert Berns took over.

But Leiber and Stoller had done a number of remarkable things. They had written some brilliant songs; they had become the first independent producers in rock history; they had made the producer's role in rock similar to the director's in movies. After their pioneering some producers could put their 'names above the title'. In other words, just as there are 'Hitchcock films' and 'Truffaut films' and 'John Ford films' so now there would be 'Leiber and Stoller productions', 'Spector productions' and 'George Martin productions'. They had brought black groups into the mainstream of pop, and once black artists had a toehold in the charts, they were not going to relinquish it. The role of black artists became increasingly creative and important to rock in the years that followed.

But Leiber and Stoller did one other important thing. They recognised the need for really first-rate pop songs. Songs of equivalent quality to those they wrote themselves. As we have seen, the general standard of pop performance

and writing was low; production-line songs for robotic singers. They had to find the talent to supply the right material. And find it they did in a shabby office block on Broadway – the Brill Building.

The Brill Building was pop's answer to Tin Pan Alley. It was, to use a terrible cliché, a 'hit factory'. Inside, it was divided into little boxes with a piano. Into these boxes writers were put, either individually or in teams, and they wrote songs. Most of them wrote songs for a man called Don Kirshner whose remarkable ability to pick hits and sign hot writers to his companies earned him the title 'The Man With The Golden Ear'.

Contracted to Kirshner's Aldon Music at that time were the incredibly successful and talented (the two didn't necessarily go together in those days!) teams of Sedaka and Greenfield, Goffin and King, and Mann and Weill, as well as Jack Keller. As a slight indication of their worth, it is interesting to note that these seven, in one combination or another (Keller, for example wrote with Goffin and Greenfield and/or Sedaka), were responsible for 58 songs that appeared in the British Top 20 between 1955 and 1973. (The bulk falling between 1958 and 1966.) In addition, a list of the writers who appear most frequently

on the labels of hit records for the period lists Goffin as third and King as fourth most successful, only after Paul McCartney and then John Lennon. In those years Goffin's name had appeared on 30 hits and King's on 27, with the bulk, of course, written with each other. (The source for these figures is *Rock File Vol. 3*.)

Kirshner was a pop entrepreneur *par excellence* and took the industry a step further by combining three aspects of it. At one time or another during this period he managed Bobby Darin (one of the most consistent hitmakers of the period) and Connie Francis. He signed his songwriting teams who supplied songs to his artists (for instance Greenfield and Sedaka wrote *Stupid Cupid* for Connie Francis) and then he set up his own label, Dimension. On this he recorded Little Eva (who, it happened, had been babysitter to Goffin and King's children!) singing Goffin and King's *The Loco-Motion* and Carole King's solo debut as a singer, *It Might As Well Rain Until September*. (This togetherness got a bit claustrophobic on occasions. Little Eva's debut album *Lllllloco-Motion* was produced by Gerry Goffin, co-arranged by Carole King who also conducted the orchestra; seven of the 12 songs were written by Goffin

classics as *He's A Rebel*, *Da Doo Ron Ron*, *Then He Kissed Me* and *Uptown* (all by the Crystals) and *Be My Baby* and *Baby I Love You* (the Ronettes).

Spector relied upon the Kirshner songwriting teams but even more heavily on another talented husband and wife partnership–Jeff Barry and Ellie Greenwich. The latter told Roy Carr, of the *New Musical Express*, about Spector's unique recording methods that produced such staggering aural results. 'Phil had this way of swimming everything into itself until it became one gigantic wall of sound. And, as he got more and more into studio production he just about went crazy with his overuse of echo. Sure, he got the effect that he was looking for, but in the process he drove the sound engineers mad.'

There may have been a degree of madness in Spector's method but it drove him to produce two of the greatest singles ever made–the Righteous Brothers' *You've Lost That Lovin' Feeling* and Ike and Tina Turner's *River Deep, Mountain High*. One is tempted to say that they are the perfect pop creations, the very pinnacle of mono art. So good that they defy description.

This was the very best of pop. The

and King. In fact, only one was from writers *not* signed to Kirshner! The back cover carried a message from Kirshner and his partner Al Nevins and an endorsement from Bobby Darin!)

It is evident from all this that the Brill Building, and particularly those parts of it rented by Kirshner, was a creative powerhouse. Leiber and Stoller tapped this rich vein for songs and offered these young, and often inexperienced, writers an incentive. The Drifters were con-

Little Eva.

sistent chart-denters and gave the writer who could capture their sound the chance of a big hit and lucrative royalties. Goffin and King particularly benefitted from this; they'd had little chart success before tailoring *Will You Still Love Me Tomorrow* for the group; after it they seemed unable to do anything wrong.

Other of the best young American writers gained from this association and flourished after it. Ben E. King left the Drifters to pursue a solo career. An early record of his was a beautiful song called *Spanish Harlem* which got to number 10 in the States. It was produced by Leiber and Stoller and written by Jerry Leiber and Phil Spector.

Spector–who had written and recorded *To Know Him Is To Love Him* (under the group name the Teddy Bears) some years earlier–went on to take black group music in another direction by creating the female counterparts to the Coasters and Drifters with the Crystals and Ronettes. For them he made such

Above: *The Ronettes.*
Left: *An insecure Phil Spector, whose originality set new recording standards.*

rest was inferior. Jolly enough, but inferior. It was in the main simply to dance to or smooch by. You could dance to Bobby Vee, you smooched to and over Ricky Nelson.

The thing that marked this breed of pop singers was their youth. They were no older than the people who bought their records in uncounted millions. Ricky Nelson – one of the prettiest and most successful – was just 17 when his first record *A Teenager's Romance* (what title could typify the era and the style better?) went into the Top 10 in 1957. (As if to prove just how typical Nelson and his records were, the flip was a cover of Fats Domino's *I'm Walkin'* which also sold its way into the Top 20).

followed up with such offerings as *Lonely Boy* and *Puppy Love*, hymns of teenage anguish and yearning.

The greatest howl of adolescent agony belongs not to Anka, but to Dion (Di Mucci) and the Belmonts. 'Each night I ask the stars up above/ Why must I be a teenager in love?'! God it was Hell and Dion went through it all. He was the *Lonely Teenager*, who fell for *Runaround Sue* (a perfidious tease) and became *The Wanderer.*

Neil Sedaka also had his problems but he approached them in a rather jauntier style. He was correct in insisting that *Breaking Up Is Hard To Do* but he accompanied it with the immortal chant 'Doobie doobie dum doobie dum doo wah, cumma cumma dum doobie doo dum dow'! Sedaka was terrific, a really bouncy performer who seems irretrievably good humoured no matter what perversity he faced. Hits poured from his cubicle in the Brill Building—*Oh, Carol* (directed at his colleague Carole King who responded with the less successful *Oh, Neil*), *Calendar Girl*, *Happy Birthday Sweet 16* (a hymn to pubescent awakening; you could not help thinking that the young lady who had so recently reached the age of consent was about to lose rather more than her teethbrace!) and other such opera.

The pop era was a merry enough time—except, of course, for the odd wails of frustrated love—and mostly undemanding of performer or listener. In the later years, between about 1960 and 1962, the most that was expected of you was that you turn a nifty ankle: 'You broke my heart, 'cos I couldn't dance/You wouldn't even have me around/But now I'm back/To show you I can really shake it down . . .' So started a big hit of the time, *Do You Love Me* ('now that I can dance . . .'!) which equated the ability to athletically execute the steps of that week's dance craze to sexual desirability.

The progenitor of these dance crazes was, again, *American Bandstand*. One of the features of Dick Clark's show were the teens who

Nelson was already well-known to the American public, having grown up in their full gaze on his parents' TV show *The Adventures Of Ozzie And Harriet*, consequently it was not too difficult for his singing career to lift off. This it did with spectacular rapidity, scoring hit after hit like *Stood Up*, *Poor Little Fool*, *It's Late*, *Travellin' Man*, *Hello Mary Lou* and *Teen Age Idol*—in all, over 20 hits between 1957 and 1964.

All, as can be judged from their titles, were the trite teen fare of the pop formula machine. Songs of love, for, of and by the young. Some younger than others. Paul Anka made Nelson look like a veteran. When he had his first, biggest and best remembered hit he was but 15! But that first hit, *Diana*, said it all: 'I'm so young and you're so old/This my darling we've been told'. Quite gruesome but utterly engaging. This pint-sized *wunderkind*—he had a hand in writing most of his hits—

regularly appeared, danced and soon became national celebrities. In living rooms all over the States, kids watched intently what steps Carmen and Mike were doing, and what refinement Joe and Mary Anne had added, and then aped them. (Girlfriend dancing with girlfriend, of course, rehearsing the steps so they could dazzle their dates at the Saturday hop.)

The ability to dance well, and to do the dance of *this* week (it was death to be seen Hully-gullying in Mashed Potato week), was paramount. Dance crazes swept the States via *Grandstand* and, of course, the invention of a weekly terpsichorean style became an industry. Records came out that created their own dances–you danced the Wah-Watusi to the Orlons' *Wah-Watusi*, the Bristol Stomp to the Dovells' *Bristol Stomp* and so on. If the dance creator got it right, he had a long-running series of hits based around his first record/style. Thus, Dee Dee Sharp did well with her *Mashed Potato Time* and followed up with *Gravy (For My Mashed Potatoes)*!

Inmates of the Brill Building: Paul Anka (above), Neil Sedaka (below left), Dion (below centre) and Carole King (below).

Dance crazes flourished in the pop era, whether they were performed to the rhythms of rock & roll (above) or were more artificial concoctions such as the Mashed Potato, Wah-Watusi or Swim (below). Since little of their music was available on the radio, the teens made the local juke-box (centre) the focus of their leisure activity.

The undisputed king of the dance crazes was Chubby Checker. And the undisputed dance craze of the time was the Twist. Although Checker and the Twist are coupled inextricably in the memory, neither the dance nor the original record was his creation. Received wisdom says that Hank Ballard wrote a record called *The Twist* in 1959. Tony Cummings (in *The Sound Of Philadelphia*) points out that another performer, Little Joe Cook, claims he had a song called *Let's Do The Twist* around 1958 and that Ballard 'borrowed' the tune and adapted it. Whatever the truth, the number was picked up by shrewd men in Philly and given to an ex-chicken plucker called Ernest Evans to record. (Evans had been rechristened Chubby Checker in a sort of homage to Fats Domino. Fats–Chubby; Domino–Checker.)

In the convention of the day he was told what to record, when and under what name. He was lucky. The Twist took off in a way that exceeded the wildest expectations and Checker, a plump, likable chap with a small talent for impersonation, got very, very famous. He gyrated rather sweatily and proved that the Twist was so cretinously simple to perform that *everyone* started doing it. Yes, everyone from the geriatric to the infant, from heads of state to the unemployable. They did it on yachts in Monte with the same ease (but rather more portly decorum) as the dripping teens in a damp cellar in Manchester or Pittsburgh. It was the first truly international, truly classless, dance craze. It required little physical fitness and no expertise. It didn't even require a partner so there was no worry about synchronizing your movements to another.

The Twist went on and on. Checker scored even bigger with *Let's Twist Again*, Sinatra made a

Twist record and Petula Clark revived a flagging career in her native Britain with a French disc called *Ya-Ya Twist*. There were even Twist movies – abysmal, of course – ripped off in both title and style from Haley's efforts a few years before – *Twist Around The Clock* (which was advertised as being 'Twist-errific!' and featured – Heaven forfend – *Merry Twistmas*!) and *Don't Knock The Twist*.

Twist king, Chubby Checker.

The Twist was the last of the great dance crazes – even though Checker went doggedly on trying to repeat his lucky strike with the Huckle-buck, the Hitchhiker and even the excruciatingly difficult Limbo – and in many ways it marked the end of an era. It was, like so much else of the time – entirely contrived. It was

manufactured, promoted and sold like a can of beans. Its perpetrator had little above an amiable personality and a light, not unpleasant, voice to commend him. In the final analysis, he – and his ilk – were as much a product as the song and dance he performed.

People still twisted long after Chubby Checker had hung up his dancing shoes, but now they twisted to a new and far more spontaneous beat. Pop was not overthrown overnight, but it was radically changed, almost entirely by one group. But that group – who did for the likes of Checker – had an enormous hit with a twist record. It was one of the few hit songs they recorded that they did not write themselves. Ah, the times they *were* a-changin' . . .

The Beatles

THE BEAT BOOM

THE BEAT BOOM
1962-1967

The bottom line of the mid-Sixties can be summed up thus. In 1962 98 records appeared in the American Top 10; two were by British artists. In 1964 the balance had shifted; 68 records appearing in the American Top 10 were home-grown; 32 were by British artists.

Such figures tell you everything – and nothing. They tell you that the tide had turned and that American rock dominance had been broken. But they don't tell you how, or why, or by whom.

The answer to that is short as well. The Beatles.

The Beatles were to the Sixties what Elvis Presley had been to the Fifties. They epitomised a rock style and an era. They gave rock its second great surge forward. In fact, they took the music from being gimcrack tunes performed by pretty puppets and turned it into a sub-culture. They changed the role of the pop performer, they expanded the scope of rock, they brought respectability – even intellectual respectability – to the raucous, squalling brat that Haley, Presley and others had begotten.

It is barely credible, in retrospect, that four working-class young men from the provinces should wreak so much change, in so many areas, in so little time. Once, like kingfishers, they had flashed gaudily through the decade, leaving their brilliant iridescence upon it, nothing was quite the same. Before them it had been short-back-and-sides; after them even bank managers wore their hair over their ears. Before them pop had been sung by wooden little Pinnochios; after them Pinnochio had cut his strings and danced to his own, self-written tune. Before them pop films had been exploitative crap; after them they *could* be considered as *cinema*.

The Fab Four at the height of Beatlemania; shaking their fringes on TV (below) and mugging happily (top right).

They fundamentally impressed their personalities on everything they attempted and they mostly changed our perception of it.

What made them so different? If you were 16 or less in 1962 you could hear it and feel it. You didn't try to analyse it. You just *knew*, through your pores and your senses, that here were four very different young men. For a start, when you saw them playing you could hear and see that they were integrated. They were, truly, a group.

The line-up was conventional enough–three guitars (lead, rhythm and bass) and drums. Nothing new in that, the Shadows had been clicking up hits with just such a combo for nearly three years. But the Shadows were strictly an instrumental outfit, not one of their hits since *Apache* went to number 1 in 1960 had featured a vocal. That changed, of course, when their boss, Cliff Richard, joined them on stage or disc. But then they became, strictly, a backing group. They stepped into the limelight's gloaming and contributed only musical accompaniment and the occasional vocal back-up.

The Beatles were really very different. Three of them could sing as they played, frequently together. There was no instantly identifiable lead singer; in fact, they often swapped lead vocals between them *during the same song*! And they sang in unison and harmony. Furthermore, the songs they sang and played in this individual manner were, more likely than not, ones they had written themselves. In consequence, the ear was struck both by the individuality of every song and the 'togetherness' of its performance.

Perhaps the most noticeable feature of the Beatles, and the major contributory factor in their truly astonishing rise to rock pre-eminence, was their pursuit of excellence. It was as if they simply could not do, or be involved in, anything shoddy. They were always looking to make things better, to push forward the frontiers of taste and achievement.

Whatever they tackled–as a

Cliff & the Shads in the '60s: Marvin, Bennett, Rostill and Welch behind Cliff.

group or individually–they seemed to change or improve. To start with, they created their own image. It was a distillation of several elements (as were many of their 'innovations') but by bringing these together in a certain way, they made the result entirely their own. Shortly before the Beatles burst upon the public awareness they had led a wild, uninhibited and not scrupulously sanitary life in the rougher districts of Hamburg. As Hamburg has a reputation of being, at best, a pretty

rough port, it may be understood that the Beatles played to a section of the community that was, to be discreet, raffish.

They learnt their craft by sweating out rock & roll, loud, hot and dirty for eight hours a night, seven nights a week. They fell in with a bohemian crowd, sported leather, imitated Gene Vincent and Jerry Lee Lewis, and were as noted locally for their outrageousness on and off stage as their music.

Only a few months later, they were popping up on TV, looking freshly-scrubbed, cuddly and entirely inoffensive. How had the change been wrought, from whence had come the deodorant? How had they created this remarkable image?

The hair – the most instantly notable feature of their appearance because of its length – had been styled by the German photographer girlfriend of Stuart Sutcliffe (a member of the original group who died in Hamburg of a brain tumour) and owed a great deal to the 'Existential' youths of the Paris Left Bank.

The suitings had been at the insistence of manager Brian Epstein. Previously the Beatle uniform had consisted of leather jackets and jeans – filthy, unwashed, begrimed. It had summed up their irregular, yobbish attitude and they deserted it with reluctance. They were bullied into suits but, typically, soon turned an imposition into an advantage by wearing Pierre Cardin jackets that carried no collars or lapels! They followed the rather conservative American custom of shirts with button-down collars and turned them into a fashion craze. They matched these to straight, knitted-silk ties (sometimes Ringo did not complete the knot, but wore the long end of the tie *over* rather than through the knot at the throat and consequently provoked another, minor trend).

The physical image, therefore, was constructed from elements borrowed from many sources. The result, however, was undeniably and unmistakeably *Beatles*.

And so it was with the music. The most remarkable thing about the Beatles' invasion of America was the fact that they were, in essence, re-exporting America's own music to its land of origin! Long after rock & roll – in its raunchiest and rawest form – had been superseded in the public taste by pap-like pop, the Beatles had remained faithful to it. 'We're just happy little rockers,' Paul said, years later and John always swore allegiance to its honesty and strength. The German taste in music (like that of young Liverpool) had been for hard, slogging, loud, spikey rock & roll. That was the fare they demanded in the basement clubs and that was

Beatle breeding-ground, Hamburg's Star Club where they played songs by groups like the Shirelles (above).

what the Beatles provided in abundance. But at the same time, they were always listening to contemporary American music, particularly that of the new wave–sophisticated black groups who were just breaking through on a variety of smallish labels but most noticeably on two based in Detroit, Motown (founded June 1960) and its sister Tamla.

The Beatles' first two albums–*Please Please Me* (released in April 1963) and *With The Beatles* (released in November the same year)–showed just how much and with what a discerning ear the Beatles had been taking in the American scene. The two albums contain 29 tracks of which 16 were written by the group (15 by Lennon and McCartney, one by George Harrison); the remaining 13 were all of American origin. One was a rock & roll classic–*Roll Over Beethoven* by Chuck Berry–two were rather out-of-place 'easy listening' offerings that grated on the teenager's ear but delighted his parents and contributed to the Beatles' cross-generation appeal. The songs were *A Taste Of Honey* which had been a US Top 50 hit for Martin Denny in '62 and an instrumental British Top 20 hit for Acker Bilk in '63 and *Till There Was You* from the hit Broadway musical (and later movie) *The Music Man*.

That leaves ten other tracks all of which were by black American artists, few of whom had ever been heard of by the majority of Britain's record buyers. Interestingly, half these tracks were by girl vocal groups–the Marvelettes' *Please Mr Postman*, the Donays' *Devil In Her Heart*, the Cookies' *Chains* and two by the Shirelles, *Boys* and *Baby It's You*. Three emanated from Tamla and/or Motown–*Please Mr Postman*, *Money* (previously a hit for Barrett Strong) and *You Really Got A Hold On Me* by Smokey Robinson and the Miracles. And the last two were *Twist And Shout*–with which the Isley Brothers had had a hit–and Arthur Alexander's *Anna*.

Every one of these were unfamiliar to British audiences and every one suited the Beatles' vocal style. They allowed harmony; they gave opportunity for switching vocals, chanting responses or plain, raucous blues shouting. It was thanks to this introduction that Tamla and other labels managed to get a toehold in the United Kingdom.

The influences were evidently American and by the fourth album, *Beatles For Sale*, they were reinforced. Six of the 14 tracks were non-Beatle songs and five harked back to rock & roll with Berry's *Rock & Roll Music*, Leiber and Stoller's *Kansas City*, Buddy Holly's *Words Of Love* and two by Carl Perkins *Honey Don't* and *Everybody's Trying To Be My Baby*. (Incidentally, the third album was the first to include all-Beatle material, mainly

The Isley Brothers.

because the first side was the soundtrack from their debut film *A Hard Day's Night*. These details about tracks included on albums apply to British releases. In America albums frequently appeared under different titles and with different tracks.)

They sang songs by American negro groups; their own work showed the influence of American music. And they sold this music first to Britain and then right back into the States!

This is not to say the Beatles lacked originality, nothing could be farther from the truth. They *were* the best, they *were* the most original, it's just that they never tried to hide their musical roots. The fact that they took American music triumphantly back to its home only increases their credit and further proved that the rock world had never seen anything quite like the Beatles.

It started reasonably quietly in late 1962. On 5 October a song called *Love Me Do* was released on Parlophone R4949. It received no great welcome from the critics. One of the few who bothered to mention it noted: 'Harmonica again starts off *Love Me Do* and then this strangely-monikered group gets at the lyrics. Fairly restrained in their approach, they indulge in some off-beat combinations of vocal chords. Though there's plenty happening, it tends to drag about midway, especially when the harmonica takes over for a spell. Not a bad song though . . .'

Although that might seem dismissive at first sight, it's actually rather perceptive. Remember, the Beatles were completely unknown outside Hamburg and Liverpool. And at that time the British music business was so concentrated around London that Liverpool might just as well have been Hamburg. The reviewer was ploughing doggedly through a mass of offerings from the record companies who worked then, as now, on the mud-against-the-wall principle, ie if you throw enough some must stick. He was right in saying that the use of the harmonica was unoriginal. Even Lennon agreed: 'It was true that the harmonica had become a bit hackneyed in the new pop discs. But what was forgotten was simply that our record had not been released as soon as we made it. There was a long delay. We'd certainly produced that sound before, for instance, Bruce Channel had got his harmonica bits on *Hey Baby* into the charts. We thought we were right up there setting new trends, but by the time it all happened, we were about the sixty-eighth set of people to use harmonica'.

(To put the record absolutely straight, John may be right in asserting that 'we'd certainly produced that sound before . . . Bruce Channel' but NOT on record. *Love Me Do* and its harmonica had come out of recordings held on 11 September 1962. Channel's *Hey Baby* had entered the British chart in March that year, some six months before.)

The Beatles may not have been first with it, but they certainly used harmonica to good effect and it's worth noting that their producer, George Martin, later told Hunter Davies in the Beatles' official biography, that he'd chosen *Love Me Do* from a number of Lennon and McCartney compositions because 'it was John's harmonica which gave it its appeal'. The British public seemed to agree.

However, the harassed reviewer quoted above had acute enough hearing to recognise that vocally, at least, there was something interesting going on and that the song had merit. Both absolutely correct.

Love Me Do was a 'sleeper'. That is, it took off slowly and it is generally recognised that had fanatical Liverpool supporters not bombarded the few available radio request shows with sackloads of mail, it may never have reached the charts at all. It took nearly two months to enter the Top 30, at number 21 in the week of 1 December 1962. It dropped five places the following week and finally entered the Top 20 in January, peaking at 17. It was not a big hit but substantial enough to get an odd name known.

The Top 20 they entered so early in 1963 was pretty typical of the state of British rock. Nine of the 20 discs were by American artists. But of the 11 by British artists (actually two of these – Rolf Harris and Frank Ifield –

Mark Wynter, UK answer to Fabian et al.

were Australians!) 4 were covers of American hits – Ifield's *Lovesick Blues* was a re-make of Hank Williams's 1949 hit but the other three – Mark Wynter's *Go Away Little Girl*, Susan Maughan's *Bobby's Girl* and Kenny Lynch's *Up On The Roof* – were virtually note-for-note lifts from American hits of the previous few months. At least one other – Joe Brown's *It Only Took A Minute* – was by American writers. In other words, 14 songs out of the 20 were either performed by Americans or written by them or both. America still held dominance.

Just as a small indication of the Beatles' impact after *Love Me Do*, it is salutary to take a look at the Top 20 in Britain exactly one year later.

The Beatles again featured, of course. At number 1 with *I Want To Hold Your Hand*, at number 5 with the descending *She Loves You* and as writers at number 12 having given *I Wanna Be Your Man* to the Rolling Stones. Of the 20 records only five were from foreign artists, four Americans and the Singing Nun from the Continent. Therefore 15 records were by British artists and at least nine were by British writers and, even better, five of those nine were performed by the people who wrote them. It was as if, spurred by the Beatles, British writers and/or performers had suddenly found a mighty self-confidence. And all in one year.

But back in early '63 none of this was apparent. The Beatles now needed to follow-up *Love Me Do*

with another hit and George Martin, like the good A & R man (Artists and Repertoire) that he was, set about matching a repertoire or, rather, song to his artists. He came up with a song by British writer Mitch Murray called *How Do You Do It?* He was sure–as sure as you can ever be–that it had hit potential.

The Beatles turned it down! It is difficult to convey now the full enormity of that. No artist–especially not one with only a single, middling hit–ever turned down a song that his producer–just one remove from God–gave him. It was the producer's job to pick hits and wed them to performers. But the cocky, arrogant Beatles didn't like *How Do You Do It?* It had nothing to do with whether they thought it would be a hit, it was just that they didn't like it.

So George Martin, taken aback, told them to come up with some-

thing better. They came up with *Please Please Me* and it is to Martin's eternal credit that he recognised it as being better and *admitted* that it was better. He let them record *Please Please Me* and watched it go to number 2. It is also to Martin's credit that he was right on two counts–*How Do You Do It?* was a number 1 hit for another Liverpool, Epstein-managed group, Gerry and the Pacemakers.

It soon became evident that the Beatles were not, as so many critics had predicted, one- or two-hit wonders. In 1963 they followed *Love Me Do* by charting with *Please Please Me*, *From Me To You*, *She Loves You* and *I Want To Hold Your Hand*, the last three all going to number 1. In addition they released two albums–*Please Please Me* and *With The Beatles*–both of which went to number 1 and three big-selling EPs (Extended Players

containing four tracks which had, generally, been released in other forms)–*Twist And Shout*, *The Beatles' Hits* and *Beatles No. 1*.

As if that was not all, the pro-digious songwriting talent of John Lennon and Paul McCartney was supplying a steady stream of mat-erial to other artists, mostly those signed to Brian Epstein's NEMS management stable. And they were astonishingly successful. Billy J. Kramer and the Dakotas hit the Top 20 with three Lennon and McCartney songs that year–*Do You Want To Know A Secret* (2), *Bad To Me* (1) and *I'll Keep You Satisfied* (4). The Fourmost (another Liverpool/Epstein band) did nearly as well with *Hello Little Girl* (9) and *I'm In Love* (17) and the Rolling Stones got their first Top 20 hit with *I Wanna Be Your Man*. Others benefitting from a Beatle song that year but failing to make the charts were Cilla Black

Merseybeat rules! Gerry & the Pacemakers (above left); Billy J Kramer at the Cavern (right) and the Beatles with producer George Martin (above).

with *Love Of The Loved* and Tommy Quickly with *Tip Of My Tongue* (both Epstein protegées), Duffy Power had a crack with *I Saw Her Standing There* and Kenny Lynch a near-miss with *Misery*, a song that had originally been intended for husky-voiced, teenage chanteuse Helen Shapiro.

It's doubtful that anyone in rock history has made such a comprehensive impact within a year as the Beatles did in Britain in 1963. But that wasn't all.

You can pin an exact date on the start of Beatlemania: 13 October 1963. That's when Beatlemania became an official phenomenon. 'Official' in the sense that the national newspapers recognised it and

67

The Beatles under John Lennon and Paul McCartney were the first group to write their own songs, their high-quality delivery and surrealistic humour making them pre-eminent. The Beatles 'in person' in *Yellow Submarine* (above); Apple's psychedelic boutique in Baker Street (below).

trumpeted the news to the general populace by way of splash headlines on their front pages. In effect, most people of 16 and under had been aware of it for some weeks. The Beatles had spent most of the year touring, working their way up the bills from being fourth listed under Helen Shapiro, Danny Williams and Kenny Lynch on 15 dates in February and March to sharing top billing with Roy Orbison during May and June and then headlining in their own right during November and December.

NEMperor Epstein and protegés Tommy Quickly, Cilla Black and Billy J Kramer.

During the Orbison junket around the provinces from the Hippodrome Brighton to the Gaumont Hanley and from the King George Hall, Blackburn to the Tooting Granada, it had become evident that the Beatles were getting more than average crowd reaction. The din that greeted them as they ran onstage was deafening, the crush forward of frenzied young female bodies, alarming and the scenes outside the stage door as teenies lunged for the group's speeding car, positively suicidal.

These incidents had passed largely unremarked. Typically, it wasn't until something happened on

Fleet Street's doorstep that the national press took any notice. On 13 October 1963, the Beatles were booked to appear on TV's premier variety showcase, *Sunday Night At The London Palladium*. The Palladium is in Argyll Street, only a short cab-hop from Fleet Street and so reporters could rush across town to report the astonishing scenes being enacted before the venerable showbiz institution.

The street outside the theatre was jammed with teenagers, mostly girls, pressing and screaming and making an impenetrable crush of bodies so noisy that they interrupted rehearsals inside. The

reporters scratched their heads and wondered whether there had been scenes like this before. They decided, probably rightly, that there hadn't. They noted how the police were having trouble controlling the crowds and yet how good-tempered the young people seemed to be. They found the whole episode inexplicable, dubbed it Beatlemania and decided to investigate these four tousle-headed young men ('Hey, fellers, let's call 'em Mop Tops! And what's that word they keep using? Fab? Well, why not the Fab Four?!') who were the cause of the bother.

They and their colleagues in the electronic media did not have long to wait for their next big Beatle story. The next week it was announced that the Beatles were to appear before royalty–in the personage of Queen Elizabeth the Queen Mother–sharing the bill with Marlene Dietrich, among others, at the Royal Variety Performance. This is frequently held to be the highest accolade that British show business has to confer upon its performers and it is seldom that artists so new to the top ranks get invited to appear.

The Royal Variety Performance is important to the story of the Beatles and, indeed, British beat in the Sixties. Not because of the glittering event in itself, but because it was at that show in front of a television audience of about 26 millions, and with one throwaway remark that the Beatles, and particularly John Lennon, won the heart of the adult nation.

They had balanced their act–one huge, familiar hit in *She Loves You*, a middle-of-the-road, easy-on-the-ear-for-Mum-and-Dad number in *Till There Was You* and an out-and-out rocker in *Twist And Shout* just to prove to the kids that they hadn't sold out completely, even though they were wearing evening dress. They were going across well, impressing a lot of people who would be automatically antagonistic to pop musicians. They were clean and had nice smiles and could evidently sing in tune and were not as loud and noisy as might be expected . . . And then John clinched it. He stepped forward, a roguish

twinkle in his eye, and asked 'The people in the cheap seats to clap your hands' in time with the next song. And added, in a remark aimed towards the occupants of the royal box, 'The rest of you just rattle your jewelry'.

It was a daft remark but timed and aimed just right. It was cheeky without being offensive. Very important as the British are touchy about their royals. It was an intimate joke, shared among millions of friends on this cosiest of evenings. It made the adult nation smile benevolently. The Beatles became favourite nephews who were sometimes a little naughty but had such twinkling eyes and charming smiles that you really couldn't be mad at them for long. Just as they admitted to taking drugs and upsetting you, they'd come along with a song like *Yesterday* just to show that everything was all right, really.

This rapid acceptance of the Beatles by both the show business establishment and the generations above adolescence fixed them into a level of popularity that few had ever reached before. It also put them and those like them into a context. It laid down a demarcation line that divided 'good' pop stars from 'bad' stars. In the same year as the Beatles took off, another group rose, rather more slowly, to prominence and started grabbing the headlines. The members of this group were 'bad' pop stars. And they did very nicely out of it, thank you.

Compare the deep and favourable impression made by the Beatles when they appeared on *Sunday Night At The London Palladium* in 1963 with the one made by the Rolling Stones when they appeared on the same show in 1967. It was part of the show's format that, at the finale, all the guests climbed aboard a carousel and mugged and waved asininely at the cameras. The Beatles had ridden the roundabout. The Rolling Stones . . . well, here's a report from the *Daily Mirror* of 23 January 1967: 'A bitter row flared at the London Palladium last night when the Rolling Stones broke a show business tradition by refusing to 'revolve' at the end of the Sunday

night television show.

'The rumpus began at rehearsals, two hours before the show was due to go on . . . "They're insulting me and everyone else", shouted the show's director, Mr Albert Locke. Mick Jagger said later: "That revolving stage isn't an altar; it's a drag".'

Could this surly, offensive young man be very nearly as popular as Paul McCartney? And his group second only in success to the Beatles? And could they manage this by *distressing* adults, antagonising authority and generally not caring less? They could and they were.

The Rolling Stones were the other face of the double-headed pop creature of the Sixties. Compare these two reactions from the same newspaper, the *Daily Mirror*, then the biggest-selling daily in Britain (if not the world). When Beatlemania was frowned on by the stuffy, right-wing *Daily Telegraph*, the *Mirror* leapt into print to defend its Fab Moptops: 'You have to be a real sour square not to love the nutty, noisy, happy handsome Beatles'. (And giving itself away for the bandwagon-jumper it was, by use of woefully outdated 'hep' talk!)

A year later, in August 1964, the *Mirror* was being fairly sour and square when it lambasted the Stones with ' . . . if ever parents of Britain are almost united, it must surely be in their general dislike of those shaggy-haired discoveries . . . They are the anti-parent symbol'. The Stones and the Beatles were at two ends of the spectrum and the press attempted to play one off against the other, toning down any Beatle transgressions and inflating the tiniest slip in etiquette by the Stones. It must have galled them to learn that, in reality, the Stones and Beatles were good friends and that the Beatles had given their 'rivals' an important early boost with *I Wanna Be Your Man*.

But right from the start there had been a dichotomy between the two groups. When the Beatles looked to rock & roll and rather smooth black music for their inspiration, the Stones had sprung from an early, rawer tradition. They looked to the blues and, particularly, rhythm &

DECCA

TONES LET IT BLEED DECCA

The Rolling Stones

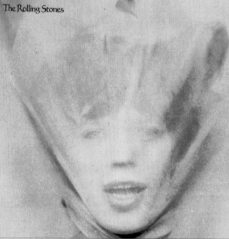

Simon AND Garfunkel Bridge Over Troubled Water

THE DRIFTERS
Love Games

Featuring: LOVE GAMES, DOWN ON THE BEACH TONIGHT, LIKE SISTER AND BROTHER, KISSIN' IN THE BACK ROW OF THE MOVIES.

SURREALISTIC PILLOW
RCA

JEFFERSON AIRPLANE

THE MOODY BLUES

IN SEARCH OF THE LOST

Laughter & Tears
The best of *Neil Sedaka* today.

The Moody Blues
On The Threshold of a Dream

THE SURFARIS PLAY
JACK THE RIPPER
POINT PANIC
WAIKIKI RUN
SURF SCENE

LOOK AT US
SONNY & CHÉR
INCLUDES THEIR BIG HIT
I GOT YOU BABE

IT'S EVERLY TIME! THE EVERLY BROTHERS

THERE'S A BOND BETWEEN US

THE GRAHAM BOND ORGANIZATION

BLUES BREAKERS
JOHN MAYALL
WITH ERIC CLAPTON
DECCA

FLEETWOOD MAC

THE PRETTY THINGS

ROAD RUNNER · JUDGEMENT DAY · 13 CHESTER STREET · BIG CITY
UNKNOWN BLUES · MAMA, KEEP YOUR BIG MOUTH SHUT
HONEY, I NE... · DON'T LIE TO...

KINKS

Five Live Yardbirds

JULIE DRISCOLL,
BRIAN AUGER
& The Trinity

READY-MOUNT

THE FREEWHEELIN' BOB DYLAN

Anti-Beatles: no matching suits or cheeky grins for the Rolling Stones; even on TV they refused to be repressed or groomed.

blues for their roots.

The two groups had trod much the same road in their early days, playing small clubs packed with an enthusiastic clique, picking up a wider audience slowly and by word of mouth. But the Beatles had started a bit earlier and learned a bit quicker. They had also been reluctantly willing to compromise—if not musically then at least in appearance. The Beatles had climbed into suits even though they never felt truly comfortable in their uniform. As John said: 'We felt embarrassed in our suits and being very clean. We were worried that friends might think we'd sold out. Which we had, in a way'.

When the Rolling Stones' manager, Andrew Oldham, suggested that his newly-signed group wear neat checked suits for their first appearance on TV—on the highly influential *Thank Your Lucky Stars*—to plug their debut disc, *Come On*, he met with a spirited resistance. Wearing matching clothes was exactly what the Stones were NOT

had first attracted him to the Rolling Stones. He replied: 'Music. Sex. The fact that in just a few months the country would need an opposite to what the Beatles were doing . . . It registered subconsciously that when the Beatles made it, another section of the public were going to want an opposite. The Stones were that opposite. It was just an instinctive thing and that's the way it worked out. In the early days, the way the media was running was that you could invite the Beatles for tea but you couldn't invite the Stones'.

Working on that shrewd supposition, Oldham projected his group, with their willing co-operation, in as bad a light as possible. And Mick Jagger was the focus for adult disgust, dislike and resentment. Years before Johnny Rotten and his Sex Pistol colleagues were outraging 'public morality', Jagger, Bill Wyman and Brian Jones were summonsed, tried and fined for insulting behaviour, to whit urinating against the wall of a service station.

During '63, while the Beatles were soaring, the Stones garnered more attention for their 'neanderthal' appearance and general anti-social demeanour than their music or even Jagger's electrifying stage presence, quite the most exciting to emerge since Presley's pelvic thrusts. The first single had been a competent, rather raw version of a lesser-known Chuck Berry song, *Come On*. They had problems finding a follow-up. The truth was that they needed a hit, something to establish them in the Top 20 and get them out onto the road to reach a wider audience. Nothing in their R & B-dominated repertoire was suitable, and despite some pretty harsh comments from Jagger about the Beatles 'selling-out' and his own determination not to 'kowtow to fancy folk who think we should start tarting ourselves up with mohair suits and short hair', they were grateful enough to take a song from their 'bitter rivals'.

I Wanna Be Your Man was a fast, rather contrived rocker from the *With The Beatles* album that had been given to Ringo—as something of a sop—to sing. It was a

about. He resorted to pleading: 'You've got to make some compromises. The TV people are used to dealing with groups like the Searchers and Swinging Blue Jeans. If you dress the way you do in a club, they won't even let you inside the building'.

He eventually prevailed upon them, but even so a letter appeared in a newspaper as a result of their

performance which protested: 'I have today seen the most disgusting sight I can remember in all my years as a television fan–the Rolling Stones'. As a result Oldham began to realise that you might as well be hung for a sheep as a lamb and make a virtue out of authoritarian resistance.

He later admitted as much when he was asked by a reporter what compromise – of the type they'd sworn they'd never make – but it worked. The Stones hit the Top 20 and started a long, controversial, sometimes tragic, always exciting career that outstripped in longevity that of the Beatles, and established the Rolling Stones in the very top echelons of fame.

In February 1964 they released their third single, the one that was to really establish them nationally and in their own right. *Not Fade Away* was a Buddy Holly number – it had been the B-side to *Oh Boy* – and was intriguingly abrupt in its lyrics – for example: 'A love for real not fade away'. Holly's original had been performed in his familiar bubbling rather hiccoughing style but the Stones altered that considerably by chopping the tune into staccato chords, adding a wailing blues harmonica (still popular, despite the comments of certain reviewers!) and emphasising the rawness with Jagger's slurred, don't-care voice.

The sound attracted the ear but what created the excitement was Jagger's performance. For the first time the fluid body movements, the extraordinary posturings and the overt sexuality of his interpretation became obvious.

It disgusted many, delighted more. It was the prototype of a thousand impersonations by any third-rate comic desperate to get an easy laugh. It brought Jagger and the Stones vilification as they were mercilessly pilloried in the press

The Searchers brought Mersey sounds to US songs with great success. Left to right: John McNally, Tony Jackson, Chris Curtis and Mike Pender.

Typical Stones on TV in 1966.

and media. Stones-hating fever seemed to grip adult Britain–and later the States–and Maureen Cleave, columnist and chronicler of the Sixties scene, once wrote perceptively of Jagger: 'With his outlandish personal appearance, his long hair, his huge mouth, his minute hips, his girlish face already a caricature, he came to mean all sorts of different things to different people. He was uncommunicative, unforthcoming, uncooperative; nobody knew anything about him; all he had to do was stand there for the theories to form'.

The image was there; aggressive, unpleasant, churlish but highly attractive to kids and hugely successful. The hits started coming– *It's All Over Now* and *Little Red Rooster* followed in 1964, both revamps of American R & B numbers. The Stones lagged behind the Beatles only in one major respect– they were not writing their own material. But in 1965 Jagger and Keith Richard put that right with *The Last Time* and then the brilliantly incisive and wickedly perceptive *(I Can't Get No) Satisfaction*. (There have been few more concise swipes at the advertising industry than: 'That man comes on to tell me how white my shirt can be/But he can't be a man 'cause he doesn't smoke the same cigarettes as me'.)

This and subsequent Jagger and Richard compositions put them in the forefront of rock writers and rounded-off the Stones' claim to being second only in importance and popularity to the Beatles. With these two groups as its spearhead, British Beat was set to conquer first America and then the world.

1964 saw the first landings on American soil of what was to be an invasion. It was almost as if the Beatles, Stones, Hermits, Searchers and cohorts were getting back for the humiliation of 1776!

The Beatles' first visas issued by the Americans for entry into the States in 1964 specified that they were valid 'as long as unemployed American citizens capable of performing this work cannot be found'. Under those conditions the work permits would be valid for years!

But their ascent in the States was slower in its early stages than in Britain. Three singles–*Please Please Me*, *From Me To You*, *She Loves You*–and an album–*Introducing The Beatles* (which was the British *Please Please Me* LP without its title track and *Ask Me Why*)–had been released in 1963. Of them *From Me To You* had done best reaching 116 in the *Billboard* charts. They had, therefore, made no musical impact.

However, the US press could not ignore the clamouring of their colleagues across the Atlantic, nor the incredible scenes of teen pandemonium that they carried. The weekly news magazines– *Newsweek* and *Time*–and the TV channels had passed these onto their audiences. Awareness of the group was growing, and in November 1963 Epstein went to New York–ostensibly to promote Billy J. Kramer, who was closer in looks and style to the current US pop heroes of the day–but with the real intention, in his own words (from *A Cellarful Of Noise*), 'to find out why the Beatles, who were the biggest thing the British pop world had ever known, hadn't "happened" in America'.

Thanks to increasing media attention, he did manage to talk to some astute people and immediately landed two Ed Sullivan TV shows (and secured his 'unknown' band top billing!). Furthermore, an agent called Sid Bernstein had been particularly percipient and taken a great chance by booking the Beatles into Carnegie Hall– probably America's ultimate venue. All that was needed was some chart action. And Epstein thought he had found the key.

'Moving around New York,' he said in *A Cellarful Of Noise*, 'I found that there was without question an American "sound" on disc which appealed to the American public. If you have an instinct for this sort of thing–and I believe, modestly, that I have–you can sense these things . . . I felt that there was a certain American *feeling*. This feeling, I was certain, existed in *I Want To Hold Your Hand*'.

Capitol records in the States had the options on any product from EMI in Britain but had not taken it up on Beatle material. (The '63 releases had come out on Vee Jay with the exception of *She Loves You* which appeared on Swan.) Now, seeing the way the trend was moving, Capitol not only picked up their options but started promoting the

77

Beatles very actively. They spent
$50,000 pre-selling their group,
billsticking five million 'The Beatles
Are Coming' posters all over New
York. Capitol pulled whatever stunt
they could – urging their staff to 'Be
A Beatle Booster' – to bring the band
to the attention of teens. A company
vice-president, Voyle Gilmore,
admitted, 'Sure there was a lot of
hype'. And added, 'But all the hype
in the world isn't going to sell a bad
product'.

The combination of Capitol's
hype, Epstein's self-avowed instinct
for a hit and the Beatles' exceptional
talent paid dividends. *I Want To
Hold Your Hand* entered the *Billboard* Top 100 on 18 January 1964 at
position 45. The next week it had
leapt to number 3 and the week
after, the first week in February and
one week before the Beatles were
due to fly into Kennedy Airport, it
was number 1. It stayed there for
seven weeks only to be replaced by
She Loves You which was, in its turn,
toppled from that spot by *Can't Buy
Me Love.*

By the time the Beatles landed on
American soil on 7 February the
teen population of New York had

fallen before them – 10,000 turned up
to welcome them. Their appearances on Ed Sullivan and at Carnegie Hall were triumphs and soon
all America was at their feet. As the
New York *Daily News* said: 'Not
even Elvis Presley ever incited such
laughable lunacy among the
screaming generation. The Pres-
leyan gyrations and caterwauling, in
fact, were but luke-warm dandelion
tea compared to the 100-proof elixir
served by the Beatles'.

In 12 days, two TV shows (one of
which had gained the largest
viewing figures ever known for an
entertainment programme in New
York), and concerts in the
Washington Coliseum and Carnegie
Hall, the Beatles had blazed a trail.
The obvious group to follow them
were their rock alter egos, the
Rolling Stones.

The Stones reached the States in
June 1964 (while the Beatles were
conquering Hong Kong, New
Zealand and Australia) but they
didn't receive exactly the same
welcome. They were booked into
Carnegie Hall (which venue had
once turned down Elvis Presley and,
only the year before, Chubby
Checker) but Sullivan would not
allow them on his show because he
didn't like their image, thought

they'd offend his audience and
anyway they'd never even had a hit
in the States.

Instead, they got *Hollywood
Palace*, a variety show hosted by
Dean Martin who mined the rich
vein of abuse with a will. 'Their
hair's not that long,' he told his
audience, who were, no doubt,
curled double by his wit, 'it's just
smaller foreheads and higher
eyebrows'. And when a trampoline
act came on he quipped: 'That's the
father of the Rolling Stones – he's
been trying to kill himself ever
since'.

These jibes symbolised the
reception the group got almost
everywhere. It could not have been
in greater contrast to that accorded
the Beatles, except in New York
where audiences were rather more
aware. In Omaha, Nebraska a
policeman aimed his firearm at Keith
Richard's head and told him to pour
his Coke away because he sus-
pected it was laced with whisky, the
drinking of which was illegal in a
public place. (The nearest the cops
had got to using their pistols on the
Beatles' tour was when one used two
bullets as earplugs!) At the concert
in that city, the Stones played to an
audience of 637 (50 of them police)
in a venue that seated 15,000.

America was not to be indifferent and hostile for long. In October 1964, the Stones flew back and although they still hadn't achieved a Top 20 hit, their reputation was growing fast. This time Sullivan *did* book them onto his show but after some girls in the audience had 'rioted' he asserted to the press: 'I promise you they'll never be back on our show. If things can't be handled, we'll stop the whole business. We won't book any more rock & roll groups and we'll ban teenagers from the theatre if we have to. Frankly, I didn't see the group until the day before the broadcast. They were recommended to me by my scouts in England. I was shocked when I saw them . . . It took 17 years to build this show and I'm not going to have it destroyed in a matter of weeks'.

It almost goes without saying that the Stones appeared regularly on *The Ed Sullivan Show* over the next few years!

The tour helped because in November that year *Time Is On My Side* entered the US charts and peaked at number 6. The Stones were launched upon a wave of popularity that was to continue, unabated and despite some horrific incidents, into the late Seventies.

In the wave of the Beatles and Stones came many of the groups that had poured out of the British provinces and scored successes in their home country. Perhaps the most popular, after them, were Herman's Hermits, the Hollies (both from Manchester), the Dave Clark 5 from London (who had 14 Top 20 US hits), Gerry and the Pacemakers and the Searchers (both from Liverpool).

It's easy to give the impression that these and other British groups just marched into America and swept all opposition before them. In truth, there was very little opposition from native artists. The pretty boys from Philadelphia went under quite quickly. Some, like Bobby Vee, attempted a change in style to accommodate the guitars-and-

Liverpool didn't entirely dominate; Manchester offered Herman's Hermits (top) and the Hollies (centre) while London responded with the Dave Clark Five.

drums beat of the British boom but mostly they failed. If anything, it was those who remained true to themselves who survived.

Some even did better in Britain, the source of the upheaval, than in their own country. Roy Orbison and the Everly Brothers were among those who didn't change style too drastically and who flourished in the UK. Both had country roots–Orbison's very similar to those of both Presley and Buddy Holly in that he recorded both at Sun and Petty's studio in New Mexico, while the Everlys were hillbillies from Kentucky.

The Everlys–Don and Phil–specialised in country-tinged, uptempo harmony numbers, occasionally interlaced with rather lachrymose songs of lost love and even death. (*Ebony Eyes* being a classic example of the latter.) From their first hit, *Bye Bye Love*, in 1957 they could do little wrong. An impressive string ensued, most notable among them, *Wake Up Little Susie*, *All I Have To Do Is Dream*, *Bird Dog*, *Cathy's Clown*, *Walk Right Back* and *No One Can Make My Sunshine Smile.* They were enormously popular in Britain and although they suffered briefly from the onslaught of the Beatles they bounced back in 1965, hair brushed forward and clothes re-styled, with two songs as good as any coming out of Liverpool or Manchester– *Price Of Love* and *Love Is Strange* (the latter, interestingly, a remake of a 1956 hit!). Both did well in Britain, although not in the States, but were, sadly, something of a swansong. However, it was not Mersey-beat that finished the Everlys so much as their own deteriorating relationship.

Orbison, a contemporary of Presley, had started out as a rocker but had, frankly, been unsuited to the role. His forte was strong, dramatic, tragedy-struck ballads which he delivered in a highly-charged voice, dressed in black and with no part of his body moving except the lips. In a sad stroke of irony, Orbison's private life reflected the mournful subject matter

of his songs, his first wife was killed in a motorcycle accident and, two years later, two of his three sons died in a fire at his home. This just went to throw his songs like *Only The Lonely* (his first big hit in 1960), *Runnin' Scared* and *It's Over* into greater tragic relief.

Because Orbison's style and material were so uniquely his own, he was about the only solo American star to last the beat inundation, continuing to belt out his soulful ballads and score hits–*In Dreams*; *It's Over*; *Oh, Pretty Woman*; *Too Soon To Know* and others–right through to 1966.

Although it is true that during those heady days of '64 any young male with a British accent, hair over his collar and bell-bottom trousers could get mobbed in public and laid in private by nubile American girls just for *being* British, so violent was Anglophilia, there were three pockets of musical resistance in the States. And none was in the music capital, New York, which had surrendered without a fight.

The first was right across the nation in California and neither the group nor the music owed a thing to the Beatles or British beat. In fact, at first the music, or rather its subject matter, owed nothing to anywhere but California. The music was about surfing and, as the Beach Boys said in their first Top 10 hit, *Surfin' USA*, 'if everyone had an ocean 'cross the USA/Then everyone would be surfing like in Californ-i-a'. But not everyone did have an ocean and even those who did on America's East Coast found that it was not suitable for California's cult sport. Therefore, it was rather surprising that anthems about this esoteric activity should become national, and then international, hits.

Dennis Wilson had two loves–music and surfing. His brothers, Brian and Carl, shared the former but not, at least to the same degree, the latter. Together with their cousin Mike Love and a close buddy, Al Jardine, they formed a group that featured close harmony singing married to a diluted rock & roll beat.

Another survivor, both of Merseybeat and personal tragedy, was lugubrious Roy Orbison.

Within this group of relatives there nestled a man who was to become one of the giant writing/producing talents in rock. The word genius is too lightly thrown around in the music business. Brian Wilson has often been called a genius. He may not strictly qualify, but he must come very close.

Brian looked for subject matter to the things that he and his brothers and their friends loved. He looked at the life-styles and leisure of those golden, privileged Californian kids. And he wrote it all down; put it all into songs that were little descriptive essays. He wrote about surfing, of course, in *Surfin' USA* (the format depending heavily on Berry's *Sweet Little Sixteen*), and

Surfer Girl; about freewheelin' in *Fun, Fun, Fun* and *I Get Around*; about cars in *409* and *Little Deuce Coupe*; about . . . well *California Girls* says it all; about the uncertainties of adolescence in *When I Grow Up To Be A Man* and *Wouldn't It Be Nice*. Someone once described Brian Wilson as 'a journalist: absorbing and reflecting the emerging lifestyle of teenage California'. Certainly all these songs are vignettes of an enviable world.

It was a world that a lot of teens would have liked to have shared; failing that, they could enjoy it vicariously through the words, the easy-rolling music and the smooth, charming harmonies of the Beach Boys.

Motown breakthrough; careful grooming and a distinct sound brought success to artists like the Marvellettes and the Four Tops (below).

The Beach Boys flourished during exactly the years that the Beatles dominated. They broke through nationally in the States with a Top 20 hit, *Surfin' Safari*, in 1962, and had five further hits there before cracking Britain in 1964 with *I Get Around*. From that point the Beach Boys and the Beatles vied for ascendancy, the Californians losing out to the Liverpudlians until 1966. In this year Brian Wilson came out with two masterworks that projected rock forward, took the initiative away from the Beatles and gained acclaim in Britain. They were the *Pet Sounds* LP (which went virtually unnoticed in the States) and *Good Vibrations* single and both must wait to take their turn in the story.

The other two pockets of musical resistance were, significantly, both black. One was based around Detroit and was released via the Tamla and/or Motown labels. The other was centred around Memphis, Tennessee (Stax records) and went under the confusingly broad title of soul.

The Motown story pivots around Berry Gordy Junior who was one of those men with the determination, drive and vision that ensured he would one day succeed at something. After a couple of false starts (including work on the Ford assembly line—cars being Detroit's major industry, gaining it the nickname 'Motortown' of which Motown is a contraction) he started writing and producing records. He did pretty well and got ambitious. He wanted his own record label and so, in 1960, he set up with borrowed money two labels, Tamla and Motown.

His first signings were the Miracles and their lead singer, who was also to become one of black music's major writing talents, Smokey Robinson. The labels had the early advantages of two excellent writers (Gordy had co-written *Money*, a US Top 30 hit for Barrett Strong in 1960 and included on the Beatles' second album) and a promising group. This accumulation

Motown fostered many talented ladies: Gladys Knight (here with the Pips) turned '60s success into '70s superstardom; Mary Wells faded after My Guy.

of assets soon paid off and within a twelvemonth the label and the group had two big hits with *Shop Around* (which reached number 2) and *Way Over There*. Hits followed with the Marvelettes' *Please Mr Postman* (which made number 1 in '61), and *Do You Love Me* (which reached number 2, sold gold, was written by Gordy and appeared on his Gordy label in '62) and Top 50 entries from Mary Wells and Eddie Holland. Gordy's Motown Corporation started buying in small, ailing Detroit labels and their artists rosters which gleaned him talents like the Ruffin brothers, Jimmy and David, Lamont Dozier (then a singer, but he became one of Motown's, and the world's, most successful songwriters in partnership with Eddie Holland and his brother Brian), Junior Walker, the Temptations and others.

Very quickly Motown was establishing itself as a force to be reck-

Heatwave by Martha (Reeves) and the Vandellas, *Mickey's Monkey* by the Miracles and *Two Lovers* by Mary Wells.

As we have seen, few people outside the States had heard of the Motown sound and its stars except, of course, the Beatles. By 1964, and thanks to the boost given to it by the Beatles, that had changed. The breakthrough was made by the Supremes who had three gold discs in the States that year with *Where Did Our Love Go?*, *Baby Love* and *Come And See About Me*, the first two of which were also monsters in Britain, reaching numbers 3 and 1 respectively. In the same year Mary Wells's *My Guy* reached number 5 in Britain.

The great Motown sweep into Britain was not to come until 1966, but by '64 it was a national label of note in the States and fast becoming international. Its rollcall of stars included some of rock's greatest masters–Smokey Robinson and Stevie Wonder in particular–and others who were going to be consistent and huge hitmakers like Marvin Gaye, the Four Tops, the Temptations, Martha and the Vandellas and, of course, the

oned with. There had been other small independent labels, of course. Perhaps there had been other labels that had been run by, exclusively

The growth of discos in the '60s increased the popularity of smooth dance music; and Motown helped fill the gap.

staffed by, and featured the talents of, black people before. But there had never been a black, independent label that produced hits with such regularity. In 1963 the Motown complex registered four million-selling gold discs with *Finger-tips* by the then 'Little' Stevie Wonder,

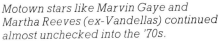

Motown stars like Marvin Gaye and Martha Reeves (ex-Vandellas) continued almost unchecked into the '70s.

Supremes. Furthermore, the last contained, in embryo, one of the biggest female superstars of the Seventies, Diana Ross. Couple these performers to writers like Holland/Dozier/Holland and Norman Whitfield, strict discipline in artist grooming, the legendary Motown 'sound' and you start to understand how Motown grew through the Sixties into one of the leading record companies in the world.

Motown can be easily pinned down to a place, a group of people, a label, and—far more difficult to categorise—a sound. This does disservice to the wide variety of styles and performers that have appeared under the Motown umbrella but it will do as a rough guide for the purposes of identification. But what, as a Ben E. King song of the time so stridently demanded, is soul?

I must confess that I can't answer that question. But then I do not claim any expertise in this particular area of rock music. I bow to students of black music and find that they have as much trouble with definition as me. Ian Hoare in his introduction to *The Soul Book* shows the difficulty.

What is soul? 'Historically it can be pinned down with reasonable accuracy: the word came into wide use as a broad generic musical term in the mid-Sixties, when heavily gospel-based vocal and composing styles began to bring success consistently to R & B artists; when new kinds of instrumental arrangements were developed to complement these styles; and when recording techniques became increasingly seen as part of the music-making process.'

What he is implying in that—or rather, what I am inferring from it—is that soul was a smoothed-out R & B. R & B with the jagged edges knocked off, with properly charted arrangements, disciplined backings—frequently using brass—and the full technology of the recording studio brought into play to give the most refined product possible without loss of excitement.

The excitement of voices raised on gospel singing in churches that rocked to the joyful sound.

In other words, instead of getting a rhythm & blues artist into a studio with his own group or a scratch selection of sessionmen and hoping to capture his earthy electricity cold onto tape, this black music was being treated the same way as commercial, mainstream pop. The same way as Motown was doing it up north.

So far so good. But, as Hoare points out, as time went on 'soul' – ever a loose term – became so overused as to become almost meaningless. It was used, as he says, 'to cover styles as diverse as the driving dance sound and machismo of James Brown; the cool sophistication of Roberta Flack; the high-flying exuberance of teenybop heroes the Jackson 5; and the improvisation of jazz-orientated bands like the Ohio Players'.

Amid this confusion can one draw any sort of conclusion? Hoare thinks so, but it doesn't help us. 'The significant common factor of these performers is, quite simply, that they are all black: as a category, ''soul'' now seems to serve much the same purpose within the workings of the music industry as previous labels like ''race music'' and ''rhythm 'n' blues''.'

So 'soul' has become just another synonym for 'black', just as 'coloured' used to be. In which case, and risking general disapprobation, I'm going to make so bold as to describe the music that a young white kid loved and danced to in the Sixties and called 'soul' because he didn't know any better. Soul back then fell into two broad types – the 'Sock-it-to-me', dance-yourself-into-a-lather, bop-to-the-sax numbers like *Mr Pitiful*, *Respect*, *Fa Fa Fa Fa Fa* by Otis Redding (although, of course, the second was a bigger hit for Aretha Franklin), *In The Midnight Hour*, *Land Of A 1000 Dances*, *Mustang Sally* , *I'm A Midnight*

Mover by Wilson Pickett, *You Don't Know Like I Know* and *Hold On I'm Coming* by Sam and Dave, Eddie Floyd's frantic *Knock On Wood* and Arthur Conley's *Sweet Soul Music*.

Interleaved with these 'ravers' were the 'smoochers'. Having proved our terpsichorean abilities to our partners, we would move in for a clinch and general sensual reconnoitre to the strains of Otis Redding's *My Girl*, Percy Sledge's *When A Man Loves A Woman* or Solomon Burke's *Down In The Valley*.

All of *those* were soul to us. We could hear and feel soul. And they were bound together by something more tangible – all were recorded on either the Atlantic or the Stax labels. Which, in effect, meant they all came from the same source.

To put it rather crudely, Stax was to Memphis what Motown was to Detroit. (Although it should be said that Sledge's hit was recorded at the Muscle Shoals studios in Alabama.) It had been started by Jim Stewart and his sister Estelle Axton as Satellite, but a name change had become necessary because another label was trading under that name. Taking the first two letters of their

surnames, Stewart and Axton created Stax. In 1959 they had put out a single, *Deep Down Inside*, by a duo called Rufus and Carla. Up in New York, the shrewd Jerry Wexler – overlord of the Leiber/Stoller/Coasters/Drifters teamings – had picked it up on his sensitive antennae, got the licensing rights on it and Atlantic and Stax started a loose relationship that, as the Sixties progressed and soul gained greater public acceptance and popularity, became closer. (Rufus and Carla, incidentally, were father and daughter Thomas. Rufus had hits with *Walking The Dog* and *Do The Funky Chicken* while Carla scored with *Gee Whiz* – Stax/Atlantic's first US Top 10 hit – *B-A-B-Y* and *Tramp*, a duet with Otis Redding.)

One of the great advantages of Stax was its house band – Booker T. and the MGs (the initials standing for Memphis Group.) These extra-ordinary musicians – Booker T. Jones on keyboards and a multiplicity of other instruments, the astonishing guitarist Steve Cropper, Donald 'Duck' Dunn on bass and Al Jackson on drums – laid the basis of the Stax or Memphis sound. They played on virtually every hit that emerged

The Who (Roger Daltrey, John Entwistle, Keith Moon and Pete Townshend) were the only group to rival the Beach Boys, Beatles and Rolling Stones in the '60s. They combined electrifying stage performances with high-quality records and albums such as *My Generation, Won't Get Fooled Again* and *Tommy* (the first successful rock opera).

from the studios during the successful Sixties, laying a solid foundation (and some brilliant, electrifying guitar work from Cropper that helped many a record into the charts on its own) upon which vocal performers could build. In addition, they produced considerable hits in their own right, most noticeably *Green Onions* in 1962 and continuing with others like *Soul Limbo* and *Time Is Tight.*

With this talent as its nucleus, Stax and Memphis—ever a music centre and, remember, the scene of Presley's first successes on the local Sun label—became a gathering point for soul stars. It lasted through the Sixties, surviving even the death of its biggest star, Otis Redding, in an aircraft crash on 10 December 1967; an exit which ensured him immortality and a number of posthumous hits of which *Dock Of The Bay* was the biggest. The truth is, however, that by the end of the decade the sting had gone out of sweaty soul music and the molasses of its smooch had turned sickly. Its greats like Redding and Pickett had taken to revamping Beatle hits. In the Seventies, despite a massive hit by Isaac Hayes with *Shaft*, times were lean. A succession of co-deals with other companies failed and the company was wound up in 1976.

If soul had a King and Queen in the Sixties then they surely must have been James Brown and Aretha Franklin.

Brown was a most extraordinary man. He was, undoubtedly, the most popular and successful black singer of the late Fifties and Sixties. If a white person had caught his act in, say 1963, he might have been tempted to describe him as a black Mick Jagger because of his flamboyant and extrovert stage act. In fact, the reverse would have been nearer the truth, because in his exuberance and choreography Jagger was a white James Brown. Brown took showmanship to a degree never before seen in rock. He had much of Little Richard's theatricality but everything—every movement he made or his band

The Stax house band, Booker T & the MGs (above); backbone of the Memphis Sound and the label's biggest male star Otis Redding moving with typical verve.

made, every step, every stunt, every helper rushing from the wings to wrap a royal cloak around his master's sweating, lathering body – was timed to a second and rehearsed to perfection. Any deviation from the routine by a member of the roadshow, any tardiness in timing, any bum note was punished by a system of fines.

For years, Brown and this meticulous, magnificent, overblown and mind-boggling show were 'underground' at least as far as white folk were concerned. But the success of Motown and Stax in white markets opened up a whole new audience. And anyway, this swaggering, cocky, completely self-confident braggadocio (he came on like a musical Muhammad Ali) was not to be contained; he would have broken through to a world audience one way or another.

Strictly, Brown's was brassy, belting dance-tempo R & B, but, by God, he had the feel and the impact of soul. Or, more accurately, Brown

had soul and then some. He earned his title–Soul Brother No. 1. He broke through into the national charts in 1963 with *Prisoner Of Love* and really made a huge impression two years later with the barely comprehensible–at least to white ears–*Papa's Got A Brand New Bag*. (Mind you, the words didn't matter– viz *Tutti Frutti*–the performance and sound assault did the work.) He followed with other, equally amazing, discs like *I Got You (I Feel Good)* and *It's A Man's Man's Man's World* and proceeded to leave anyone who saw his shows either speechless with energy loss or apoplectic at the mechanical, feelingless roboticism of it all.

He had always been something of a campaigner–a sort of rock hot gospeller–warning kids against taking the same adolescent route as him, towards crime and imprisonment. With the stirrings of black militancy in the late Sixties he came out with an anthem–*Say It Loud (I'm Black And I'm Proud)*–but after a brief flirtation he returned to his more conventional themes as exemplified by *Get Up I Feel Like Being A Sex Machine*. He kept on the road, rich, bizarre, a one-man tornado taking his unique show across America and still earning the tag of 'The Hardest-Working Man In Show Business'.

Aretha Franklin once came up with her own definition of soul. 'If a song's about something I've experienced or that could've happened to me, it's good. But if it's alien to me, I couldn't lend anything to it. Because that's what soul's all about.' And if that's her personal philosophy of soul, it certainly works in her case because she's always been at her best when she seems to be mining her own emotions to project a song–just listen to *Respect*.

Aretha's roots were firmly embedded in gospel being the daughter of a man who might be described as a 'superstar preacher'. So successful was C. L. Franklin and in such demand that Aretha grew up in a great deal of comfort, not to say

Above: *The astonishing James Brown in hyper-energetic action.*
Below: *Aretha Franklin onstage with youthful influence Ray Charles.*

luxury. But there always seems to have been a shadow on her spirit– she had some very difficult times after success which some commentators attribute to tragedy in her childhood–and she veered away from the joyous affirmation of God in her teens. She was drawn towards the gospel style of Ray Charles.

Charles may seem to have been neglected in this narrative, but that is simply because he has so many facets to his talent and his career has covered so many years and taken so many changes in direction, that he's a difficult man to categorise. There's no doubt that he was a strong, vital and influential force in black music. He crossed-over from the strictly black market into the US national charts in 1959 with the great *What'd I Say?* but the splintered, rough-edged quality of that R & B classic was soon eroded. *Hit The Road Jack* two years later was a good song but lacked the raw power of the first. Next he essayed and succeeded, commercially at least, in wedding country to black idiom with songs like *I Can't Stop Loving You* and *Take These Chains From My Heart.* He seemed to be drifting from his roots to a cabaret approach.

Nevertheless, Charles was an important influence on many younger performers and Aretha Franklin was one. She started singing in a more commercial style, like Charles keeping her gospel-taught fervour but allying it to secular themes. She signed to Columbia in 1960 and threw away several years as they tried to find a 'style' for her, not realising that the lady was her own stylist. As an indication of the contrived image that was imposed on her, she had a smallish hit in '61 with a version of *Rock-A-Bye Your Baby With A Dixie Melody*! The trouble was that Aretha was not following her own rules–she was singing things that were alien to her and lending nothing to them.

The change came in 1966 when she joined Atlantic and, he crops up again, Jerry Wexler. Wexler took her to Muscle Shoals (which was fast replacing Stax in Memphis as *the* recording studio in the South and becoming the black answer to country music's Nashville) and let

Dionne Warwick, smooth soul diva.

her sing just the way she felt. The result was *I Never Loved A Man (The Way I Love You)*. Obviously the inspiration of the song's subject matter was within Aretha's experience because the song tingled and crackled and listeners just *knew* that a great lady star was emerging. She quickly ripped out a scorching set of numbers including *Respect, Baby I Love You, Natural Woman* and *(Sweet Sweet Baby) Since You've Been Gone*. She was indisputably the Queen Of Soul.

But her personal life was difficult and she seemed to lose her musical direction. For example, *Say A Little Prayer* was a good number well delivered, but it wasn't, essentially, an *Aretha* song. Almost any good female singer could have had a hit with it and, indeed, the far more sophisticated and polished Dionne Warwick had reached number 4 with it in the States the year before.

Things fell apart rather from 1968 to 1970 although the hits kept coming and Aretha's position as a very special soul performer was never challenged. However, more than a

few longed for the chill that came from first hearing her sing, say, *Natural Woman.*

Motown and Stax, Brown and Franklin, the Supremes and the Four Tops achieved something very important in rock. They gained general acceptance with white artists. They brought their black music into the mainstream of pop. They were now getting chart hits on equal terms with white artists. They were now a strong and evident force in rock's continuing progress. In America black music–in step with a growing black consciousness, politicising and radicalisation–was taking its rightful place.

In Britain, which was still the market leader through the mid-Sixties, black music was wielding unprecedented influence but, interestingly, not the new, assertive, well-buffed products of Detroit and Memphis. The great source of inspiration for most of the British second wave bands was unpolished R & B.

The second-wavers took their lead more from the Rolling Stones than the Beatles and, as a rule of thumb, came from around London

and not the Liverpool/Manchester axis. Most of them looked to a man called Alexis Korner; he was the Boss. He had pioneered R & B virtually single-handed in Britain, he had snubbed blues purists by adding electric guitars to his bands, he had idolised Muddy Waters and proselytised his work in the country. Most important, he had formed a group called Blues Incorporated through which many musicians had passed and used as their training ground. And if the musicians who were going to make such an impact on rock in the second half of the decade had not been formally members of Blues Incorporated, they had certainly jammed with the band at some time.

Among those who had played with Korner were Charlie Watts, Dick Heckstall-Smith, Graham Bond (who later split to form his own influential group, the Organisation, with two ex-Korner-men Jack Bruce and Ginger Baker), Long John Baldry, Paul Jones and Lee Jackson. Charlie Watts, who was Blues Incorporated's regular drummer before joining the Stones full-time, once said of it: 'It boils down to the fact that the first band in the field produces all the leaders'. Very true, especially when you think that two other Stones—Jagger and Brian Jones—also put in stints.

The groups who specialised, at least initially, in R & B included Georgie Fame and the Blue Flames. Georgie (né Clive Powell) had outlived the Larry Parnes stable and ploughed his own, rather solitary furrow, playing an R & B-jazz fusion to a small but enthusiastic audience at London's Flamingo Club. He was an accomplished organist (when keyboards had not really made an impression on mainstream pop) whose voice managed to catch a jazz cadence. It took him a long time to gain acceptance but *Yeh Yeh*—a jazzy number that owed a lot to his heroes Lambert, Hendricks and Ross—made the charts in 1964 and set him on a career that, regrettably, pulled him farther and farther from his original path.

This was the story for many such bands. Manfred Mann, for example, also found twin roots in jazz—Mann

Four Britons, Dick Heckstall-Smith (top), Alexis Korner (above left), Graham Bond (above right), Long John Baldry led the blues revival in the '60s.

himself had been a jazz pianist in his native South Africa—and R & B. They toured the small beat clubs playing R & B standards like *Smokestack Lightning* to enthusiastic if cliquey audiences. Two singles flopped but a third (*5-4-3-2-1* which was, for a while, the signature tune to the hugely popular TV show *Ready Steady Go*) made the Top 5 in 1964. It retained a bluesy flavour but this was soon lost as the group launched upon a series of very successful hits which were pure, good pop.

Paul Jones (né Pond and ex-Blues

Georgie Fame (top left), Yardbirds with Clapton looking uncomfortable (top right), Manfred Mann and the wayward Jeff Beck were part of the UK blues boom.

Incorporated) was a good-looking lead singer and his face seems to have pulled the band inexorably towards the chart treadmill with offerings like *Doo Wah Diddy Diddy*, *Sha La La* and *Pretty Flamingo* which owed more to the Brill Building of the early Sixties than British beat of mid-decade.

A similar story is true of the Yardbirds. They started as a blues-based band and boasted a fine guitarist in Eric Clapton but their first two R & B-inspired singles didn't make it so they turned to rather more obviously commercial material. Their third disc, *For Your Love*, was a good song, unusual for 1965 and written by Graham Gouldman who also gave hit songs to the Hollies and Herman's Hermits and turned up in the Seventies as part of the spectacularly successful 10cc. But *For Your Love* was not blues and so Clapton quit for more like-minded company.

The Yardbirds obviously felt the loss keenly and approached a top session guitarist called Jimmy Page who turned the gig down. He recommended Jeff Beck who was drafted in and proved to be an accomplished, occasionally brilliant lead. The Yardbirds continued successfully turning out some of the most unusual and experimental singles of the period–*Heart Full Of Soul*, *Evil Hearted You/Still I'm Sad*, *Shape Of Things* and *Over Under Sideways Down*. In '66 Paul Samwell-Smith, the bass player, left and Page was persuaded to join as co-lead guitarist with Beck (rhythm guitarist, Chris Dreja, taking up bass duties) but Beck experienced a breakdown on an American tour, quit and Page took up the strain.

The story of the Yardbirds high-lights one important trend that developed in the middle years of the decade–the rise of the guitarist as hero. Now, not only were groups attracting their own followings but individual lead guitarists within them were commanding the loyalty of fanatical devotees. And these were not just pubescent girls who selected their fave members because of their prettiness or 'gear eyes' or whatever, but young males who watched the 'axeman's' every move and noted every change to, improvement on and refinement of equipment.

Guitar and amplifier technology improved rapidly to keep pace with the increasing demands for new guitar effects, greater volume and crisper clarity. The technique of the best guitarists always seemed to be one jump ahead of it and soon the lead guitarist–previously just an integral but discernible part of the group sound–stepped forward to offer solo breaks in the middle of numbers–which were getting longer to accommodate them–or add telling, highly individual licks to the basic foundation laid down by drums, bass and rhythm guitars.

The three lead guitarists who served time with the Yardbirds were the first generation of guitar heroes. Each went on to greater acclaim–Clapton, of course, constituted one third of the world's first 'supergroup', Cream; Page was part of one of the Seventies dominant rock outfits, Led Zeppelin, and Beck maintained his reputation as an ace despite a series of personal and professional difficulties that beset him over the following years. If anything, his seeming inability to coalesce with others successfully enhanced rather than diminished his musical mystique.

When Clapton left the Yardbirds, he went to an oasis of electric blues music among the pop and to one of the other–after Korner's Blues Incorporated–great breeding grounds of young British musicians– John Mayall's Bluesbreakers. Mayall's devotion to his beloved music attracted the brightest and the best, most of whom played with him for a short time–say a year–and then were either tempted away by offers from established bands or split, together or severally, to form their own outfits. Renowned alumni of the Bluesbreakers include John McVie, Peter Green and Mick

Fleetwood who formed Fleetwood Mac; Clapton and Jack Bruce who formed Cream; drummers Aynsley Dunbar and Keef Hartley both of whom founded their own bands; Hughie Flint who teamed up later with Tom McGuinness, ex-Manfred Mann; and Mick Taylor who took up Brian Jones's mantle in the Stones.

While the first wave of British beat in the Sixties broke the ground and was fun, it had little lasting impact, apart, of course, from the Beatles and the Stones. The Mersey groups who had stomped south in such hordes in '63 had their hits and disbanded; most of their members– the golden days of fame over– returned home to their jobs. The bigger groups with American success–notably the Hollies, Dave Clark 5 and Herman's Hermits– plugged on in their unpretentious way, turning out the pleasantest of pop hits. Others like the Honeycombs, the Zombies, Unit 4+2, the Nashville Teens, Freddie and the Dreamers, the Fortunes had their moments and sank virtually without trace. The groups or their individual members contributed little input to the progression of the music.

The same cannot be said of those who followed. We have seen that the main impetus for R & B-based music came from groups living in or around London but one band broke this and other rules. First they came roaring out of Newcastle–boozing,

shouting, barn-storming Geordies. And next, their first huge hit, and only second release, was the longest single anyone had ever heard. In the days of the 2½ minute A-side, this magnum opus lasted fully four minutes. Furthermore, it was a hit against the trend. Some of us knew it as a bluesy folk song we'd sung, to slightly different words, in coffee shops and cellar clubs but this band had added an incredible, wailing organ and the singer was simply bursting with his effort to growl it out. *The House Of The Rising Sun*–a most magnificent single– deservedly shot to number 1 in Britain and the States. The Animals had erupted into the Sixties.

They never equalled that first effort, of course. It just wasn't possible. But their subsequent releases, although increasingly poppy, still retained traces of that spectacular anger that singer Eric Burdon let fly. He never really fitted in as your conventional pop star. For a start he could never master the art of lip-synching. He went on *Top Of The Pops*–or some similar TV pop show that demanded the artists mime to a recording of their hit–and his lips were always out of phase with the track! The trouble with Burdon was that he was a black man in a white skin; he sang as he felt and he felt differently every time and so he sang differently!

The hits followed–*I'm Crying*,

'The isle is full of noises'; the many sounds of Britain: (top left to right) blues godfather John Mayall; vulgar pop of the Troggs; early supergroup Traffic. Below: boozy blues-shouters the Animals (Burdon front centre, Chandler behind him and Price at right) and the destructive Move with Roy Wood (second from right).

Don't Let Me Be Misunderstood, We've Gotta Get Out Of This Place, It's My Life, etc.–but the band was riven with internal changes. Alan Price–the man who had arranged *Rising Sun* and contributed that distinctive organ work–left to set up his own outfit, scored early with a tremendous version of *I Put A Spell On You* and settled into a long and varied career. Burdon went through several incarnations with various forms of Animals, including a successful psychedelic phase and Chas Chandler, the beefy bass player, went into management, discovered Jimi Hendrix (and, later, Slade) and thus gave the world a guitar genius.

In step with the rise of the virtuoso guitarist, came the ascent of the rock songwriter. Among other things the Beatles had pioneered was members writing specifically for their own group. This broke the previous stranglehold of the producer imposing upon the artist a song *he* thought would be a hit whether or not it suited the performer. Now some young British songwriters of

97

note began to emerge; they wrote hits for their groups and, frequently, the subject matter transcended the intention. The intention being, at least hitherto, to produce a saleable commodity and never mind what it contained. Some young writers started excavating their own experience and that of their contemporaries for subjects. In short, they were doing in London and about London kids what Brian Wilson was doing in California about Californian kids.

Two groups in particular were lucky enough to boast writers of considerable, and expanding, talent. The Who had Pete Townshend and the Kinks had Ray Davies.

'The kids are alright', Townshend had said on a Who single in 1966. The kids to whom he was referring in particular were those exotic effete, narcissistic creatures called the Mods. Mods were sharp dressers, wore their hair short and neat—against the trend—appeared entirely homogenous, very nearly asexual (the boys wore eye make-up and sometimes discreet pan on their faces), rode scooters (as opposed to the motorbikes of their hated and oft-fought enemies the Rockers), popped pills, mostly uppers to get them through their all-night raves, and followed the Who and, to a lesser degree, the Small Faces with an unswerving devotion.

Townshend was their voice. If you must, he was the closest anyone ever came to being their poet. He articulated the fact that they were inarticulate with *I Can't Explain* and later, the great anthem, *My Generation* in which our hero stutters at adult authority 'why don't you all f-f-f-fade away?' He did exactly what he claimed in that song—'I'm just talking 'bout my generation'. And his generation, as he pointed out so tellingly in *Substitute*, were like him—'I was born with a plastic spoon in my mouth'.

The inner tensions between the members of the group—Pete Townshend, Roger Daltrey, an unusually exciting vocalist, John Entwistle, a stoical, rock-steady bassist, and Keith Moon, a certifiable drummer of quite phenomenal

Mods and Rockers: the great Mod heroes were the Who (top) and the Small Faces (below). The great Mod enemies were greasy, leather-clad, bike-riding rockers. Mods preferred scooters and few looked as uncomfortable as this mini-skirted dollybird.

ferocity – gave the performances a crackling excitement coupled with a sense of the unpredictable. It seemed as likely, during one period, that the group would assault one another as soon as launch one of their much-publicised attacks upon their equipment in which Townshend would smash his guitar into the stage and then plunge its neck through his speakers. There was undoubtedly some well-played hype in this – the Who's managers were very shrewd with the media and convinced several people for a while that the Who were Pop Art – but there was also genuine anger and agony, especially from Townshend who seems to have been bedevilled by internal demons.

The Who, like the Stones, just seemed to grow in stature and influence as the decades changed. (Indeed, as good a way as any to start an argument in the late Seventies was to speculate which of the two *really* deserved the title of The Best Rock & Roll Band In The World!) Townshend developed from his early songs – which were finely-brushed miniatures – to the much wider canvas of *Tommy*, the first and only true rock opera. He expanded the bounds of rock, remained totally committed to it and thrust it into a new dimension.

Ray Davies trod a similar path. He seemed to have the same promise but never quite managed to pull his most ambitious projects off. The Kinks started conventionally enough in 1964 revamping *Long Tall Sally* for their first, unsuccessful, single. Another flop followed and then came *You Really Got Me* which went to number 1 in Britain and into the Top 10 in the States. It was simple, almost cretinous. Ray Davies sneered it out, a look of distaste curling his fastidious lip, as if outraged by the rubbish he was singing, the stupid name of his group and the utterly ridiculous pink hunting jacket he'd been forced to wear.

He followed this with what was essentially exactly the same record but with a different title, *All Day And All Of The Night*. Next came *Tired Of Waiting For You*, not terribly different and delivered in an even more bored and languid voice, but it still got to number 1, their second in three records. Things dropped off slightly after that for a couple of records. Then came a rather odd number called *See My Friend* which seemed to have the vaguest homosexual undertones . . . no, couldn't have, not in 1965. There was another little oddity called *A Well Respected Man* which did well in the States but not in Britain. It was about hypocrisy, how behind the facade of respectability, lurked dark and corrupt forces.

Davies' songs were changing rapidly and dealing in subjects that had previously been outside the pop 'tunesmith's' bailiwick. Next he scored bang on target with a delicious piece of pop satire – *Dedicated Follower Of Fashion* – that debunked the rampant narcissism of the Mods, Carnaby Street and the British fashion boom. This was followed by a remarkable run of 'poperettas' (ghastly word but it makes the point, I hope), each chronicling a fragment of life and society – *Sunny Afternoon* about the aristocracy in decline, *Dead End Street* crashing right to the other end of the class spectrum, *Waterloo Sunset* a finely-cut little cameo of working class kids in love in a city, full of flashes of insight, an unalloyed delight and finished with a scrapbook song *Autumn Almanac* that dripped heavy with nostalgia.

There were other hits after this but that streak was astonishing and, perhaps, creatively exhausting. Davies went on to essay the sort of works Townshend had pioneered with *Tommy* producing concept albums like *Village Green Preservation Society* and other such ventures but always seemed to fall just short of success.

The middle Sixties were enriched by the efforts of people like Davies and Townshend, the continuing brilliance of Lennon and McCartney, the increasing maturity of Jagger and Richard. A turning point, another one, was coming. But this time it originated not in Britain, powerhouse of so much new in the decade, but 6,000 miles to the west, in California.

Ray Davies (bottom) and his group the Kinks with brother Dave on the left.

Bob Dylan

The Age of ROCK

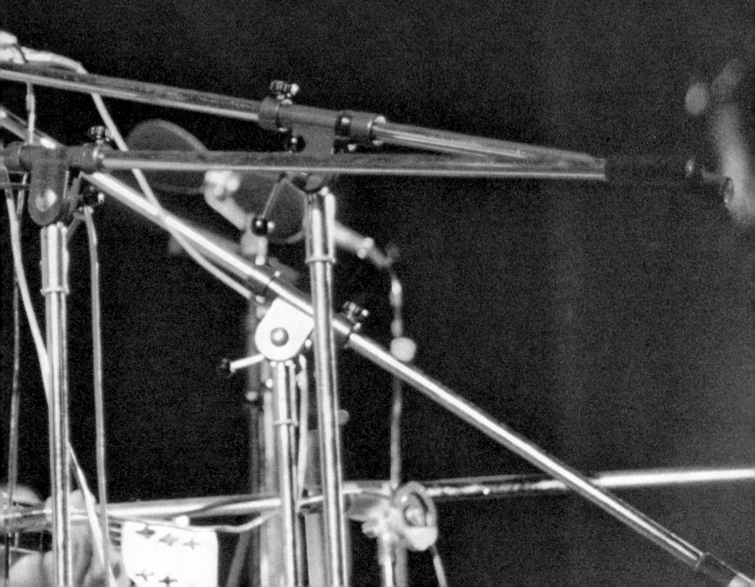

The Age of ROCK
1967-1970

The music had changed fundamentally and in many ways. It was, by 1966, no longer simply pop – the best of it had become rock. Rock – it's a harder, stronger, more firmly-rooted word than pop. It denotes permanence and history. And, at its most superficial, that was the difference between rock and pop. Pop fizzed and burst very quickly. Rock stayed.

One of the most significant pointers to the new age of rock was that not only had the music changed, but other people's perception of it had altered as well.

For example, what is this man referring to? And where did it appear? '(It) is expressively unusual for its lugubrious music, but harmonically it is . . . most intriguing, with its chains of pandiotonic clusters. . . .' He's referring to a modest song entitled *This Boy*, written by Paul McCartney and John Lennon. (It was the B-side of *I Want To Hold Your Hand*.) And he's writing about it in *The Times* of London!

What? Are we talking about rock & roll here? 'Shoobie-doobie-wah-wah-doo!' and 'Dooby-dum-dooby-doo-dum-dow?' and 'She loves you-

The Beach Boys were the Beatles' greatest rivals in the '60s.

yeah-yeah-yeah' and 'Tutti-frutti-o-rutti'?

The very same. But now – and this is as early as 1963 – Lennon and McCartney are being compared to Beethoven and Schubert and the man from *The Times* goes on to say: 'Harmonic interest is typical of their quicker songs too, and one gets the impression that they think simultaneously of harmony and melody, so firmly are the major tonic sevenths and ninths built into their tunes, and the flat submediant key switches, so natural is the Aeolian cadence at the end of *Not A Second Time* (the chord progression which ends Mahler's *Song Of The Earth*)'.

Dear God! Are we talking about the four 'happy little rockers' whose expressed ambition was 'to end up sort of famous'? Well, some of us are. The Beatles and their ilk wrought that. As the man from *The Times* concluded: 'They have brought a distinctive and exhilarating flavour into a genre of music that was in danger of ceasing to be music at all'.

Beach Boys (left to right) Dennis, Al Jardine, Brian, Carl and Mike Love.

Blimey! That needs some thinking about. It would appear that in a few years the music, *our* music had become . . . er . . . *Valid, Meaningful, Worthy Of Study And Consideration.*

It was all down to the Beatles of course. But that Brian Wilson didn't help. He started getting ideas above his station in 1966.

Through 1965 and 1966 the Beach Boys and Beatles had recognised in each other friendly rivals who would act as a spur to greater things. The air during those years was alive with new music. The Beatles had pushed songwriting and recording forward in very late '65 with the, then, extraordinary

Rubber Soul (even the punny title raised startled eyebrows). Alongside such charmingly romantic numbers as *Michelle* and *In My Life* could be found such an abrupt departure from the general subject matter for pop songs as *Norwegian Wood*.

This is songwriting pared to the bone. A boy and a girl; a boy trying to pull a girl. So what's new about that? Not a thing except that the song is so damned oblique, everything is hinted at, it teases the mind. The girl is single, free and very, very hip. Her house is stark and modern and individual. He is bewildered, a sexual aggressor who has lost the initiative.

They drink and they talk into the small hours. He's sure they'll end up in bed. She gives every indication that this is the inevitable conclusion to the evening. Suddenly she says: 'It's time for bed'. But what happened? 'She told me she worked in the morning.' His look of frustration and disappointment must have been marked because she 'started to laugh'. Or was she a sexual tantaliser who got her kicks from leading lads on and then dashing their hopes? He 'crawled off to sleep in the bath'. In the morning she was gone and her lovely, clean-edged, Scandinavian-style home – 'Isn't it good?/Norwegian wood' – is deserted. And what does he do? 'So I built a fire/Isn't it good?/Norwegian wood.'

We'd never heard anything like this before. Never. It was obviously about sexual predation and sexual frustration and, ultimately, arson used as a weapon of sexual revenge. It *was* about all that, wasn't it? You couldn't quite be sure because it was so elliptical and in those days we were used to understanding every song in every detail. (Most were so undemanding that this was not difficult!)

Norwegian Wood started us thinking anew about popular songs. It was another milestone. Richard Goldstein in his book *The Poetry Of Rock* claims that 'The new music starts here'. It's a big statement to pin on one song. Too big, really, even if the song did mark the first time the sitar had been used in western popular music. But with *Rubber Soul* the Beatles DID serve notice that they were hustling rock along in directions it had never previously been.

In California, Brian Wilson was both inspired and depressed by these innovations. He had dropped out of touring and performing with the group, a first indication of the increasing reclusion that was to remove him from the world over the next few years. He now concentrated his considerable creative energies on writing and producing for his brothers. But he was aware that the pressures on him from without were to continue the gold disc formula of success that had

marked the past few years. The public – at least in America – and his record company loved *California Girls* and others like it and wanted more of the same.

Wilson's internal drive was to race ahead with Lennon and McCartney, finding out just what could be done. He was no longer interested in being the King of Surf Music, and he wasn't going to churn out the hits just because they were copper-bottomed guaranteed hits. 'I've never written one note or word of music simply because I think it will make money,' he declared later.

He took himself into a solitary world. The world of the recording studio and attempted to direct what was in his head onto tape. The result was an album called *Pet Sounds*. In so doing he produced a masterwork of rock. The subject matter of the songs wasn't all that different; love yearned for and love lost still played an important part. It was the setting, the structure, the sound, the arrangements of the songs that were so new.

In Britain it was instantly recognised as being important. As Richard Williams later said in *Melody Maker*: 'It was immediately obvious that Brian had travelled further than anyone in popular music, extended its scope beyond a fantasist's wildest dreams. *Pet Sounds* was a massive elaboration on the more interesting aspects of his earlier work; the harmonies were denser, structured in myriad layers, achingly lush, yet . . .pure'.

'The words assumed a newly mature view of emotional relationships . . .' (exception can be taken to this statement. The words still betray a teen's naiveté – 'Wouldn't it be nice if we were older/Then we wouldn't have to wait so long' exhibits none of the lyrical advances made by *Norwegian Wood* and the other best-known songs – *God Only Knows*, *Here Today*, *Caroline, No* for example – are not much more profound.)

'But,' Williams continues, correctly, 'it was the arrangements that blew minds. Brian had used a bewildering array of resources, more than Spector and the equally

iconoclastic Burt Bacharach combined.'

Britain embraced the album. Britain – used to Lennon and McCartney – knew what Brian Wilson was attempting, understood that there were no rules any longer in rock and recognised that Wilson had extended the frontiers yet again. In America the record was ignored by the public. It's difficult to know why. In fact, there's no logical explanation. Perhaps it was simply that this surf bum had had the effrontery to consider himself a serious musician. Perhaps the American public was suffering from an uncharacteristic loss of self-confidence – the invaders, the Beatles and their ilk, could pull off musical ground-breaking but home-grown pop groups like the Beach Boys just weren't up to it. If the latter *is* the case, it is just the sort of inferiority complex that the British had experienced before the Beatles had demonstrated its patent falseness.

Anyway, *Pet Sounds* bombed in the States. Even Brian's severest critic – and yet, ironically, strongest supporter – came out on the side of the record. This was Murry Wilson, the brothers' father, with whom Brian had had a difficult, tense, often rather bitter relationship during his years of fame. Murry, himself an unsuccessful songwriter whose frustrated personal ambitions had been channelled through his sons' careers, declared: '*Pet Sounds* is a masterpiece of accomplishment for Brian, even though the public doesn't realise it . . . Brian took a lot of the masters, approached the music in his own way, and put a rock & roll beat to it. He even got Stephen Foster in there – phrases that we used to sing when he was a baby, you know? And it's twisted around with his beautiful approach to rock & roll, and his bass root; his bass root figurations of the bass guitar are quite fantastic!

'*Pet Sounds* has been copied, chewed up, renewed – Negro artists have used it in band arrangements, commercials have used it. Every day you hear a commercial that has a Beach Boys sound in back of it'.

Murry Wilson was right in suggesting that *Pet Sounds* was influential even though, in the States at least, it was not a commercial success. The perceptive–on both sides of the Atlantic–realised it was pioneering new musical territory and felt liberated by it. However, as Marilyn, Brian Wilson's wife, told *Rolling Stone* years later: 'Pet Sounds was not a big hit. That really hurt him badly, he couldn't understand it. It's like, why put your heart and soul into something?'

Pet Sounds was so extraordinary that Wilson could have been excused for bowing out–at least temporarily–after it. But he had something else, something more, he needed to produce. He was fighting with a song. It is said that he intended it for *Pet Sounds* but couldn't get it right. Then he rejected it as Beach Boys' material and thought that only a black vocal group could handle it. Later, apparently, he was tempted to give up on it altogether. But, thank God, he persevered. 'I wanted to see what I was capable of doing,' he said later. 'I tried to reach a personal pinnacle of writing, arranging and producing with *Good Vibrations*.'

He succeeded. We had *never* heard a single like it. It was the most curiously structured thing that had ever hit our ears. It sounded like it was composed of different 'movements' that merged and mingled and separated and remixed again. And we'd never heard an instrument like the one that wailed at the end. (It was a theremin.) And we'd never heard a vocal arrangement quite so complex. We didn't quite know where the voices ended and the instruments began and vice versa. And the words seemed disjointed. When you saw them cold on the page they made no sense. Look: 'I hear the sound of a gentle word on the wind that lifts her perfume through the air'. But when they were wedded to that other-wordly music they conveyed a mysterious, sensual impression.

With *Good Vibrations* Brian Wilson had crashed through another rock frontier. This time the public in both America and Britain recognised it and Brian was satisfied that he had succeeded. But there

had been a great deal of trepidation along the way.

'It took six months to make,' he told *Rolling Stone* in 1976. 'We recorded the very first part of it at Gold Star recording studio, then we took it to a place called Western, then to Sunset Sound, and then to Columbia. We wanted to experiment using four different studio sounds–every studio has its own marked sound. Using the four studios had a lot to do with the way the final record sounded. So it took

After Brian retired into seclusion Bruce Johnston (far left) stepped in.

quite a while.' (It reportedly cost a lot too. An unprecedented $16,000! No single had had so many resources, such a long time, such a huge budget lavished on it.)

Lyrically, Brian was aware of the contrast between what he described as the 'extra-sensory perception' of

The burly Brian whose many problems forced him to leave stage work.

the good vibrations of the title and the extremely sensual, erotic feel of the words. He was going for something quite new. It was a sound montage combining the mystical with the sexual.

'*Good Vibrations*,' he said, 'was advanced rhythm & blues music, but we took a great risk. As a matter of fact, I didn't think it was going to make it because of the complexity, but apparently people accepted it very well. They felt it had a naturalness to it, it flowed.'

Frankly, it left us—the unwitting recipients—slightly stunned and rather breathless. And we were only listening to it! What did it do to Wilson's musical rivals? Some must have felt like giving up. Rock was now a whole new ballgame. It was no longer about 2½ minutes of

hummability that would sell. Now the clever-ass critics could bring classical analysis to bear on popular music and almost make it stick convincingly.

Many musicians, of course, were inspired by *Good Vibrations* and *Pet Sounds* and rose to their challenge.

While Brian had been in the studio making them, the Beatles had also been busy. At the end of 1966 they came up with their by now–annual album, *Revolver*. They had not been sitting still, there were more strides forwards on this. George Harrison followed up the promise of the sitar on *Norwegian Wood* by offering a song based on an Indian raga called *Love You To* that puzzled us considerably at first because our ears were just not attuned to its rhythms. McCartney produced a blinder in *Eleanor Rigby*. (It was by now obvious that, increasingly, Lennon

and McCartney were writing separately and only collaborating at a late stage of a song, offering each other help when they got stuck on their own. By and large, McCartney's songs were lighter, more romantic, occasionally mawkish. Lennon's were tending to be grittier, raunchier, harder-edged and occasionally invoked some most unusual phrase-making.) There was a rather bitter song of breaking up called *For No One*, a nursery-rhyme (but with concealed undertones and symbolism?) in *Yellow Submarine*, a eulogy to *Dr Robert*. *Revolver* was a constantly-changing kaleidoscope. You just could not predict what would be coming next.

And, furthermore, in 1966 you just did not understand the two tracks that finished the two sides. The closing cut on side two was called *Tomorrow Never Knows*. Nothing had prepared your ear for it. You

came out of the rocky, brassy *Got To Get You Into My Life*, the foot involuntarily beating time, and then there was this harsh, strident, ugly sound.

There were odd snatches of seemingly unrelated music – scratching strings and whining electrical screams intercut with symphonic chords that crashed in and then disappeared. It was like running along the dial of a radio and catching brief snips of foreign stations, hearing an orchestra here, an announcer there, some drama in an unrecognised language, a screech, a roar, a crackle of static.

Once over the initial aural shock, and groping desperately for something familiar, something upon which the ear could latch and the mind grasp and comprehend you picked out the words that Lennon was – well – singing? You queried it because he sounded like he was vocalising through a comb and

tissue paper. And he was saying the most extraordinary things: 'Turn off your mind, relax and float downstream/It is not dying/It is not dying/Lay down all thoughts/Surrender to the void . . .'

Couple these verbal puzzles to that unearthly 'music' and you got an aural picture of the utmost bleakness. It was discordant, menacing. These were not the happy Moptops we knew and loved.

At the end of side one there was a similarly enigmatic song called *She Said She Said*. The music was more accessible. It was hard, harsh but nowhere near as disconnected as *Tommorrow Never Knows*. But the words were disturbingly unreachable. What do they mean by: 'She said "I know what it's like to be dead . . ."/And she's making me feel like I've never been born'?

And: 'I said "Who put all those things in your head?/Things that

*The Fabs in psychedelia; the glories and hubris of '67 and post-*Sgt Pepper.

make me feel like I'm mad?"' '

Indeed, that was a question we could level at our lovely Beatles. Who DID put all those things in your head?

A good question, but we didn't know at the time that it was wrong in one respect. We should not have been asking who but what? What put all those things in your head?

The brief answer is drugs. Or rather one drug – LSD. Lysergic acid diethylamide is a hallucinogenic drug. It had been known for years before it gathered its cult following; Dr Albert Hofman had synthesized it way back in 1938 but did not realise its effect on the mind until he took some by accident about five years later.

The existence of hallucinogenic drugs had been known and studied

Can this be THE Robert Plant of Led Zep? It is, in '67 and as 'leader of the Midlands Flower People' he parades outside a court.

for years. They had been taken and incorporated into religious observance by the natives of Mexico and other Central and Southern American areas. Aldous Huxley – preoccupied by mysticism in his later years – had written about a hallucinogenic 'trip' in *The Doors Of Perception* and an increasing interest had started to develop in LSD and other drugs that seemed to be – in the phrases of the time – mind expanding or perception altering.

Clinical tests had been carried out since about the mid-Fifties in America and it was thought at one time that the LSD 'trip' produced the symptoms of schizophrenia in controllable form and that a study of LSD trips could contribute to the cure of schizophrenia. It was even used in an attempt to cure alcoholics

and as a part of psychotherapy by some psychiatrists.

LSD produced the most extraordinary mental and perceptual experiences, and some people thought they were the key to unlocking the subconscious. It was claimed that acid (as it was widely known) obliterated the ego, transforming the taker into a better, sweeter, more loving, more beauty-conscious, more creative person. The apostle of LSD was a Harvard man called Dr Timothy Leary who strongly advocated it and, together with a psychologist colleague named Alpert (who had been sacked from the university for giving his charges acid) he set up the International Federation for Internal Freedom in Mexico. Leary told his acolytes – and, indeed, anyone who would listen; there were many in those days – that 'It becomes necessary to go out of our minds in order to use our heads'.

A lot of exaggerated claims were

made for and against LSD. Those in favour told you it would change your life and alter the way you looked at society. Some said that it could actually change society, make it a better place to live. Some promoted it as simply a happy drug, liquid sunshine and carried out a mission by slipping it to unwary victims.

R. D. Laing, British campaigner against psychiatric orthodoxy, author of *The Politics Of Experience* and once described by *Esquire* magazine as 'Pop-Shrink, Rebel, Yogi, Philosopher-King', was in California in 1966 when the word about acid's 'magic' qualities was being spread. In a 1978 interview he recalled that 300,000 trips had been manufactured – quite legally then – and distributed in San Francisco's Haight-Ashbury District over a period of three days!

Others, like Ken Kesey and his Merry Pranksters, were also proselytising acid, handing it out like GIs distributing chocolate to liberated Continental kids in the Second World War. In the general euphoria nobody knew or thought of the consequences. It was, as Laing has said, 'an extraordinary thing to do. But it was the way some people were thinking at that time. They believed in a chemical revolution; that the human race had gone psychotic, that we were racing towards a nuclear confrontation that would be the end of everything, and that a stabilising chemical would help us to regain our balance'.

For a while LSD poured, unchecked, around San Francisco and California and seeped outwards towards New York and London. It was not, however, simply 'happy juice'. As it spread out of the laboratories and psychiatric clinics it became obvious that LSD's effects on the brain were not just charming and whimsical. Increasingly the newspapers carried reports of young people dying under its influences—a recurring scare was of 'trippers' thinking they could fly and launching themselves off roofs—and soon LSD was recognised as a dangerous drug and declared illegal in the States and Britain.

Not that outlawing it meant any diminution in its manufacture or use. Quite the opposite. Illegality only granted it an added cachet for the young.

The celebrated British columnist Cassandra (William Connor) wrote in the *Daily Mirror* in June 1966: 'LSD is a clear, tasteless, odourless liquid that is easy to make, cheap, and convenient to use.

'By pouring a few drops on a lump of sugar you may take temporary leave of this world and all its conventional measurements and sensations and experience an unknown part of the mind that has never been fully explored before . . . It is the prince of the chemistry of madness and hallucination'. LSD was, he asserted, 'The stuff of dreams as only madmen know'.

It is unlikely that Cassandra ever tried LSD—he was 56 when he wrote that and would die the next year—but he was perceptive enough to see what made it different from other drugs and therefore, in his

Captain Beefheart who was born with the less intriguing name of Don Van Vliet and pushed forward rock frontiers.

opinion, more dangerous. This was 'the introduction and spread of a type of drug that has an intellectual and almost religious backing'. And in a time of exploration and questing by the young, those two properties—the 'intellectual' and the 'religious'—made it very attractive indeed. (Incidentally, Cassandra and others who warned against the dangers of LSD were considered as extremely boring old fools by the youth of the day. In the event they were far nearer the truth than Leary and his 'scientific'/'mystic' brethren.)

People like the Beatles were looking for the novel, the profound. They were young, unbelievably rich, had experienced just about everything that the sensual imagination could invent or enjoyed everything that money could buy. Now they were seeking something deeper. They were trapped in a spiritual vacuum. George Harrison looked to the East for his philosophy and so, for a while, did the others. But why do that when there was

'instant bliss', synthetic nirvana, blinding revelation for a mere 30/- (£1.50) per sugar lump dose?

The Beatles first encountered LSD in 1965 when a dentist (was it *Dr Robert*?) introduced John and George to it, who soon were happily dropping the stuff and revelling in its effects. Next they wanted to propagandise it, but had to be discreet. They could not just come out straight, call a press conference and exhort their fans to 'Turn On, Tune In, and Drop Out' as Leary was doing. So they wrote songs that attempted, clumsily at first and then with growing expertise, to re-create, aurally, the mystical experience of an acid trip.

I shall not attempt to describe this; Peter Laurie in his book, *Drugs – Medical, Psychological and Social Facts*, tells us what the drug does to the brain and then sums it up in this way: 'A physical analogy for this ''mind enhancing'' drug would be spraying salt water inside a television set'. He also notes a particular phenomenon of acid: ' . . . the transference of impressions from one sense to another. Thus LSD subjects can hear clapping as showers of sparks, or feel a mild electric shock on the forearm as a bolt through the whole body'.

This phenomenon–the altering of perception–is important because it accounts for the many bizarre words and associations in many of the songs of the time. Thus: 'Turn off the mind, relax and float downstream' and, particularly, the importance of colours in songs because, under acid, colours could be 'felt'.

In late '66 *Good Vibrations* and some of the songs on *Revolver* delighted but puzzled us. We did not understand them at all. In the most incredible year of 1967 we were to comprehend precisely and look back on some other songs with a knowing smile. Because we realised at last that there was a growing rock elite, a jet set who mingled together when they happened to be on America's West Coast or passing through London, and who shared experiences together and told each other of their newfound knowledge and revelations. They introduced each other to their pet mystics and gurus, recommended savants and books full of esoteric learning. And when they weren't together they made their records which contained code words that, if you understood them, made you smile at a secret shared. Before 1967, acid and its effects were limited to a golden few who whispered of it and gave it names and euphemisms and then incorporated these into their songs. In 1967 acid was common knowledge and in common use. And that, principally, is what made 1967 one of the most extraordinary years in modern history.

1967 was amazing because, for one glorious summer, we really *did* believe that all you needed *was* love. And that love was everything. And that love was going to change the world.

By 'we' I mean every young person who bought a kaftan, or wore beads, or hung a tinkling Indian bell around the neck, or played Scott McKenzie's *San Francisco (Flowers In Your Hair)*. 'We' included those who dropped acid, stuck flowers into the barrels of the rifles of soldiers guarding the

Scott McKenzie faded, like flowers, after his '67 anthem San Francisco.

Pentagon, attended Be-Ins and Love-Ins, coupled gently under the stars and to the strains of Procul Harum's *A Whiter Shade Of Pale*. Or wandered around Monterey, at pop's first great festival and tribal gathering, stoned on pot or merely the 'natural high' of being young, loved and loving and accompanied by music.

It didn't matter that, for example, a London kid hadn't done all or any of those because this was a collective experience. As Jerry Rubin–later a revolutionary, yippie and defendant in the notorious Chicago 7 court said in 1978: 'You really felt that everyone on earth was your brother and sister. And that you *could* change the world . . . In the Sixties we said 'love'–thinking that a joint or LSD or saying the word could produce love . . .'

It was a time for idealism, anti-materialism. A time for forging an alternative society based on sharing. The centre of this new society was that area of San Francisco formed around Haight Street and Ashbury Street. Here young middle-class drop-out kids flocked to smoke dope, barter at the 'head shops', make leather-work gee-gaws, drift from one sexual encounter to another and put on their best Madras cotton gladrags at the weekend to share in the communal experience of youth tribalism at one of San Francisco's vast ballrooms.

The dance halls were very important to the explosion of music in–and later out of–San Francisco in the mid- to late Sixties. In 1965 an arts/community group calling themselves the Family Dog started putting on dances–featuring the Lovin' Spoonful from New York as well as 'Frisco's homegrown bands like the Warlocks (who would

Summer '67: a love-in where LA flower children undoubtedly dance to the music of Procol Harum (bottom).

become the Grateful Dead), the Charlatans, Jefferson Airplane– at the city's Longshoremen's Hall.

Ralph J. Gleason, writing in *Rolling Stone* in 1968, called these 'the first adult rock dances' and considered them significant because they allowed the audience to dance, to be a part of the performance, to express physically what the music meant to them. The pop shows of previous years had been 'concerts', parades of performers who stood their turn before a seated, controlled audience. However much the girls watching them squirmed and squealed and, according to reports, relieved themselves sexually and in other ways ('There wasn't a dry seat in the house,' ran the joke), there was still a barrier between the band and the audience. The audience was supervised by stewards who equated dancing in the aisles with hooliganism.

But, starting with the Family Dog's events–which became, in the parlance of the day, 'happenings'– there occurred what Gleason described as the 'San Francisco dance renaissance'. These were followed by a benefit held by the San Francisco Mime Troupe to raise funds. It was organised by Bill Graham who, over the next few years, was to be a central figure in the SF scene. He soon graduated to hiring–and then running fulltime– the Fillmore Auditorium which became a mecca for groups.

Looking back on those two years Gleason concluded: '. . . the Fillmore and Graham have brought an incredible list of great and important music and performers to San Francisco. Its presentations have been, in effect, a crash course in American popular music without which San Francisco and (to the heavy extent that San Francisco has set the pace for the rest of the country) the US would have been a great deal poorer culturally'.

The Fillmore concerts, the local bands, the communards on Haight-Ashbury, the acid that wasn't illegal until late '66, the pot, the posters

Politics and rock merged in opposition to the Vietnam war. Yippie-clown Jerry Rubin arrives for a hearing on the '68 Chicago riots; West Coast bands like Jefferson Airplane (with Grace Slick) stirred awareness in their audience.

advertising the dances, the artists like Robert Crumb, the paper started in November '67 and called *Rolling Stone* that chronicled the scene – all of these helped create a San Franciscan community. And binding it together was the music.

The musicians had been around for a while. In 1963 there was a band called Mother McCree's Uptown Jug Champions. By '65 a nucleus of that struggling outfit became the Warlocks and the members were dropping acid with Ken Kesey and playing his Trips Festival at the Fillmore. The acid started affecting the music. It started getting strung out, it lost its conventional rock structure and splintered. This was the start of West Coast Acid Rock.

Soon San Francisco had wrested the title of Music Capital of the World from London. Jefferson Airplane, formed in '65, were recording by the next year – the album *Jefferson Airplane Takes Off* – and were the first group of the new wave to reach the charts. *Takes Off* sold gold. The next album *Surrealistic Pillow* (even the titles of the two LPs show the direction in which things were going) did better still and contained two songs that would become big US chart hits: *Somebody To Love* and *White*

Rabbit, the latter leaning heavily on Lewis Carroll for inspiration and being a thinly-disguised anthem to drugs. (It just goes to show how naive and unschooled in such matters people were then. *White Rabbit* made the US charts without trouble. When the Beatles released *Sgt Pepper* in mid-67, people were so aware of drugs that the BBC banned *A Day In The Life* from the

air. They particularly objected to the lines: 'Found my way upstairs and had a smoke/Somebody spoke and I went into a dream'. Paul insisted they were referring to cigarettes, the BBC was convinced that the cigarettes contained, in the language of law officers, 'certain substances'. But Grace Slick's references caused no flurry even though to the aware they were

The death of the hippie movement; funeral rites conducted in Haight-Ashbury in '67; the obsequies were premature.

unsubtle–'And you've just had some kind of mushroom/And your mind is moving low' or 'Remember what the dormouse said:/"Feed your head/ Feed your head/Feed your head"'.)

Out of the Haight-Ashbury creative cauldron also emerged Big Brother and the Holding Company which featured the most arresting and, ultimately, tragic lady singer of the period–Janis Joplin. She, like most of the groups in the musically turbulent Bay Area at the time, was firmly grounded in blues and folk.

But as the summer of 1967 progressed, the music changed from reworkings of blues numbers to the sunny whimsy of soft rock and then to a heavier, more strident sound.

A sound that was well-captured by the Doors. Not one of the reported 1,500 bands in and around San Francisco, they came from Los Angeles down the California coast, but in spirit and content and form and attack the Doors were part of the San Francisco movement that later became the so-called West Coast sound. Their first album,

The Doors, rock anarchists under their lead singer, the late Jim Morrison.

released in '67 and called, simply, *The Doors*, was a tour de force. It featured a swirling, crashingly-erotic number called *Light My Fire* that smashed to number 1 in the States as a single. In addition there was a version of the Kurt Weill/ Bertold Brecht *Alabama Song (Whisky Bar)*, the forceful *Break On Through (To The Other Side)* an exhortation for the listener to pursue the Doors' own taboo–and consciousness-busting course. (Lead singer/cult figure Jim Morrison was continually kicking down the frontiers of behaviour. This flaunting and gesturing at authority met its apogee in Miami in

1969 when he was accused of taking stage sexuality to its ultimate point—he allegedly dropped his trousers and exposed himself. He was later found not guilty of the felonious charges of lewd and lascivious behaviour and guilty of the misdemeanour of indecent exposure.)

The second side on the album includes an $11\frac{1}{2}$ minute track called *The End*. It was an extraordinary rambling nightmare of a song, filled with dark imagery, 'a tale of madness, patricide and incest'.

While '67 and drugs were, to many, *Mellow Yellow* and full of sunshine supermen, the Doors pointed the other side. The side of LSD, for instance, that had led early researchers to believe that it could reproduce the symptoms of schizophrenia. While some groups were warmly embracing love and peace and flower power and dropping out and setting up alternatives, the Doors were crashing into confrontation. 'Think of us as erotic politicians', Morrison told *Newsweek*. 'I'm interested in anything about revolt, disorder, chaos, especially activity that seems to have no

meaning. It seems to me to be the road to freedom.'

As Scott McKenzie was singing of *San Francisco* and wearing flowers in your hair, while the quaintly-named Flowerpot Men (does the name cover two of the fashionable trends of the day – flower power and pot? Or was it simply named after a children's TV show featuring inarticulate puppets?) were ripping-off the sentiments in England with *Let's Go To San Francisco*, Jim Morrison was showing us the way that youth and rock were going. He was pointing the road to rock politics, to radicalization, to rock as propaganda.

Morrison cast a shadow across the sun of that glorious summer. A summer that blazed brilliantly with the Beatles' answer to Brian Wilson's thrown down gauntlet of *Pet Sounds*. The summer of *Sgt Pepper's Lonely Hearts Club Band*.

Sgt Pepper was extraordinary. It was, to the best of my knowledge, the first time any group had printed the lyrics to the songs enclosed on the sleeve of an album. (Previously this would have given the publisher apoplexy because he earned considerable revenue from the sale of sheet music.) Was it the first

gatefold album sleeve ever? Perhaps. It was surely one of the earliest, at least in rock. It was the first to have a giveaway sheet of cut-outs. It was perhaps the first to use 'proper', 'real', 'genuine' or 'legitimate' artists (albeit 'pop' artists, Peter Blake and his wife Jann Haworth) to design a cover. It was the first to carry a design – swirling gradations of red – on the inside sleeve.

All these innovations and we haven't even talked about the music! These were just the surface trimmings but they indicated the attitude, the progression, the streets-ahead thinking of the Beatles. (Incidentally, it was the first public acknowledgement by the Beatles of Apple, a concept that was to loom large in their collective lives over the next few years.)

Sgt Pepper is frequently cited by critics as being the Beatles' great recording masterwork. It is undoubtedly one of the greatest albums ever made. It was a giant leap forward in technique, in concept, in care devoted on a rock work. Most observers, most knowledgeable commentators will award the gift of laurels to *Sgt Pepper*; most will say that it is the Beatles'

Lennon's psychedelic Rolls. Love. Peace. And conspicuous consumption!

greatest ever album.

I have to stand aside from this. It is a technical masterpiece. It broke just about every rule around and some that weren't. The Beatles made up new rules just so as they could break them! Song ran into song, image spun dizzily on top of image, sound effects merged into melody. The listener hearing it for the first time was stunned by the barrage of new sounds, new effects, new instruments. It was – is – an astounding achievement. But it is, above all, a triumph of technique. Of recording technique, of writing technique, of production technique.

At bottom there is little heart, little soul to *Sgt Pepper*. It moves the admiration to gasp in delight at its cleverness but it rarely moves the emotions to laugh or to cry. (It is, I suggest, a less complete work than the second side of *Abbey Road*. Here, great writing, ambition in creating a musical unity – a broadly 'symphonic' structure in which different 'movements' contribute to the whole work – and highly sophisticated recording and production combine with humour and humanity to produce the finest piece of sustained work the Beatles ever achieved.)

Nevertheless, the impact it had upon its time was incalculable. No one, but no one, had ever conceived of such a project in rock. The songs were quite extraordinary. Even the ones that were instantly accessible. If *Sgt Pepper* lacks heart and humanity in general, it does, however, contain a song that is deeply moving, astonishingly well-observed, acutely sensitive. *She's Leaving Home* is a dramatised documentary put to music; it tells of a girl running away from her parents to live with a man who will give her love. It switches from objective observation of the girl's 'escape' – 'She's leaving home after living alone for so many years' What a line! All the barrenness of non-communication between generations and all in 10 words! – to the wailing chorus of the middle-aged couple who are shattered and bewildered by her absence. 'We gave her everything money could buy', they bemoan, not realising that what their daughter needed has no

price. It is love, warmth – that 'something inside that was always denied for so many years'.

It is a thrilling song. One of those rarest of songs that expresses true and deep-felt emotions within a few lines, using the music as a perfect sympathetic accompaniment. Many novels have said less about what another of the album's songs – Harrison's *Within You Without You* – calls 'the space between us all'.

This and a few others – *Lovely Rita* a perverse little hymn of love to a traffic warden; *Being For The Benefit Of Mr Kite* taken from an old circus poster; *When I'm Sixty-Four* a eulogy to marital bliss set to a music hall tune; the gimmicky show-opener of the title track – are all good songs. All instantly accessible, easily understood.

But what was one to make of *A Little Help From My Friends*? 'I get high with a little help from my friends'. Another drug reference, surely? Wasn't one always advised not to take an acid trip unless accompanied by a good friend or lover? What was one to make of *Lucy In The Sky With Diamonds*? **L**ucyinthe**S**kywith**D**iamonds. It was code, wasn't it? More secret language for acid. And, of course, the words confirm it – 'tangerine trees and marmalade skies . . . rocking horse people . . . newspaper taxis . . . plasticine porters with looking glass ties'! What could be trippier than that?

Utter nonsense, of course! But was it greater gibberish than the stream of consciousness of *Good Morning, Good Morning* with its accompaniment of farmyard noises? And then there's George's rather fey philosophising, his curious mixture of Kharma and the New Testament, *Within You Without You*.

This all says nothing of the record's biggest puzzle, the vexation of the BBC, *A Day In The Life*. 'Four thousand holes in Blackburn, Lancashire/And though the holes were rather small/They had to count them all/Now they know how many holes it takes to fill the Albert Hall'! Now WHAT is that supposed to mean? It HAS to be about drugs. After all the whole strange mélange, with its menacing vortex of tortured

sound, is punctuated with the wistful desire – 'I'd love to turn you on'.

An unprecedented album. A strange album. A curious mixture of Northern working-class warmth and mysticism; of traditional forms and pioneering techniques; of simple sentiment and complex wordgames. A milestone album. But a work of transition.

A cliché, but rock really was never to be the same after *Sgt Pepper*. Rock really did become significant and, more important, the musicians thought of themselves in a different way. *Sgt Pepper* crashed through so many barriers and signposted so many possibilities that it profoundly changed the thinking of rock musicians. They began to get a new opinion of themselves and their work. Sadly, this opinion was often overblown.

After the Beatles had proved themselves divine with *Sgt Pepper*, had produced what has been dubbed – injudiciously in my opinion – rock's first true work of art, the rock star changed. He was no longer just a very popular human being who entertained. Now people talked about Eric Clapton as 'God', damn near deified Bob Dylan (of whom more shortly), raised the Beatles and, especially, Lennon onto a pedestal. Or perhaps an altar.

Maybe I'm going too far to say they were elevated to gods. The most celebrated were demi-gods, half divine. The rest were canonised and became temporal saints.

Two major themes coalesced in rock over the next few years – drugs and the rock musician as superstar and super-hero.

These strands met in Mick Jagger.

The Rolling Stones had continued to be the *enfants terribles* of international rock. They'd caused a flap in Britain – which had been blown up out of all proportion by the press – by refusing to ride the carousel at the end of *Sunday Night At The London Palladium* in early '67. Jagger had replied to the near-hysterical outrage felt by members of show business in typically forthright terms: 'The only reason we did the show was because it was a good national plug – anyone who thought we were changing our image to suit

Waiting to shoot Abbey Road *cover;*
his shoeless feet 'proved' Paul was dead!

---

a family audience was mistaken . . . It
was a mediocre show and it made us
the same. It was all terrible. I'm not
saying we were better than the
other acts – it was just too depress-
ing . . .'

At about the same time they'd
released a single that had also been
controversial. The barriers sur-
rounding sexuality were falling
slowly but fairly steadily. This trend
was viewed with alarm by many.
They were horrified by what seemed
to be a blatant incitement to
adolescent promiscuity – *Let's*
Spend The Night Together. (This
howl of outrage might have been
even louder if the objectors had
heard rumours current in rock that
Ruby Tuesday – the B-side – was
about one of the more successful
groupies on the scene!)

The single ran into potential
trouble and there was talk of it being
banned from some of the most
important airplays. Premier among
these was the *Ed Sullivan Show* in
New York. To save the plug, Jagger
consented to compromise and it was

reported that he'd sung 'Let's spend
some time together'. He later
denied that. 'I never said "time", I
really didn't. I said "mumble".
"Let's spend some mmmmm together." They would have cut it off if
I'd said "night".' (Five years or so
later he had the decency to feel
abashed about the incident. 'I'm
ashamed of doing that,' he said. 'We
should have walked off . . .')

Despite this admittedly minor
compromise, Jagger was still an
adult *bête noire*. He still seemed to
be spitting in the face of authority.
And there was almost an inevit-
ability about him being the first big
drug bust in rock. (Donovan had
been arrested previously but it was
a fairly low-key affair.)

The Jagger/Richard drug bust in
February 1967 was dirty and juicy
and just the thing a slavering gutter
press relished. There were stories
of a naked girl wearing a fur rug
which, it was maintained in court,
'from time to time she allowed to fall,
disclosing her nude body. She was
unperturbed and apparently
enjoying the situation'. (The stories
about this famous young lady's
activities that night that circulated in

Fleet Street in the weeks immediately following the arrest were
considerably more colourful and
lubricious.)

The charge against Jagger was
actually rather trifling. He was
accused of being in unauthorised
possession of four tablets containing
amphetamine sulphate and methyl
amphetamine hydrochloride – in
other words, pep pills. Keith
Richard was accused on a rather
more complicated charge of allow-
ing his house to be used for smoking
cannabis resin. (One other, Robert
Fraser, was also charged with
possessing heroin and eight cap-
sules of methyl amphetamine
hydrochloride and pleaded guilty at
the subsequent trial.)

When the case came to court –
amid much media ballyhoo – both
Jagger and Richard pleaded not
guilty. Jagger said he had bought
the pep pills quite openly and
legally in Italy. The trouble was that
while they were easily obtained in
Britain on a doctor's prescription, to
possess them without such medical
authorisation was illegal. However,
Jagger entered into evidence the
fact that he had telephoned his doctor

on return to Britain to check whether they were safe to use. The physician told the court that he had advised Jagger that they were safe if used properly but that he must not take them regularly.

Jagger's doctor also testified, in response to a question from the judge, that had Jagger not had these tablets he would have prescribed something similar.

Such exchanges made the charge seem trivial and not worth the court's time. Jagger's offence seemed, at worst, technical. But the judge ruled that 'In law these remarks [by Jagger's doctor] cannot be regarded as a prescription by a duly authorised medical practitioner and it therefore follows that the defence open to Mr Jagger is no longer available to him'.

He turned to the jury: 'I therefore direct you that there is no defence to this charge'. The jury returned after five minutes with a verdict of guilty against Michael Philip Jagger.

He was remanded in custody until after Keith Richard's trial and taken by van to a nearby prison. In the following days he travelled back and forwards between the court and the jail *handcuffed* to warders!

If this treatment seemed extreme, the sentence handed out when Richard was eventually found guilty was outrageous. Richard was

'Who breaks a butterfly on a wheel?' Jagger suffers police overreaction on way to trial on minor but notorious drugs charge.

sentenced to one year's imprisonment, Jagger to three months.

The furore was instantaneous and great. The rock world reacted with shock and disgust. The Who took out an advertisement in an evening paper to say that they considered Jagger and Richard 'had been treated as scapegoats for the drug problem'. This sort of response was perhaps predictable from prominent rock musicians who thought that they too might come in for unwelcome attention from an overzealous and headline-grabbing drug squad. (One way to become a famous policeman in those days was to nick a very famous rock star on a drugs charge.) What was more significant was the reaction of weighty, establishment opinion that had previously been inimical to Jagger, rock and all both stood for. There had clearly been a miscarriage of justice and it is to Britain's credit that there were a great many people who loathed both Jagger and his lifestyle and yet were ready to shout, 'Foul!'.

The most significant and influential broadside was a long, thoughtful editorial, penned by the editor himself, that appeared in the London *Times* on Saturday, 1 July 1967. Under the heading WHO BREAKS A BUTTERFLY ON A WHEEL the old 'Thunderer' thundered yet again.

The editorial dealt with the charge against Jagger, insisting it was 'an offence of a technical character' and

pointing out that it was one that any unfortunate and unwitting citizen might commit. It then went on to deal with the severity of the punishment meted out and the deep suspicion that Jagger was harshly treated simply *because* he was Mick Jagger. 'There are many people who take a primitive view of the matter . . . They consider that Mr Jagger has ''got what was coming to him''. They resent the anarchic quality of the Rolling Stones' performance, dislike their songs, dislike their influence on teenagers and broadly suspect them of decadence . . .'

It concluded: 'There must remain a suspicion in this case that Mr Jagger received a more severe sentence than would have been thought proper for a purely anonymous young man'.

At the end of July, an appeal against the sentences was heard. Keith Richard's conviction was squashed and Jagger's reduced to a conditional discharge – if he kept out of trouble for 12 months what had gone before would not count as a conviction; it would only become a conviction if he committed another offence.

After the appeal the TV current affairs programme *World In Action* flew Jagger by helicopter to the peace of a country house garden. There waiting to enter into discussion with him – this 24-year-old popular entertainer – were William Rees Mogg, editor of *The Times* who had written the closely-reasoned

editorial, Father Corbishley, the eminent Jesuit, Lord Stow Hill and John Robinson, the forthright and controversial Bishop of Woolwich.

Distinguished men, all. Debating matters of import before a television camera with a pop singer. As the TV critic of *The Times* said: ''They led him gently into a discussion as to whether or not society was corrupt and the extent to which absolute freedom was desirable. As television the idea was good, although the discussion was not very rewarding . . .'

Hardly surprising! But the point was that suddenly Jagger and the rock he represented were of enough consequence to rate such a forum. Rock had gone far beyond mere entertainment. Now it was in the public arena. Rock stars were no longer mere performers, but were politicians, propagandists, spiritual gurus, pundits, artists. And a stripling youth who sang for his, admittedly lavish, supper had occupied centre stage in the national news and commanded a fair section of the international press. It was a sign of things to come.

A further straw in the wind was the fact–slightly overshadowed by Jagger's coverage–that during the trials and appeals of his two colleagues Brian Jones was also arrested and charged with a drug offence, possessing cannabis. He was also tried, also found guilty, also sentenced to prison–this time for nine months–also lodged an appeal and was also set free as a result. But the difference was that for Jones there was no TV debate with great men, no campaign, no glory. Three days after his sentence was set aside, in December '67, Brian Jones was admitted to hospital for the second time that year. He was again suffering from strain and exhaustion. For some the pace was already too great.

If Jones saw the dark that year, he also saw the light. Because he was at Monterey. Jagger wasn't there. Richard wasn't there. The Beatles

were not there. But Brian Jones
made it, along with Association, the
Animals, Buffalo Springfield,
Grateful Dead, Simon and Garfunkel, Jefferson Airplane, Big
Brother and the Holding Company,
the Mamas and the Papas (Papa John
Phillips had been instrumental in
setting the festival up), Canned Heat,
Otis Redding, Jimi Hendrix (guitar
ablaze) and the Who (instruments
splintering; this was their–and
Hendrix's–big breakthrough in
America). They were all there as
were 60,000 spectators (among
whom stars mingled untroubled,
sharing the communal euphoria)
and 1,100 of the world's press.

Monterey was the world's first
rock festival. It was an affirmation of
youth's togetherness, of its unity, of
its oneness under rock.

It also established the international brotherhood of rock stars.
Or rather, rock superstars. As
Roger McGuinn of the Byrds remembered (to Tony Palmer in *All
You Need Is Love*): 'It was the first
time that all the pop groups had
gotten together in one place to see
each other personally and discuss
their views on music and everything
else'.

Rock was establishing an élite.
Certain groups recognised each
other as peers. They were pre-
eminent in popularity and/or
creativity and they banded together
into a loose federation. Certain
performers were acknowledged as
masters of their instrument, as
supreme vocal stylists or brilliant
writers.

This musical magnetism transcended the boundaries that had
previously limited intercourse. It
did not stop at nationality, or even
loyalty to a group. Certain performers began to feel stifled working
within the constraints of a hit band.
They felt that their colleagues were

The Spencer Davis Group.

The Jimi Hendrix Experience.

holding back their development and they wanted to join together with other, more compatible musicians. It did not matter that these musicians were already contracted to other groups nor, indeed, that they were halfway across the world. The international brotherhood of superstars did not recognise such frontiers. They wanted to start their own new groups. Better groups. Made up entirely of virtuosi. Supergroups.

In September '67 *Melody Maker* – then Britain's most aware, thoughtful and serious music weekly – featured a Magnificent Seven of the best guitarists in the world. Six were British and one an American who had had to come to Britain to find acceptance. They were Eric Clapton, Pete Townshend, Jeff Beck, Jimmy Page, Stevie Winwood, Peter Green and Jimi Hendrix. Of them, Clapton, Beck and Page had all been part of the Yardbirds, Townshend, of course, was with the Who, Winwood had been in the Spencer Davis Group and had recently founded Traffic (one of the first instances of a band 'getting it together in the country' – as the cliché became) and Green, ex-John Mayall, was starting to find success with Fleetwood Mac.

Of these superheroes – many of whom would form the bases of supergroups – Jimi Hendrix was the odd man out. He was also the greatest and most innovative.

Hendrix was a magician. Anyone who saw him in 1967 would tell you that. He looked like a magician, an afreet. He was a black Heathcliff, wild, maniacal, soaring. He laughed madly on stage as he conjured magic with his guitar. His guitar was his familiar. He made sex magic with it. The notes spun, shot, tumbled, cascaded, pitched, flew, glided, spat, whined, snarled, stuttered, sang and whistled from that guitar. Hendrix made music that no one had heard before. He took ugly tones and made them beautiful. He loved the guitar, he balled it right there on stage and then flung it from him in disgust, crashed it into the stage. He caressed it, picked its strings with his teeth. He tossed it carelessly over his shoulder and still played it!

He had complete mastery over it

Hendrix making musical magic.

and on stage he was all-powerful. He was the high priest at a pagan ritual. He conducted the perverse liturgy, orchestrating the responses of us his acolytes, building us to a peak of fervour, calming us down, incanting and casting spells, stimulating us to another climax, wringing out our emotions, demanding our utter involvement. He brought us to an orgasm of sacrilegious worship and then he offered his guitar – his magic wand, his staff of life, his phallus – as sacrifice. He set fire to it and abruptly quit the stage with all the amplifiers howling like tormented djinns. We subsided into

our seats. Drained, exalted, emptied, triumphant.

Offstage he was diminished. Reduced to merely human proportions, I suppose. A shy, inarticulate man who had said everything he had to say through his music on the stage. A man who giggled behind a long, beautiful hand and spoke – when he did speak – in a voice so soft as to be barely distinguishable.

Perhaps even in 1967 as we watched him ignite, as he tore into us with *Wild Thing* (a pop song of almost unprecedented banality that he somehow turned into a sexual hymn), perhaps even then we knew that he was too incandescent to last.

Cream were three of rock's elite: Ginger Baker (drums), Jack Bruce (bass, vocals) and Eric Clapton (guitar, vocals). They appeared first at the 1967 Windsor festival and by 1968 had had three immensely successful albums

(*Fresh Cream, Disraeli Gears, Wheels of Fire*). Nevertheless they had then begun to question their progress and on 26 November 1968 played their final concert. Their last album was *Goodbye* in 1968.

Cream, the first true supergroup.
Top: *Baker on drums backed by Jack Bruce on bass (also in bottom shot) and the 'god-like' Eric Clapton on lead.*

Hendrix would never just glow, steadily and surely. He would flare, briefly and intensely.

When Hendrix played, say, the Savile Theatre in London (where Brian Epstein held a series of memorable Sunday night concerts in summer 1967) the rock world turned out to see him. The super-heroes acknowledged that he was *primus inter pares.* The first among equals.

And at these and other occasions—at the clubs for Olympians like the Revolution, the Speakeasy or the Bag O'Nails—the Great Ones mingled and talked and formed plans. And from the plans came groups.

The first supergroup was Cream. Not a modest name but then the three people involved were not noted for their modesty. And they could be forgiven their vanity because, for some time, it had been common knowledge among discerning observers that there was no more forceful or powerful drummer than Ginger Baker, no more incendiary guitarist than Eric Clapton (this was before Hendrix came on the scene) and no more creative bass player than Jack Bruce. (Before Bruce the terms 'bass player' and 'creative' were mutually exclusive!)

Everyone told them they were virtuosi and so you cannot blame them for believing it. If they WERE the three best why not form into a group? A trio—now that, in itself, was unusual—no rhythm guitar, no keyboards. A trio that was inclined more towards instrumental than vocal work.

Well, they did it. They took a bold step forward and they succeeded. At their best they were magnificent. Dazzling in their musicianship. At their worst—and later, in retrospect, they were to accuse themselves of being bad more often than good, routine more often than electrifying—they were boring, self-indulgent, laboured. Improvisation was replaced by sheer stamina—who could play longest, loudest. They set out to break down the

The well-named, ill-fated Blind Faith were Baker and Clapton with Winwood and Rick Grech. Family with Roger Chapman (bottom) were underrated.

conventions that had hedged rock. No song had a set time to it, they played as long as they felt they were bringing something to the number. The trouble was that their judgement was sometimes lacking and that they'd forgotten the need for self-discipline. But this is to cavil too much. At their very best they were unbeatable. It was not their fault that audiences were so besotted that they became uncritical. It was said that Clapton only had to fart on stage to get a standing ovation.

The idea of the supergroup was initially exciting. The trouble was that it was also élitist and smacked of fascism. Luckily, human nature intervened before it got too far out of hand. These were some of the world's biggest egos attempting to work together and the results were inevitable.

Cream broke up eventually, as it had to do. Three such talents and personalities and egos could not long be bound together. Baker and Clapton, not having learned their lesson, then became half of the nadir of supergroups–Blind Faith. If Cream was a group named out of over-confidence, Blind Faith was named with an ironical aptness.

Joining our two superheroes in 1969 were the young prodigy of the early Sixties, Stevie Winwood, by now a veteran of cult worship after his highly successful stint with Traffic, and Rick Grech who'd won his spurs with the much-rated but under-achieving Family. The attempt was a failure. It just didn't jell, and after one album (probably better remembered for its contentious cover–showing a barely-pubescent girl displaying her budding breasts and clutching a bronze phallic symbol–than its music), a free concert in London and some American dates, the members bowed to the inevitable and gave it up.

The international brotherhood of superheroes found its best expression in a supergroup formed in 1968. If the story is to be believed,

three friends were at Joni Mitchell's house. All were in successful groups and all were feeling oppressed by the strictures imposed by those groups. So they decided to get together on their own account. David Crosby was on the run from the Byrds, Stephen Stills was still clinging onto a disintegrating Buffalo Springfield (one of the best groups to come out of Los Angeles when everything was happening in San Francisco, and creators of at least two classic songs in *For What It's Worth*—about the confrontations between the hippies and the police, 'the heat', on Sunset Strip—and *Rock 'n' Roll Woman*) and Graham Nash was extremely disenchanted with what he considered to be the meaningless pop formula pursued so successfully by the Hollies.

Together Crosby, Stills and Nash produced a beautifully soft, rather fey album called *Crosby, Stills and Nash* which was occasionally spiced by Crosby's slightly cross polemicism. It looked like this was a supergroup that really could work. Next they drafted in another ex-Springfield refugee, Neil Young, who added a rather more jagged edge to the music and set off on a very successful chain of concerts. The problem was that they were still four individuals doing four different types of songs. The albums became mélanges that were only occasionally successful, and before too long antipathies, rivalries and

personal differences boiled up. In a way, C, S, N & Y never truly broke up because they were never truly a group. Over the years they'd get together in various combinations for various chores and then drift off. A supergroup like other supergroups—never *really* super, never *really* a group.

THE group continued. The Beatles were going through changing times. They were—as they had been for much of the decade—instrumental in the changes. But in mid-67 one major change was forced upon them. In August Brian Epstein—their manager throughout all the years of their fame—died, alone, from an overdose. The Beatles, whom he loved and cherished, and of whom he was so jealous, were away in Wales, sitting at the feet of their spiritual mentor, the Maharishi Mahesh Yogi.

The Beatles no longer depended on Brian Epstein. Had not done so for some time. He could no longer console himself with the thought that he was 'the fifth Beatle'. He took care of business, a routine chore, and watched, helpless, as they developed into four strong, determined, resourceful individuals. Perhaps it is well that he died when he did because what happened over the next few years would have been unbearably painful for him.

Epstein's death forced a decision on the Beatles. One that they had perhaps deferred during his life for

fear of wounding him. They must now be self-determining.

The *Sgt Pepper* album sleeve had borne the words: 'Cover by MC Productions and The Apple'. They wanted to make a film their own way and they wanted it to go out on television. (Their two movies—*A Hard Day's Night* and *Help!*—had been, like everything they essayed, far better than any film made by any pop/rock group/star before.) They *had* to do it themselves. Brian was dead and so Paul stepped in and organised it. It was the first major Apple production. It was called *Magical Mystery Tour*. It was premiered on BBC TV on Boxing Day 1967 and it was the Beatles' first public failure. The press leapt on it and them with ill-disguised glee.

Apple's second venture was a boutique in Baker Street, London selling the exotic, rainbow, magical, troubadour clothes in silks and satins that adorned the slim and pampered bodies of rich flower children. The outside walls of the tall building were painted in a vast trippy mural by a group of young, excessively unworldly, artists—led by a Dutch husband and wife named Simon and Marijke—who called themselves The Fool. (They also adorned guitars owned by Clapton and Hendrix and supplied artwork for an Incredible String Band cover.) The Beatles lasted about seven months in the rag trade before closing the place down in a fit of disgust and giving about £20,000-worth of merchandise away.

Neither disaster deterred them from their idealistic course. In between trips to India to study Transcendental Meditation they formulated plans to set up Apple Corps Ltd—a record/retailing/movie producing/electronics developing company-cum-arts foundation. The Beatles were going to use it to back the work of young artists/poets/writers/designers/musicians/actors/inventors who could not get funding through conventional sources. It was also going to handle the Beatles' own business and recording projects. It

was absolutely typical of the woolly-headed thinking of the time. And it was absolutely typical that the Beatles actually got it off the ground. But this WAS the Sixties in England and ANYTHING could happen. (Sadly, 20th century London wasn't *quite* 15th century Florence and the Beatles, as arts patrons, weren't *quite* the de' Medici!)

It served to show the way that rock stars were thinking about themselves and their place in the world. Apple was doomed to failure, of course. It was a grandiose idea. But neither the Beatles nor anyone working for them had any notion of what they were *really* trying to do or how to make it work.

Apple and its artistic/socialist dream sprang directly from the events and love and dreams of 1967. A lot of good things came out of that year and stayed—the Pink Floyd, for example. Some sprang up, flourished and withered, like Hendrix. And a lot of nice thoughts and theories and pipedreams (the pipe contained something more than tobacco!) were brutally crushed the very next year.

Ten years later—and after he'd been arrested 14 times in five years, imprisoned in California for possession of ½ ounce of marijuana, escaped from gaol, taken asylum in Algiers and then returned to the States on parole—Timothy Leary was asked if anything had come of the flowers that had blossomed in that extraordinary, extravagant summer. He cited the young, enthusiastic staff of President Carter's administration, the fact that 'today banks are run by long-hairs' and concluded: 'Flowers produce seeds and there are millions of seeds from the flowers of the Sixties'. He might also have added that there are a great number of acid casualties from the Sixties.

That silly, wonderful, hope-filled, brain-befuddled, impossible year ended with Graham Nash pronouncing flower power dead. And

Donovan, the prototype flower child and minstrel, making a plea: 'I call upon every youth to stop the use of drugs'.

Nash was right. Nobody was listening to Donovan.

On 20 January 1968 a Woody Guthrie Memorial Concert was held at the Carnegie Hall, New York. Guthrie—who had died on 4 October 1967—had been the great inspiration of a generation of performers. A generation who had turned their political anger, their bitter outrage at the iniquities of American society, their implacable hatred of nuclear weapons and Cold War brinkmanship into a musical crusade. They had sung, accompanied by guitars, wherever young people had congregated to protest. They had sung American folk songs. They had sung Woody Guthrie's songs of the Thirties. But increasingly they had found that Guthrie's howls against the Depression, the Dust Bowl and fascism were not directly relevant to the fights—for Civil Rights, against segregation in the southern states, against war and nuclear proliferation—that they now faced.

They needed their own songs. Their own writer. Someone who could distil the bile and the fury, the moral indignation, the sense of frustration into a scathing satiric song. Into an anthem.

But Woody had been their inspiration and they were all gathered at Carnegie on this Saturday. They sat on the stage and got up in turn to sing one of Woody's songs in tribute. Many of the major figures in the so-called protest movement of the early-Sixties were there—Pete Seeger, Judy Collins, Arlo Guthrie (Woody's son), Tom Paxton, Jack Elliott and Odetta.

Each rose and sang, generally

accompanied by the others. Then a slim, rather frail, young man got to his feet. He wore a beard and moustache that made him look Rabbinical and contrasted quaintly with the grey suit, blue shirt, be-jewelled cufflinks and suede boots. He was joined on stage by two guitarists (one playing electric bass, the other on acoustic guitar am-plified via a pick-up) and drums. Together they roared into *Grand Coulee Dam*, *Mrs Roosevelt* and *Roll On Columbia*. The performance brought the crowd to its feet, yell-ing, stamping and applauding.

Bob Dylan was back. He was alive. He was sane. His face was not disfigured by mutilating scars. He could sing, he could play just as well as before. To some misguided devotees this return to performing was comparable only with Christ's resurrection.

It *was* a form of resurrection but, despite the best efforts of some self-appointed 'Dylanologists', this was no miracle and Dylan was not, nor did he claim to be, divine. It is true, however, that a year-and-a-half before he *had* come very close to death. In July 1966 he had been thrown from his motorcycle near his home in Woodstock and broken his neck.

The injuries were serious and had forced him to recuperate quietly, away from the hectoring idolatory that had surrounded him for so many years. As he got better he extended the exile, brought in a few old friends, re-thought his attitudes to everything especially his music. And he kept his head down as increasingly alarming rumours about his fate circulated among the large, loosely-formed tribe that saw Robert Allen Zimmerman as a Messiah. Correction, THE Messiah.

Bob Dylan is the third towering talent in the history of rock. The only other man who ranks in sheer fame and influence with Presley and the Beatles. He took his musical roots from the same sources as these, but deliberately rejected them for a number of years. His path to fame was entirely different as were his goals, at least at the start of his career.

He was born in Duluth, Minnesota on 24 May 1941. The family moved upstate to Hibbing and during the late Fifties, while at high school, he formed a group and performed a startling impersonation of Little Richard.

His rock & roll days were short-lived and he soon traded his interest in rock for a fascination with folk, the music of the campus coffee houses and, increasingly, of student unrest and protest. He became obsessed by Woody Guthrie and by a dream of going to the folkies' mecca, Greenwich Village in New York, playing the coffee houses and becoming a great folk singer.

Dylan as God and as the angular, spikey youth who influenced a generation with his angry songs. Judy Collins (right) shared similar but tenderer folk roots.

In 1961 part of the dream came true. He got to New York. He even got to meet Guthrie. And he started singing around the folk haunts. Already he was fascinating people with his curly hair (a very early form of the later-popular 'Afro'), crammed under a cap, and his harmonica wired to his guitar. But most of all it was the directness and rawness of his delivery. He sang and played in a harsh, untutored manner. The rasp of his harmonica was a reflection of the cold, angry edge on his voice.

Many found his delivery so stridently atonal as to be beyond music but for others – eventually the majority – the voice and the words and the music sawed their way into the attention.

He started off with a conventional folk repertoire of Guthrie songs and traditional ballads and his unusual performance of them started gathering audiences. He earned a name and reputation around the Village. It seems he was dead set on doing well and, supported by a huge self-confidence, he was therefore ready to take any opportunity.

This soon materialised when he was signed to Columbia records (CBS in Britain) and cut his first album *Bob Dylan* which was released in 1962. It caused some comment and a small interest but was not sufficiently different from the staple folk fare to make many waves.

The Freewheelin' Bob Dylan changed that. Now Dylan emerged as a writer. In fact, *the* writer that the amorphous 'protest movement' had been needing. He gave them an anthem – *Blowing' In The Wind*; he gave them a song of disgust – *Masters Of War*; he gave them a nuclear nightmare – *A Hard Rain's A-Gonna Fall*; he gave them 'song-journalism', musical reportage of the black struggle in Mississippi – *Oxford Town*; he gave them songs of love – *Girl Of The North Country* and *Corrina, Corrina*; songs of love gone sour – *Don't Think Twice, It's All Right*; and songs that seemed

just plain crazy – like *I Shall Be Free*. This album was a revelation. And, in many ways, a liberation. It changed the nature of what popular songs were trying to do. It broke down the format and structure of songs. It made words into weapons or into sound patterns. After *Freewheelin'* a song could be as long as you wanted, as obscure as you wanted to make it. It could be a dart of love or a barb of hate.

It would be easy to summon up some rock pundit to show the importance and impact of Dylan; to testify to his worth as a writer. The eulogies, the phrase-making and the adjectives would fill another book. I prefer to take the opinion of someone from another generation. Writing for another audience. Springing from a different and generally hostile (at least to rock) cultural background.

Bernard Levin is a distinguished British journalist, a witty, sharp-brained columnist for *The Times*, a lover of opera, a slave of Wagner. He wrote an acerbic book about Britain in the Sixties called *The Pendulum Years*. In some 430 pages he dismisses popular music in five and gives the Beatles a scant two! He is, as you can see, no fan of rock.

But of the five vouchsafed to the music, two are devoted to the words of *A Hard Rain's A-Gonna Fall*. And Levin has this to say of its creator: '... Bob Dylan sang in the tones of a medieval flagellant charging the sins of mankind with responsibility for the ravages of the plague ... one of his best known songs [*Hard Rain*] consisted of an unmistakable, and far from comforting, vision of the apocalypse ... Not many ... groups' songs had the genuinely poetic quality of that. But very many of the players and singers, and huge numbers among their audiences, would have sensed something of what Dylan, and the movement he somehow led, meant by his vision'.

The truth is that any concerned adolescent – and there were plenty filling the coffee houses, scuffling round the campuses and marching under banners urging bombs banned and blacks freed in both Britain and America – knew exactly what Dylan and the (not his) movement meant by that vision.

The important point, though, is Levin's comment about the song's 'genuinely poetic quality'. Poetry! The Beatles' music had been talked of in terms of classical analysis. Now Dylan's lyrics were compared to poetry. Oh, rock was going a long way down the cultural road!

And Dylan was hustling it along fast. He moved on from being a propagandist and musical documentarist (the highpoint of that phase being *The Times They Are Changin'* album with its awful warning to adults and authority contained in the title track, its ironic comment on warmongers, *With God On Our Side*, and its three chronicles of personal injustice and inhumanity : *Ballad Of Hollis Brown*, *Only A Pawn In Their Game* and *The Lonesome Death Of Hattie Carroll*) to more personal and less political statements on the next album *Another Side Of Bob Dylan*.

He was moving so fast that many couldn't keep up. Those who'd seen him as the new Woody Guthrie, the liberal leftish intellectuals who'd been the mature backbone of the folk/protest movement were puzzled, and in some cases angered, by

a song like *Motorpsycho Nightmare* (on *Another Side*) in which Dylan's ever-strengthening surreal streak found one of its earlier forms.

This side found further expression in the next album *Bringing It All Back Home*. *Subterranean Homesick Blues* spewed words, machine-gunned images, chattered out ideas and left the unwary listener breathless. His songs were more oblique now, more elliptical. About girls you couldn't quite see – *She Belongs To Me* – about situations you couldn't precisely comprehend – *Maggie's Farm*. And about things you could only feel as mood.

I don't think any of us knew that *Mr Tambourine Man* was a drug song. I don't think it mattered to our enjoyment of the song. We were used to not quite grasping the meaning of Dylan's words but accepting that they were part of the sound mosaic of the song. Individually they didn't

The Byrds in Mr Tambourine Man *days.*

mean anything but put together in an order dictated by the artist they created a pattern, a picture, a shading of colour and tone.

I'm sure that we were not knowledgeable enough when we first heard the song in 1965 to see the meaning in a line like: 'Then take me disappearin' through the smoke rings of my mind'. (The caverns, rooms, windmills and, hilariously from the Bonzo Dog Band, wardrobes of the mind became common clichés of later drug/philosophy rock songs.) But I'm also sure we didn't worry at it. It was Dylan being Dylan and yet still touching us, arrow-straight and true with his song. I'm sure we would

The Band undoubtedly greatly helped Bob Dylan's transition to rock as well as storming to their own success.

have agreed with Robert Shelton, a critic on the *New York Times*, if we'd read his comment on the song: 'An introspective, symbolist piece that moved in and out of this listener's comprehension, but still conveyed a strong mood'.

Tambourine Man is important in a further respect; it marks the meeting of Dylan and rock. The Byrds, a Beatles-inspired West Coast band, took the song and gave it a rock treatment. It was a tremendous success and must have confirmed in Dylan's mind the way his future music was going. (He'd had the first inkling rather earlier when he'd heard what the Animals had done to a song in his repertoire – *The House Of The Rising Sun*.) The Byrds' *Mr Tambourine Man* marked the first instance of a rather ill-fitting style that was labelled 'folk/rock'.

Dylan knew what could be done with his songs in a rock idiom and he was starting to feel the tug of his rock roots. In 1965 he made a long bitter, vengeful and entirely brilliant rock single called *Like A Rolling Stone*. This was a very new, biting, rock Dylan. Dylan backed by Mike Bloomfield on guitar, Al Kooper on organ and some very sharp blues-based rock musicians.

This was electric Dylan and the single was a giant hit, finding a whole new audience among those who had previously thought of his as 'intellectual's music'. Now it was rock like the Rolling Stones, like the Animals.

Dylan played the Newport Folk Festival in July 1965 and went onstage carrying an *electric* guitar and backed by the Paul Butterfield Blues Band. Newport was the folk purists' temple and now it was being desecrated by electric vandals. Dylan even wielded the weapon that destroyed folk's integrity – the electric guitar.

His performance was met with boos. He went off and came back with an acoustic guitar and played some crowd-pleasers. The next month he played to 14,000 people in the Forest Hills tennis stadium. The first half was acoustic Dylan, the second electric Dylan. The first half was an unqualified success, the second was met with some boos and indifference.

A further month passed and Dylan tried the same routine again, this time at Carnegie Hall. And this time the audience had caught up with him. Dylan had made the transition from folk star to rock superstar.

He was also carrying a huge weight – the responsibility laid on him by members of his generation. They made him their voice. He started as John the Baptist and, as things got madder, he was transmogrified into a Christ-figure.

In this book *Bob Dylan*, Anthony Scaduto quotes Dylan. A Dylan who was threatened by the worship of his fans. 'They want me to handle their lives. That's a lot of responsibility, I got enough to do handling my own life. Trying to handle somebody else's life you gotta be a very powerful person. The more

people's lives you got responsibility for, the bigger the weight is. I don't want that. Too much for my head.'

To the people who wanted him to handle their lives, who wanted him as their mouthpiece, who raised him above common humanity everything uttered, written, sung by Bob Dylan was charged with deep symbolism. They were always demanding to know what he meant; constantly telling him what *they* thought he meant. Always looking for answers from him.

They bought his records in millions but they were so intense about him. They demanded something in return. The more they asked him to explain, the more cryptic became his answers. and the more he just wanted the songs to sit and for people to get whatever they needed out of them.

He'd made two brilliant rock albums. *Highway 61 Revisited* in 1965 with *Like A Rolling Stone* and *Desolation Row* as high points and *Blonde On Blonde* in 1966, with *Rainy Day Women No. 12 & 35*, *I Want You*, *Just Like A Woman* standing out amid excellence. He'd also put out the quite incredible *Positively 4th Street* as a single.

And still they were pressing him for explanations. Reporter: 'Do you think of yourself as primarily a singer or a poet?' Dylan: 'Oh, I think of myself more as a song and dance man, y'know'. Reporter: 'Why?' Dylan: 'Oh, I don't think we have enough time to go into that'.

In 1966, Dylan crashed on his

The Rolling Stones' original line-up : Mick Jagger (top left), Keith Richard (top middle), Brian Jones (top right), Charlie Watts (opposite top left) and Bill Wyman .

motorbike. Or he didn't. Depending on which version/theory you believe. Either way, he dropped out for damn near 18 months. And some say that if he did crash, well like Freud says 'there are no accidents' and the crash was subconsciously self-induced to get the weight off his back for a while.

Whatever the truth, Dylan needed those 18 months of rest and recovery and recuperation. Needed to work unpressured by contracts and deadlines, in the quiet of his home in Woodstock. Needed to play with his band, The Band who used to be the Hawks and were fierce rockers, in their rented house, Big Pink.

In 1968 he returned to live performing and issued *John Wesley Harding* on which he sounded less angry, more mellow. His voice had lost its jaggedness. But it was a sad album with a feeling of spiritual questing. It confirmed his greatness, however. And that his powers were undiminished by the two year lay-off.

One year later came another abrupt change of direction. And of

On stage the Band and Dylan with help from Joni Mitchell and Neil Young.

mood. *Nashville Skyline* was exuberant country music. Much lighter, much happier in tone. A revelation. Dylan was a country singer! He, like so many American bands that followed, was going back to America's musical bedrock, to its indigenous forms. (Interestingly, he was following the Byrds in this journey of rediscovery. They had pre-empted everyone in 1968 by making the country-inspired *Sweetheart Of The Rodeo*. To our ears, then, it seemed as if they were committing suicide. Country was something only sung by hicks, middle-aged drunks in working men's clubs, maudlin crooners and middle-of-the-road Irishmen with a pleasant lilt and a winning smile!)

He twisted yet again and defied categorisation by producing the unclassifiable *Self Portrait* in 1970. This was an odd mix of his own and other people's songs and only partially successful. By now, Dylan had jinked so many times in so many directions that even the maddest of his acolytes were bemused. He'd taken the heat out of the idolatory and, as he entered the Seventies, seemed to have lost some of his own fire.

Through the Sixties he had ploughed his own furrow. He had taken the music, his music, where *he* wanted it to go and had waited only briefly for us to catch up with his coat tails before striding off again.

Bob Dylan rewrote the grammar of the rock song as James Joyce had rewritten the rules of the novel form. He was the only rock writer to whom the term poet could be strictly applied. He was rock's single greatest and most unique talent. What the Beatles did for rock music collectively, he did alone. Some song and dance man!

While Dylan was a serious musician and a serious writer, he was wary of taking himself or his work *too* seriously. Others, sadly, had no such inhibitions. From 1968 rock took itself and was taken by others very seriously indeed. Musicians viewed their own work, its purpose and intent, with a gravity that would have been hilarious to the observer if it wasn't, frequently, so pathetically self-deluded.

The infectious gaiety of 1967 couldn't last, of course. And the idealism of that summer soon turned to violent bitterness in the next. The Vietnam war was escalating and

opposition to it growing. There were violent riots in America, in Paris (near as a touch a full-scale revolution) and in London. American youth tried to influence mainstream politics in election year and got bloody heads from Mayor Daley's police in Chicago where the Democratic convention was held.

Youth and authority were, for the first time since rock & roll, coming into violent confrontation. There were some rock musicians who felt they should be leading their generation to the ramparts, others who were still trying to 'cool them out' with acid and beauty. There were revolutionaries and there were star children.

These were the days of Woodstock and Kent State University. Of hippies and yippies. Of Black Panthers and White Panthers. Of communes and draft dodgers. Of *Give Peace A Chance* and 'Up Against The Wall Motherfuckers!'. Of Black Power and *International Times*. Of Dutch Provos and American Weathermen. (Weathermen after a line in Dylan's *Subterranean Homesick Blues*: 'You don't need a weather man/To know which way the wind blows'.)

The wind was blowing hard and

cold at the end of the Sixties. It was a time of turmoil and turbulence. Of anger and frustration. Of fear and futility. What had not been achieved through love was now attempted through fists, bombs, rifles, arson.

It was a time when youth went underground. Driven underground by the illegality of its favourite

Confrontation: as the decade progressed youth clashed head-on with authority.
Above: *riot police stand between demonstrators and the White House at a peace rally.*

Below: *'Jools'—Julie Driscoll—was THE face of 1968; her cool voice and looks complemented the music of the Brian Auger Trinity and set trends.*

certain of his protégés had gone off to start their own bands.

Surfacing in '68 were groups like Savoy Brown, Chicken Shack, Fleetwood Mac and Jethro Tull (complete with lunatic flautist Ian Anderson, one of the most colourful characters of the period). The underground bands mingled and mixed, shared groupies and gigs and, commendably, staged huge outdoor free concerts in London parks or wherever the authorities were relaxed enough to allow. They continued much of the 'alternative society' idealism of 1967 but seemed to be making little headway in achieving commercial acceptance. Indeed, John Peel, the only British disc jockey to espouse their cause with any enthusiasm, was moved to comment in '68: 'The Underground is like a woman endlessly pregnant and never has a baby. So sad'.

What was sadder was that when success DID come – in '69 for Fleet-

stimulants, by the repression it felt from the police, by the regular arrests of its leaders, by the raids on its press.

The music went underground with it.

In clubs around London there were two streams of music being played by what came to be known as 'underground groups'. On one hand there was the sophisticated psychedelia – very experimental, often very free-form tending towards jazz – of bands like Pink Floyd, Tyrranosaurus Rex and Soft Machine. On the other hand there was a further resurgence in interest for the blues. John Mayall – now the Grand Old Man of British blues – was again at the spearhead of this and

The emerging underground. Ian Anderson (below and bottom right) of Jethro Tull as '60s maniac and '70s squire.
Right: *early blues from Fleetwood Mac.*

The Moody Blues 'progressed' from Go
Now *to 'philosophy' and superstardom.*

wood Mac with a massive number 1
instrumental, *Albatross* and two
consecutive number 2s, *Man Of The
World* and *Oh Well*; for Chicken
Shack with *I'd Rather Go Blind* and
for Jethro Tull with *Living In The
Past* and *Sweet Dream*—those who
had so fervently wished for it
frequently turned against their
cherished bands and accused them
of 'selling out'!

The psychedelic side of the
Underground had a rather more
curious history. The Pink Floyd had
scored two single hits in '67 with the
bizarre *Arnold Layne* (about a
transvestite and presented, dar-
ingly, in a *pink* sleeve!) and *See
Emily Play*. But the market was
changing and it took the business
side of rock a while to realise it. In
the late Sixties the main thrust of
rock commercialism was directed
behind singles. But *Sgt Pepper* had
started to change that. It had shown
the possibility of the album as a
medium for expression. Groups had
been miniaturists when working
within the discipline of the single.
The album—used properly—offered
them a broad canvas. The double
album would be equivalent to a
mural!

The new groups, Pink Floyd
among them, had far more to say
than could be contained within 2½
minutes of vinyl. They rejected the
single and concentrated their
considerable talents and energies
on the album. And their audience—
far more literate, demanding,
appreciative than any rock audience
had ever been (closer, in fact, to the
audience that had followed, understood and supported modern jazz)—
welcomed the change.

The Pink Floyd—and others—
started selling albums in large
quantities, but because everyone
was so singles-oriented it took a
while to realise the exact impact the
Underground was having. Floyd
albums like *The Piper At The Gates
Of Dawn* (in '67), *A Saucerful Of
Secrets* ('68) and the double *Ummagumma* ('69) led the way for new
groups to come to public acceptance through the medium of the LP.

For example, in '69 King Crimson
burst upon the scene with an album
full of aural fireworks—*In The Court
Of The Crimson King*—that was
extravagantly praised and established them, in one swoop, as a top-
flight band.

The album became the medium
for 'serious' musicians. No longer
was it just 12 tracks slung together.
Now it had a 'concept', was used to
tell a story, invoke a mood, as a
sound novel. The Moody Blues, for
example, used it as a philosophical
tract. They had been a good pop
group with a great image in 1965
when they had a massive and well-
deserved hit with *Go Now!* They
had failed to follow up convincingly,
and over the years the personnel
had changed (one member, Denny
Laine, went through many career
changes before finding himself a
safe and creative harbour with Paul
McCartney in Wings). The injection
of new blood, the 'revelations' of
acid, the purchase of a mellotron

(one of the many new instruments—
like the synthesizer family—that
were to create intriguing sound
possibilities in these years) transformed the Moody Blues into one of
the most successful bands of the
time.

They knew no bounds. The first of
their new-style albums—*Days Of
Future Passed* (such titles give an
indication of the sort of pseudo-
philosophy the band dabbled in)—
incorporated electronics and the
London Symphony Orchestra.
Despite a vast financial outlay and
inordinate amounts of time lavished
on it, it was a big success and
launched the band into a series of
'sound Gospels' or what someone
described as 'evangelical rock' with
each album—*In Search Of A Lost
Chord*, *On The Threshold Of A
Dream*, *To Our Children's
Children's Children* (see what I

*Keith Emerson (left) quit Nice for Greg
Lake (centre) and Carl Palmer (right).*

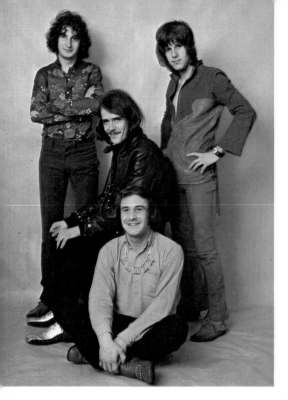

Left: *The Nice with Emerson on right.*
Right: *Sly Stone led the Family Stone and pushed black music forward.*

mean about the titles?)–getting more ambitious and pretentious.

The album and the rock/classic fusion coupled with the rock musician as 'composer' (as compared to humble song writer) brought out a lot of curios. Nice, for example, took classics and gave them a tremendously vivacious going-over. Keith Emerson's keyboard playing was full of brio and attack. (The latter adjective is used with precision–he flung himself at his unfortunate instrument, fetching a bullwhip to it and stabbing it repeatedly with daggers!) Purists were apoplectic at his rupturing of dearly-loved classics like Mozart's *Rondo A La Turque* but young audiences were ecstatic and continued to support his 'barbarism' into his next band Emerson, Lake and Palmer and their crash through such as Mussorgsky's *Pictures From An Exhibition*. (Or, as they had it, *Pictures At An Exhibition.*

Poor old Mussorgsky, he had to be content with a series of shared credits on some of his piano pieces in the cycle–thus the sleeve reads '*The Old Castle*–Mussorgsky/Emerson; *The Gnome*–Mussorgsky/Palmer' and so on! Though I suppose he should be thankful; on the same album it states: '*Nutrocker*–Kim Fowley, arranged Emerson, Lake and Palmer'. Tchaikovsky, who after all wrote the desecrated piece in the first place, doesn't get mentioned at all!)

An uneasy and generally unsuccessful attempt at rock/classic fusion continued with Deep Purple and Barclay James Harvest attempting to use orchestras as backing groups. These experiments didn't work as well as some to marry rock and jazz. The best example of this–at least commercially–was Blood, Sweat And Tears. They too were subject to the pomposity of the times. Their second, tremendously successful and really quite exciting album–*Blood Sweat And Tears*–bore this legend: 'Rebirth, regeneration and triumph. Blood, Sweat & Tears. Nine musicians–vital and diverse. Their rich musical tapestries will stun you. Brash and exciting, their music is a wedding of rock and jazz. For you and for those who have waited so long–with polished prose fancies–this album is a joy of vision and design, the freshest experience of its kind.'

What actually did stun was the sheer brass nerve of that statement.

Below left: *Deep Purple.*
Below right: *Blood, Sweat and Tears.*

Chutzpah at its finest! Nonetheless the album had some memorable and big selling (as singles) moments–*And When I Die*, *Spinning Wheel* and *You've Made Me So Very Happy*. Not to mention an arrangement of *Trois Gymnopédies* by the progressive (for his day) and highly influential (on his contemporaries) French composer Erik Satie who died in 1925. Satie used jazz elements in his revolutionary work and helped to change 'highbrow' or 'modern classical' music. B, S & T were slightly ahead of their time in acknowledging him; it wasn't until the late-Seventies that Satie's music–particularly the accessible *Trois Gymnopédies*–gained any vogue among the rock fraternity.

It can be easily seen from all this dabbling in the classics, the avant-garde and jazz that one section of rock was going very 'upmarket'. This was cerebral stuff, appealing to older teens with good education.

The diverse sounds of the British late '60s.
Top left: 'symphonic' Barclay James Harvest.
Bottom left: Love Affair who didn't play on their teeny-bop cover of Everlasting Love. Above: pop jesters Dave Dee, Dozy, Beaky, Mick and Tich.
Below: Amen Corner—from Welsh blues to teen idolatry.

What was happening to those poor benighted cretins—actually the majority of us—who still looked upon rock as an entertainment?

The rock market had started to fragment. The 'Clever Rock' of Pink Floyd and others had left many behind. The introspection of the music, the arrogant boredom of the performers (who tended to shuffle on stage in jeans, turn their backs to the audience and play long solos for their own enjoyment) left most people cold. While intellectualism was a dominant trend, it should not be forgotten that two of the most popular artists of the time were—God help us!—Engelbert Humperdinck and Tom Jones.

Pop continued virtually unabated, kept alive by teeny-screamy groups like Love Affair; Dave Dee, Dozy, Beaky, Mick & Tich; Bee Gees; Marmalade and Amen Corner in Britain. In America, the standard seemed to be better with black artists giving a refreshing input to the charts, partly buoyed by the new black consciousness/power movement in the States. Increasingly artists were pledging 'I'm black and I'm proud'. Classic songs from black artists made number 1 in the US through 1968 and 1969: Otis Redding's *Dock Of The Bay*, Marvin Gaye's great *I Heard It Through The Grapevine*, Sly and the Family Stone's *Everyday People*.

The new trend on both sides of the Atlantic was the discovery of an untapped and very lucrative market, the sub-adolescents. The teeny-

Tom Jones achieved (with group the Playboys) superstardom as a sex symbol to American matrons.

143

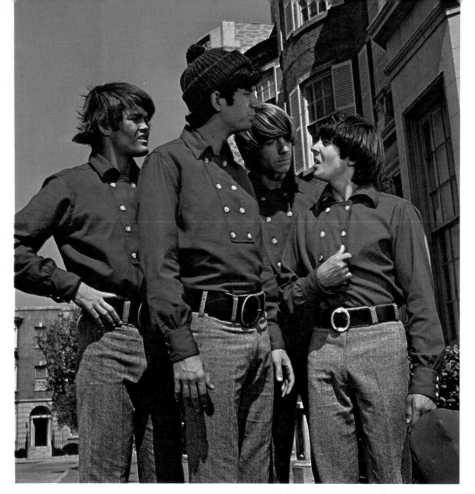

'Instant Beatles'! The Monkees.

boppers. And later, the weeny-boppers.

I will, if I may, relate a personal experience. In late 1966 I was a junior reporter on *New Musical Express* in London. Being the lowest form of journalistic life on that paper I copped all the lousy jobs and one very, very cold day just before Christmas I was sent halfway across the city to a BBC TV studio to talk to some guy nobody had ever heard of. The editor – ever a vague man – had said that he was a British kid doing well on American TV, who could sing a bit and was just home to visit his folks in Manchester for the holiday.

With no great hope of getting anything worthwhile I trudged over to the studio to learn that the kid was filming an insert for *Top Of The Pops* (then the biggest pop showcase on TV) to plug some new series about a pop group that the BBC had bought from America and would be screening in the New Year.

The kid's name was David Jones and the group and TV show were called the Monkees. He was a personable young man and, for a complete unknown, at least in

England, being given the star treatment. He gave me a lift back into town and told me about the new and revolutionary way his band had been found.

He and three other guys – Mickey Dolenz (once a child TV star playing the title role of *Circus Boy* under the name Mickey Braddock), Peter Tork and Mike Nesmith – had answered an ad in a trade paper. They'd gone for an audition with hundreds of others and been selected because they could act a bit and sing a bit and looked right.

In fact, Don Kirshner – the 'Man With The Golden Ear' from those far-off Brill Building days – together with two shrewd producers, had attempted to synthesize the Beatles. He, Bob Rafelson and Bert Schneider had watched them go up the market and knew that there remained an unsatisfied young audience who were looking for more cuddly moptops. And they knew that TV was the great medium for these kids. And Kirshner knew that *he* knew exactly the sort of pop music these kiddies liked. So these three shrewdies put it all together as a commercial package.

They made a TV series about a zany, wacky (fill in the rest of those

favourite TV adjectives yourself) group. They based the quick-cutting, the humour and the delivery on Richard Lester's direction of the two Beatle movies – *Hard Day's Night* and *Help!* Kirshner got together some of his writers from the Brill Building days – Goffin and King, Neil Sedaka, Carole Bayer (co-writer of *Groovy Kind Of Love* and later successful singer/writer of the Seventies as Carole Bayer Sager), Jeff Barry and Neil Diamond, as well as the new team of Tommy Boyce and Bobby Hart. They all turned out perfect hit songs using the structures that had been so successful pre-Beatles and the beat and arrangements that the Beatles had pioneered.

Every episode of the Monkees' TV show plugged at least two songs from this roster and, inevitably, the hits started coming – *Last Train To Clarksville, I'm A Believer, A Little Bit Me, A Little Bit You* and so on.

All that was needed were four young men to be the Monkees, to act, play the giddy goat in front of the cameras and to sing. (They didn't have to play instruments, of course, session musicians would take care of that in the studio. If they *could* strum a guitar or thump a drum, well so much the better. But it was merely a pleasant bonus.) They wanted an English kid to make the Transatlantic connection firm and just hint at the Beatles' background. (Jones came from Manchester and not Liverpool, but that's a close second and you can't have everything. After all, didn't Herman of the Hermits come from Manchester and wasn't he one of the biggest teen stars in America at the time?)

They wanted an acerbic rather sarcastic one, perhaps a bit on the brainy side to mirror the Lennon figure – slow-talking, tall, indi-vidualistic, musical and verbally cutting Mike Nesmith filled that role. They wanted a dopey, lovable, silly-ass one. He didn't have to be good-looking – Ringo wasn't – but he'd have to have charm and a soppy grin. Peter Tork took that. But what about the George Harrison look-alike?

Well, to be honest George had never really come across that

strongly as a personality, had he? He was good-looking enough but very retiring. Even in the films he'd seemed the most inhibited. Let's scrub George and go for something more American–a fusion of looks and comedy, a sort of knockabout McCartney. Dolenz won it.

So that was the Monkees. An entirely cynical operation to create, package and sell through the media a pop group. And, by God, it worked.

My meeting with Jones that cold December day paid dividends. Three weeks later the Monkees were number 1 in Britain with *I'm A Believer* and a madness took over the female population aged between about eight and twelve. Anyone who wrote about them or who had met them was subjected to a barrage of enquiries, phone calls, squeals and letters. So intense was the fervour that I must record, to my eternal embarrassment, that when I left *New Musical Express* in the middle of '67 to join a magazine called *Rave*, the mag ran a picture of me and a headline that read 'Monkee Man Pascall Joins *Rave*'!

Kirshner and colleagues had identified a new, moneyed market, and behind the Monkees there came a deluge of products aimed right at these infants. The Monkees were intelligent and really rather musical and talented young men, and it did not take them long to tire of the exploitation. The puppets started testing their muscles and then cut their strings and the venture finally broke up in acrimony, at least between marionettes and their 'masters'. But the pickings were too

rich and Kirshner tried again.

He used television again. And he relied on his golden ear–and Jeff Barry–again. But this time he was taking no chances with human ingrates. This time he had total control because this time his group did not exist. The Archies were cartoon characters! And they had a massive hit with *Sugar, Sugar*.

And so it came to pass that Bubblegum Music was born. For some time it had been known that groups had hits with records on which they had not played. For instance, there had been a colossal row in '68 when it was revealed that none of the Love Affair had played on their number 1 hit, *Everlasting Love*; the difficult chore of plucking strings and striking drums being accomplished by session musicians. But they HAD sung. Oh yes indeed!

Now came a sophistication. A producer and/or writer would take a song, record it using session musicians and singers and then release it. If it was a hit he'd put together a group under some name and send them out to promote it. If the song was a flop, well he'd only paid session fees and not much was lost–he wasn't keeping a band on the road and paying them wages.

So there came in the late Sixties and early Seventies a string of records by groups who were virtually interchangeable–*Love Grows Where My Rosemary Goes*, *My Baby Loves Lovin'*, *United We Stand* and so on by Edison Light-

Furiously sincere—Neil Diamond.

house, White Plains, Brotherhood of Man. These were in Britain and banal. They earned the sneering title of Bubblegum along with such offerings as Dawn's *Tie A Yellow Ribbon*, Steam's *Na Na Hey Hey Kiss Him Goodbye*, *Chirpy Chirpy Cheep Cheep* by the aptly-named Middle Of The Road and other such dross.

In fact, Bubblegum was a quite specific–and crass–type of music, emanating from a particular source.

It came out of the Buddah label, under the control of Jerry Kasenatz and Jeff Katz, and pure Bubblegum somehow mixed up puppy love with other juvenile interests like sweets. An exemplar is Ohio Express's abysmal *Yummy Yummy Yummy* ('I've got love in my tummy' it continued in its nauseating way). Other 'classic' Bubblegum records were *Chewy Chewy*–from the same stable as *Yummy Yummy–Simon Says* by the 1910 Fruit Gum Co., *Gimme Gimme Good Lovin'* by Crazy Elephant, and an item I offer only as a curio from an album called *Buddah '69–Bubble Gum Music* by The Rock & Roll Dubble Bubble Trading Card Co. Of Philadelphia 19141!

Left: *Tony Orlando and Dawn.*
Right: *Brotherhood Of Man in the '70s.*

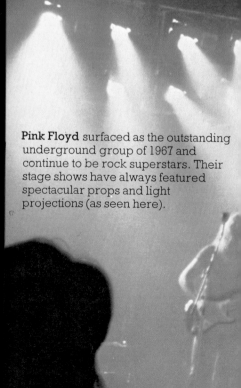

Pink Floyd surfaced as the outstanding underground group of 1967 and continue to be rock superstars. Their stage shows have always featured spectacular props and light projections (as seen here).

This frivolous music confection tapped the pockets of the huge sub-teen audience who were now demanding their own music by their own stars. This was to be a trend that expanded alarmingly in the Seventies.

The Sixties drew to a close with a clash between light and dark. The light was Woodstock, the final flowering of the peace and love movement. The hippie tribes gathered at the farm of Max Yasgur in upstate New York for three August days in '69. It started out as a commercial venture, but the half million crowd that arrived inundated the organisation and the facilities and the doors were thrown open to all and sundry for free.

The second day the heavens opened and the rain turned the site into a quagmire but peace and tranquillity/reigned and in the mud the Woodstock Nation – as they came to be known – listened to the music of Ten Years After, Sha Na Na, Santana, Richie Havens, John Sebastian, Joan Baez, Arlo Guthrie, the Who, Country Joe MacDonald, Sly And The Family Stone, Canned Heat, Joe Cocker, Jimi Hendrix, Crosby, Stills, Nash and Young, Jefferson Airplane, Grateful Dead, the Band, Blood, Sweat and Tears, Creedence Clearwater Revival, the Incredible String Band, Johnny Winter, Paul Butterfield, Janis Joplin, Melanie, Ravi Shankar, Mountain and Keef Hartley.

It was a beautiful, if rather self-conscious, event and it passed into the rock annals as the highpoint of youth's tribalism. It also lost money as a festival and gained a fortune as a movie and albums. It was celebrated by Joni Mitchell, who was not there, on the *Deja Vu* album by C, S, N & Y (who were) and became a big single hit for Matthews Southern Comfort.

It seemed to confirm that those things we'd believed in 1967 *could* actually happen. Another festival, four months later, killed such whimsical beliefs for ever.

The dark side of the late Sixties reached one of its nadirs on the night of 3 July 1969 when Brian Jones died in his swimming pool. The exact details and the truth of that tragic night will probably never be known. In the dry language of the coroner who presided over the inquest, Jones died due to 'immersion in fresh water . . . under the influence of drugs and alcohol'. There was, he recorded, 'severe liver dysfunction due to fatty degeneration and ingestion of alcohol and drugs'. He came to the conclusion that it was a case of 'death by misadventure'.

A Rolling Stone was dead.

Right: *Joe Cocker sang as if his heart would burst, flailing the air with his arms.* Below: *Ten Years After produced a considerable guitar hero in Alvin Lee (on* right*). America riposted with the excellent Creedence Clearwater Revival (bottom) and melodic rock.*

Except . . . Brian Jones was no longer a Rolling Stone. In June it had been announced that he had left the group and he was reported as saying: 'I no longer see eye to eye with the others over the discs we are cutting'. Four days later Mick Taylor, ex-John Mayall, joined up.

The Stones had already announced a free concert to be held in London's Hyde Park when the news of Brian's death came through. They decided to continue with it. They felt that Brian would have wished it.

Brian Jones was a rock & roll casualty. He was 27 years old when he died and he was burnt out. Keith Richard said: 'Brian got very fragile. As he went along he got more and more fragile and delicate. I think all that touring did a lot to break him'. He was the first of a wave of victims of the rock lifestyle. Of what Ian Dury ten years later was to enshrine in a song: *Sex And Drugs And Rock And Roll*.

Mick Jagger officiated at Jones's obsequies in Hyde Park. He wore a white frock and read from Shelley's *Adonais* – 'Peace, peace! he is not dead, he doth not sleep . . .' – and released hundreds of white butterflies from cardboard boxes. (Those that survived the incarceration, that

Above left: *Joan Baez.*
Above: *Hell's Angels in action.*

is.) And it was all filmed for TV. And there were, reportedly, 500,000 people crammed peacefully in the park. And some thought the whole thing was in bad taste and that Jagger was off into some very strange territory.

A few weeks later the Stones launched into a huge tour of the States, their first for $2\frac{1}{2}$ years. Jagger was naturally anxious that it should be memorable. He was doing his

Be-frocked Jagger in Hyde Park.

Festivals in the late '60s and early '70s grew increasingly large by attracting groups as diverse as Hell's Angels 'to keep the peace' and flower children. Later, mysticism became an important force and festivals were held at magical venues such as the Glastonbury Pyramid.

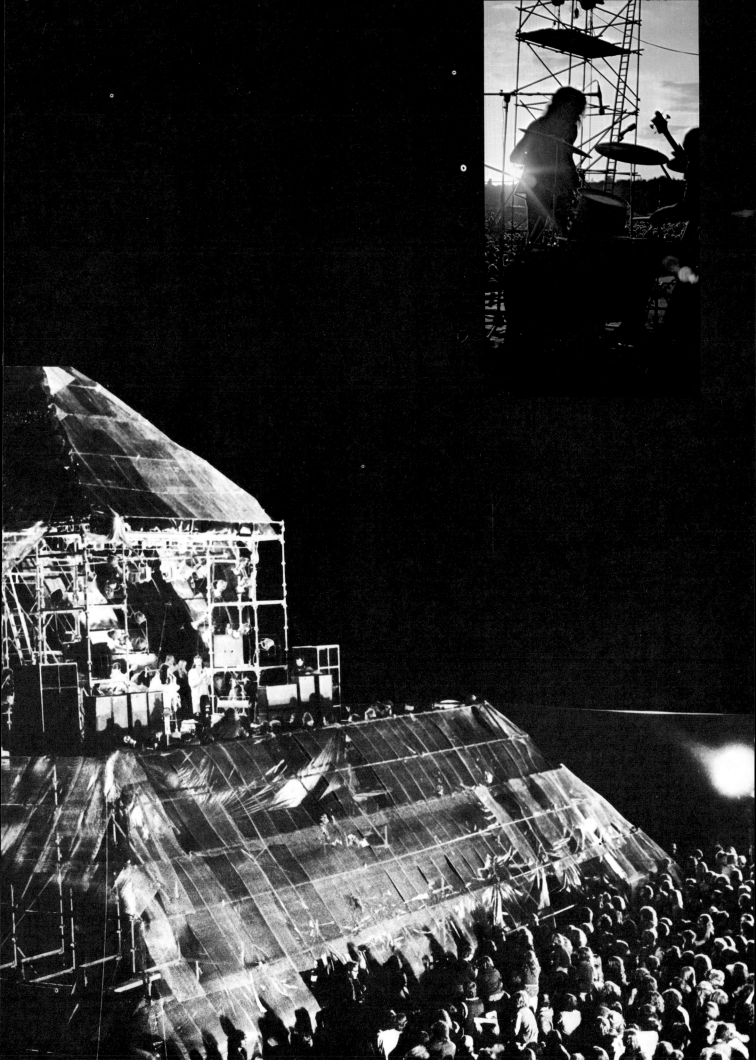

best on stage to make it memorable. He was particularly playing on his sado-masochistic, 'face of evil' persona, the one that portrayed his songs *Midnight Rambler* and *Sympathy For The Devil* so effectively, so chillingly.

The tour was a tremendous success from the start. Everything seemed to be right. Jerry Garcia of the Grateful Dead suggested that they top off the triumph by holding a huge free concert, just to say thank you. Jagger decreed that it would be so. Perhaps he was mindful of the 500,000 he had attracted to Hyde Park and ambitious to outdraw that. Perhaps it was a spontaneous gesture of affection to the fans, many of who had complained about the high seat prices at the scheduled venues.

Jagger ordered that all arrangements for the free concerts should be completed in exactly one month.

It was not possible, of course. They couldn't find a venue and when they did circumstances forced them to change it a mere 48 hours before the performance. In enormous haste they switched to a racing track a few miles outside San Francisco at a place called Altamont.

They had 20 hours to assemble the stage and the sound system and lay on facilities for a huge crowd and to

arrange some sort of security. The last problem was easily solved. The Stones were assured that the local chapters of the Hell's Angels were really quite tame and willing to undertake crowd control in exchange for plenty of alcohol.

It was a disaster from the start. The site was entirely unsuitable. It was cold and uncomfortable and you couldn't see the stage too well from the back. Dealers were pushing contaminated acid that was wreaking awful effects on takers. And the Hell's Angels were not tame. They drank their 'fee' and they took their duties very seriously as a security force.

With the accent on force. As Carlos Santana, who played early on the bill later said: 'There were bad vibes from the beginning. The fights started because the Hell's Angels pushed people around. It all happened so fast, it just went right on before us and we didn't know what was going on . . . During our set I could see a guy from the stage who had a knife and he just wanted to stab somebody . . . he really wanted a fight. There were kids stabbed and heads cracking the whole time'.

Not even the stars were immune. Jefferson Airplane's Marty Balin was so incensed by the Angels' treatment of one young man that he leapt to aid him. He was punched brutally in the face and laid out. And still the mindless viciousness continued with

bodies on stretchers being passed from out the throng, across the stage and back to the inadequate and grossly over-stretched medical team.

Many there hoped that the appearance of Jagger and the Stones would cool the atmosphere down. But as the day strayed into darkness Jagger still didn't come on. It was said that he was waiting for the theatricality of complete blackness to heighten the effect of his entrance.

'Pleased to meet you, hope you guess my name/But what's puzzling you, is the nature of my game.' So sang Jagger in his Lucifer role in *Sympathy For The Devil*. There were many that night who could not guess his game, who believed that perhaps the role had taken him over. Some say he did nothing to encourage the next sequence of events. More say that he did nothing to stop them. Some maintain that the whole colossal vanity of the event was directly responsible.

The exact details of what happened that night and in what order and for what cause are muddled. What can be squarely stated is that a young black man named Meredith Hunter was killed by Hell's Angels. He was stabbed, kicked, beaten, thrashed and clubbed. He was systematically and slowly murdered. He was killed by the people who were supposed to be offering

Left: *Carlos Santana's 'Latin rock'.*
Right: *Grateful Dead's Jerry Garcia.*

Sympathy for the devil? Did Jagger's antics provoke the horror of Altamont?

protection. For who shall guard the guardians themselves?

He did not die immediately, it seems. His battered body was lifted on a difficult journey through the people and the continuing fights to the medical tent which was, of course, ill-equipped for injuries of this sort. There was nothing the doctors, with only primitive facilities and no airlift to hospital, could do. Meredith Hunter died. One doctor declared: 'The people in charge of this concert are morally res- ponsible'.

David Crosby, who had perfor- med earlier in the day, said: 'We didn't need the Angels . . . The Stones don't know about Angels . . . but I don't think the Angels were the major mistake. The major mistake was taking what was essentially a party and turning it into an ego

game and a star trip . . . The Rolling Stones . . . are on a star trip and qualify in my book as snobs . . . I'm sure they don't understand what they did . . . I think they have an exaggerated view of their own importance. I think they are on a grotesque ego trip'.

'An exaggerated view of their own importance . . .' That was a criticism that could have been laid at the door of rock in general. The killing of Meredith Hunter was a rock tragedy. In the past, per- formers had died because of their punishing lifestyles. More were yet to die. But now the killing spread out to include the audience. Surely rock was breeding a monster that could not be contained?

In the Sixties rock had gone from harmless flippancy, music to whistle and dance along with, to high art with cultural significance. It had a gross conceit. It over-valued itself. Its performers had been placed atop

a popular Olympus. It had evolved a lifestyle to which sex and, more seriously, drugs were integral.

The Sixties had started with such promise. Rock had done so much that was good and creative and sheer fun. The Sixties ended in death, disillusion and destruction. It also ended in a great deal of dis- honesty and self-deception.

The trouble was that far too many people thought that the music and its trappings *were* life. They talked about living a 'rock & roll life' – hard, fast, drug-sped, sexually-greedy – and dying a 'rock & roll death' – premature, drug-induced, with the body ravished and mind fuddled by the effects of such a pace. They spoke of these things with admira- tion. They did not realise that rock music is not, in itself, life. It is merely an adjunct to life, an entertainment, a side-show.

The Sixties and rock showed us a dream. Both ended in a nightmare.

153

The Splintered Seventies

Led Zeppelin

The Splintered Seventies

One word sums up the decade and its music – dismal.

Don't take my word for it. Just look at any headline during any part of the decade – war, death, corruption, assassination, terrorism, kidnapping, rape, crime . . . You name it and the Seventies did it worse than it had been done before. It only lacked a global conflict.

Popular music merely reflects the time in which it is made. The Seventies were a time of fear, of poverty, – both financial and spiritual, and these led to cultural poverty – of hypocrisy, of violence. They were barren years. Bleak years. Years of exhaustion.

In rock it was as if everyone was creatively knackered after an eight-year burst of imagination and progress and work. Drugs had taken their toll, of course, they'd

Tragic rock queen, Janis Joplin.

sapped bodies and minds – witness the 'acid casualties' slouching around the streets – and robbed some of their will.

They robbed others of their life.

The decade started badly. In September 1970 Jimi Hendrix died. The next month, in October 1970, Janis Joplin died. Both were victims of drugs, both were hellions, both were ripping through life fast because they knew it wouldn't last.

Janis contributed less to the development of rock than Hendrix in musical terms. In fact, her output, both with Big Brother and the Holding Co. and on her own, was small. But she did show that women could be rock singers; could get up there and kick shit with the best of the guys. She was a 'ballsy chick', a hard drinker (Southern Comfort being her favourite tipple), a 'maniser' whose sexual conquests were famous and legion, a drug taker. On her night she exuded a powerful magic. She came on tough and raunchy. She yelled out her blues because she felt them. She'd been kicked around and shunned and ostracised and the hurt and resentment and pain exploded out of her in her songs.

The audience loved her, lusted for her, reeled with her as she blew, full-tilt, through her repertoire. On stage, on a good night, she was happy. But it's doubtful that she was often very happy off the stage. She once said – with one of those ice-lance shots of self-knowledge – 'Onstage I make love to 25,000 people, then I go home alone'.

She died in a hotel room in Hollywood on 4 October 1970.

Jimi Hendrix died in London. According to the coroner, his death

was due to 'suffocation caused by the inhalation of vomit, following barbiturate intoxication'. An open verdict was passed. The last writing Hendrix left read, in part, 'The story of life is quicker than the wink of an eye'.

The Beatles died in 1970, too. Paul McCartney left. He was blamed for the demise, but it was inevitable. Apple was a financial catastrophe. The Beatles were no longer four facets of one personality, they were four very individual people with their own lives and interests and their own music to make. McCartney made the break. If he hadn't then Lennon would have before long.

They broke up in bitter acrimony and the rancour was to continue for several years with law suits flying, accusations and counter-accusations being flung hither and yon. John Lennon said and sang some lashing, wounding things about his former partner. And Paul was scathing in his attacks on Lennon's business mentor Allen Klein. For anyone who had been young in the Sixties, the smash-up of the Beatles, their clawing at each other's throats, was a painful and almost unimaginable agony.

A less agonised but still regrettable split occurred across the Atlantic in the early days of the Seventies. Paul Simon and Art Garfunkel ended their long, fruitful and melodic partnership following their remarkable and triumphant creative and commercial pinnacle of *Bridge Over Troubled Water.*

In one way or another Simon and Garfunkel had spanned the chimerical changes in rock since 1957 when, as Tom and Jerry (oh come now!) they had achieved a US hit

Drugs took their cruel toll; both Joplin and Jimi Hendrix died 'rock & roll' deaths.

with *Hey! Schoolgirl*. They seemed set to be pop idols, New York's answer to the Everlys. But they failed to follow up and returned to school.

Simon kept trying in a series of pop groups (he also worked briefly with Carole King) but abandoned the attempt, took up acoustic guitar and folk forms and headed for Britain, where he built up a small but appreciative following. In England during the Beatles' heydays of '64 he continued writing songs and must have been re-enthused. He went back to America and Art, and together they recorded *Wednesday Morning 3 A.M.* It was an auspicious start, marrying their distinctive harmonies (which were to be such a feature of their work over the next years) to contemporary folk idiom.

Dylan was preparing the way for writers like Simon and the Byrds' rock version of *Mr Tambourine Man* showed an astute producer at CBS (Columbia in the US) what could be done with songs written originally for acoustic guitar. He took *The Sounds Of Silence*, added a soft electric and drum backing, issued it and smiled in satisfaction as it went

Beatles in the '70s: (left) Lennon's sly dig at Paul's Ram *album slipped into his* Imagine *LP. George hit gold and copyright problems. Paul soared with Wings to a second superstardom.*

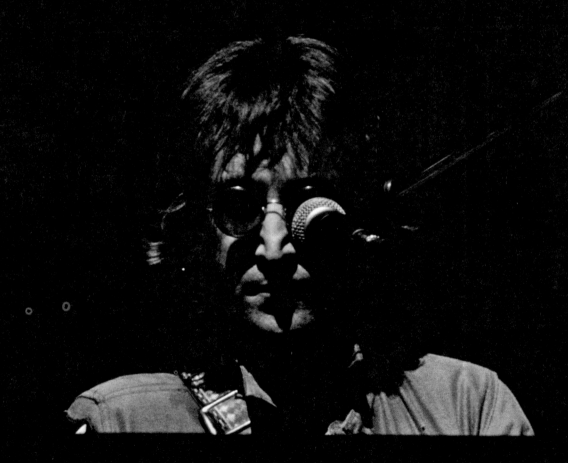

The break-up of the Beatles in 1970 was preceded by solo projects from each ; Harrison (left middle) had released the *Wonderwall* and *Electric Sounds* albums, Lennon (below) was involved with the Plastic Ono Band, McCartney (far left) had issued *McCartney* in 1970 and Starr (left) had released *Sentimental Journey*. However, only McCartney formed a regular band (Wings) while the others preferred to work with informal groups of friends to produce albums such as *All Things Must Pass* and *33⅓* (Harrison), *Imagine* and *Rock 'n' Roll* (Lennon) and *Ringo* (Starr). By 1978 all but McCartney were semi-retired from rock music.

Above: *Simon and Garfunkel.*
Above right: *Marc Bolan.*
Right: *Jackson Browne.*

right to the top of the charts in 1965.

This format settled Simon and Garfunkel's route. Some thoughtful singles (mostly taken from albums) such as *Homeward Bound* (one of the best-ever songs about a lonely performer's life on the road) and *I Am A Rock* followed. Next came the marvellous *Bookends* album with superb songs like *America*, *Hazy Shade Of Winter*, *Punky's Dilemma*, *At The Zoo*. It was a low-key collection dealing with isolation and depression, but despite the rather bleak subject matter it was handled with impeccable musical taste and distinguished by beautiful, sensitive performances.

The duo were now world stars and drawing huge and discerning audiences at their concerts. Simon was established as a writer in the first rank and the vocal interplay of the pair has seldom been equalled.

Movie director Mike Nichols cleverly used their music on the soundtrack of *The Graduate*–one of the seminal youth movies of the decade–echoing the hero's fearful ambivalence by playing *The Sounds Of Silence* over the opening sequence while holding the camera tight on Dustin Hoffman's impassive face. It was a perfect welding of music to image, and worked as well as the use of the film's main theme–*Mrs Robinson* written by Simon about the predatory older woman with whom Hoffman has an unfeeling

sexual affair–did through other parts of the movie.

Both the movie and the album taken from it were massive hits and rocketed Simon and Garfunkel to even greater heights of fame and popularity. It seemed difficult to top such success but in 1970 they achieved it with *Bridge Over Troubled Water*. It was an album packed with great songs including *El Condor Pasa* (based on a Peruvian folk tune), *Cecilia*, *Keep The Customer Satisfied* and *The Boxer*. Greatest of them all–at least in terms of sales–was the title track which became a vast worldwide hit.

Bridge Over Troubled Water was a finely-crafted song performed with great sensitivity, but it was also rather self-consciously beautiful and lush in its arrangement. It became an instant standard, covered by many of the world's finest singers (and one of the worst, Gerry Monroe, who slaughtered it) and soon a favourite in every classy cabaret and swish concert hall. Despite the care lavished on it, their version only just missed blandness.

It helped propel the LP into megasales and won audiences which had previously been inimical to rock.

Perhaps Simon and Garfunkel were aware of the dangers of being forced into a 'showbiz' image. They started drifting apart. Art Garfunkel turned to acting, first in Mike Nichols' *Catch-22* and then, more successfully, in *Carnal Knowledge*. Eventually they split entirely to pursue their own paths.

Garfunkel recorded infrequently and scored some hits (perhaps the biggest being *I Only Have Eyes For You*, a Dick Powell success from the 1934 movie *Dames*). Simon devoted himself more assiduously to music and produced at least two excellent albums in the Seventies–*Paul Simon* and *There Goes Rhymin' Simon* which yielded songs of very high calibre in *Mother And Child Reunion*, *Me And Julio Down By The Schoolyard*, *Kodachrome*, *Take Me To The Mardi Gras* and *Loves Me Like A Rock*. His position and reputation were assured and continuing. He contributed some bright, glad moments to the decade. But still the two's soaring harmonies were sorely missed.

The decade had started about as badly as any can, but one must be fair. It is most arbitrary to expect a decade–just because it is a handy time-span–to adopt its own style. But nonetheless most seem to do it. The Twenties summon visions of Gay Young Things, Flappers, the Charleston. The Thirties of bread queues, Hollywood High Gloss. The Forties of world war. The Fifties of rock & roll and so on . . .

Furthermore, the style of decade does not suddenly appear, fully-

Marc Bolan's career was patchy. The T. Rex imp (right) hit a trough until he revamped (above) shortly before his fatal car crash.

formed on the stroke of midnight of the year before. Rock & roll did not mark its presence onto the Fifties until about 1956; the Beatles did not show the way in which the Sixties were moving until 1963 and 1964.

We waited and waited. The Seventies never found a style. Unless drab can be deemed stylish.

Rock in the Seventies was splintered, fragmented. Trends emerged briefly – often reworkings of ones that had appeared years before – and then slid back into obscurity, frequently taking their protagonists with them.

The first trend of the Seventies was towards Glam or Camp Rock.

Perhaps it was a reaction against the drabness. Certainly it was a reaction against the 'heaviness–' both in sound and alleged intellectual aspirations – of the rock bands. It was frivolous, silly, amusing and, mostly, unpretentious.

The strange thing about Glam rock is that it was started by a man who had been pivotal in the underground, central to the rock mysticism and deeply involved in the idealism of the late Sixties – Marc Bolan. Bolan's group Tyrannosaurus Rex floated along on an acoustic haze producing albums with titles like *My People Were Fair And Had Sky In Their Hair But Now They're Content To Wear Stars On Their Brows*. Bolan was very beautiful and a very into spaced-out headi-

ness, man. But he also had a driving desire for stardom, a desire that had taken him from being Mark Feld, the East End kid, self-styled Mod king to underground scene-maker.

He threw away his kaftan and acoustic guitar, picked up an electric axe, sprinkled glitter dust on his make-up, wriggled his bum and turned out a load of singles that sounded almost exactly the same and sold in slews – *Ride A White Swan* (in '70), *Hot Love, Bang A Gong (Get It On), Jeepster* (in '71), *Telegram Sam, Metal Guru, Children Of The Revolution, Solid Gold Easy Action* (in '72) and so on.

He dropped the 'yrannosaurus' to become T. Rex and was the biggest star in Britain for a brief and glorious hour. The music was fairly predictable, the posturings often absurd, the clothes more and more

outrageous but Bolan brought life and glamour to rock. (He once said that people like Astaire and Mae West were his inspirations for glamour: 'I just took it and put it on *Top Of The Pops*. It's surprising how much grew out of it'.)

One of the things that grew out of it was a succession of teeny idols who got more and more extreme in their attempts to outdo each other sartorially.

According to *New Musical Express* Marc Bolan saved pop. 'He single-handedly created the teeny-bop market and dragged Pop out of its grave . . . the first major star since Hendrix to emphasise sexuality and visual image.'

(I personally do not think he created the teeny-bop market. I think he exploited it and refined it and gave it some small degree of

wore trousers at half-mast supported by twangy braces and shod their feet in brutal, great bovver boots. They failed.

They then turned to what can only be described as 'illiterate rock'! They were reacting so strongly against the brainy bullshit of the Clever Rock boys that they even spelt their songs wrongly: *Coz I Luv You*, *Look Wot You Dun*, *Take Me Bak 'Ome*, *Mama Weer All Crazee Now*, *Gudbuy T'Jane*, *Cum On Feel The Noize*, *Skweeze Me Pleeze Me!*

These were storming, stomping, stamping assaults. They were anthems, shouts and chants straight off the soccer terraces. The kids in the audience responded to Slade as if they were at the Kop or Stretford end. They held scarves up above their heads, swayed in great masses of humanity, crashed their feet into the ground in time and chorused the words. But the major difference between the Slade's crowds and football mobs was that the group—and particularly leader Noddy Holder—were tremendously good-humoured and defused any potential violence. Slade enjoyed themselves as much as their kids and they brought a very welcome smile to rock.

sophistication. I doubt if he saved pop, it's more likely that he gave it a vast dose of hormones to rejuvenate it.)

He did, however, create Glam Rock and in his wake came others, some of whom—like Sweet—locked in on the teenies and others—like Bowie—who had greater and more portentous ambitions.

Sweet produced gibberish— *Funny Funny*, *Co-Co*, *Poppa Joe*, *Little Willy*, *Wig Wam Bam*—and became increasingly androgynous as they performed it on TV. You actually could question what sex they were, so bizarre was their appearance. They tired of the nonsense and turned to some excellent, but trivial, teen screamers like *Blockbuster*, *Hell Raiser*, *Ballroom Blitz*, *Teenage Rampage*.

The great group of this time was undoubtedly Slade. Slade were self-confessed yobboes. They'd started by trying to cash in on the Skinhead cult, they had their locks razored to a literal hair's breadth of the scalp,

Glam Rock gave at least two men a last chance at stardom. The first, and more popular, was Gary Glitter. He started life as Paul Gadd in 1944 or 1940 or whatever you're prepared to believe. He became a singer in the Sixties under the nom de guerre Paul Raven and, briefly, Paul Monday. He was a veteran by the time Bolan had pioneered Glam Rock but saw a bandwagon at last upon which he might ride to success.

In fact, he was the world's most unlikely Glam star. He was—well—not in youth's first flush. Nor was he as trim as might be hoped. But he ignored all this, squeezed himself—with some pain, surely?—into the skinniest of skin-tight lurex suits (which showed some interesting bulges but not those usually associated with male sex symbols!), covered himself, as his name suggests, in sparkle and proceeded to cause havoc among sub-teen females.

He looked absolutely revolting! He primped and preened and postured; he pouted and sulked and winked. He had a serious lack of co-ordination so that his extravagant arm gestures or bum twitches or pelvic thrusts or kicks (wearing heels stacked to the height, it seemed, of 18 inches) were always a beat behind the songs' climaxes. He teetered along like a travesty of a transvestite impersonation of Mae West.

All this to songs of excrutiating and delicious cretinism: *Rock & Roll (Part 2)*—his first and one of the best—*I Didn't Know I Loved You Till I Saw You Rock & Roll*, *Do You Wanna Touch Me?* (to which he made the most ludicrously lascivious gestures and rendered himself entirely asexual), *I Love You Love Me Love* (perhaps the best of all, wonderfully dreadful!) and so on.

He retired amid tearful and stupendous farewell shows staged in the very worst of taste, handed his gold lamé cloak to his group, the personality-less Glitter Band, who went right out and had a trio of their own big hits, and, of course, re-appeared within a year. But by then the world had come to its senses. He wasn't really amusing any more, just

Glam (?) Rock: the egregious Gary Glitter (above) and mock-menacing Alvin Stardust.

a pudgy, ageing clown who'd had his glory and should have stayed quit while he was ahead.

In opposition to Glitter was Stardust. Alvin of that ilk. He too had had a checkered career. He started life as Bernard Jewry, but became Shane Fenton in the early Sixties and worked energetically round Britain making odd records like *Send Me The Pillow That You Dream On* and *I'm A Moody Guy* before being swamped by the Mersey Sound.

In the Seventies he climbed into menacing Gene Vincent-style black, sported long gloves and chains and pretended to be evil and threatening. Everybody knew that he wasn't either, but played along because it seemed to make him happy. It certainly made him successful. He hit with *My Coo Coo Ca Choo* (you see how utterly batty it all was?) in '73 and banged right on with *Jealous Mind*, *Red Dress*, *You You You* and *Tell Me Why*, all of which made the Top 20.

were very much in the Ricky Nelson/Frankie Avalon/Fabian mould of pretty boys who could sing a little.

Cassidy got his break in a similar fashion to the Monkees. He appeared in a TV series called *The Partridge Family* (in which he co-starred with his stepmother Shirley Jones) which just happened to be about a brave Mum and her talented and good-looking kids who all form a singing act. Jones and Cassidy spun off from the series to make records—as the Partridge Family, of course—and achieved considerable success in the States and Britain with songs like *I Think I Love You* and *Walking In The Rain*.

The TV exposure of his good looks, pleasant if insubstantial voice and Mr Clean personality had a powerful effect on the girls. A madness gripped them and soon Cassidy was one of the world's biggest stars. He racked up hits on his own account—pleasant ballads mostly and often remakes of other people's hits like *Cherish* (the Association) and *How Can I Be Sure?* (Young Rascals) as well as *Could It Be Forever?*, *Rock Me Baby* and others—and packed the largest auditoria with his unhinged fans. (The intensity of their dervish-like devotion was alarming and, ultimately, tragic. On 26 May 1974, 14-year-old Bernadette Whelan died of heart failure as a result of the hysteria at Cassidy's concert at London's White City Stadium.)

Cassidy, like so many others who

Stardust aka Bernard Jewry aka Shane Fenton. If at first you don't succeed . . .

All of these were pure pop stars who appealed to the eight to fifteen year olds. This was the growth market. This was where all the money could be made if you got the formula right. And fortunes *were*

Pretty David Cassidy trilled his way to temporary fame as a teen idol.

made especially if you could appeal to teens *internationally*. If you could hit these youngsters with equal impact in America, Britain and Japan, you were a millionaire.

The early Seventies produced a succession of global teen superstars—David Cassidy, David Essex, the Osmond Brothers, the Jackson 5, the Bay City Rollers.

Davids Cassidy and Essex were the most obvious teen fodder. Both

have provoked the excitement of the very young, soon sickened of the madness and the pappy music. He wanted to be taken seriously as a musician and performer. He also wanted to wreck his goody-goody image, so allowed photographs to be published of him disporting naked with nymphettes and allowed it to be known that he smoked dope. This did little to kill his image, but his attempt at being a 'serious' musician just about killed his career.

David Essex, too, tired of his teen following. But he was far better equipped to attempt a transition to musical integrity. For a start he was an able songwriter, an excellent performer and a better-than-average actor. He also moved well and had a lovely smile!

Essex served a long apprentice-ship before finding fame. He had tried to hit the top during the Sixties with a variety of groups and then switched to acting. He landed a part

Better than most teen idols, David Essex displayed style, song-writing ability and could even act in movies (bottom).

in *Godspell* (one of a spate of rock musicals that followed the success of *Hair*; both *Godspell* and *Jesus Christ, Superstar* mixed the biblical with the beaty) and soon got noticed. The next stepping-stone was a central role in the 1973 film *That'll Be The Day*. This was an evocation of youth in the Fifties (another popular theme, *American Grafitti* mined much the same vein) and gained him a wide female following. In the same year he started scoring hits with well-written, carefully-produced songs that he delivered with a cheeky charm. They were all much better than the general run of material supplied to teeny stars and their quality was reflected in the fact that they had cross-generation appeal and his first at least, *Rock On*, did monstrously well in the States where he wasn't known. He fol-

lowed this with *Lamplight* and the excellent *Gonna Make You A Star*.

In the meantime he had appeared in a very successful sequel to *That'll Be The Day* called *Stardust* (which brought the character, Jim McLain into the Sixties and superstardom only to drop out and die of an overdose) and started touring to typically hysterical audiences.

He was desperately anxious to play down the teen appeal—and undoubtedly had the wherewithal to transcend the market—but seemed unable to force himself out of the safety of unquestioning fan worship. In the late Seventies—having survived longer than most of his breed—he stood at an uneasy crossroads.

The two most extraordinary groups of the day were real-life equivalents of Cassidy's TV family, the Partridges. They were the Osmonds and the Jacksons.

The Osmonds were, are, unbelievable! For a start, there are so many of them—Alan, Wayne, Merrill, Jay, Donny, Marie and Jimmy perform, two more Virgil and Tom are in the background and parents Olive and George take care of business. They HAD to succeed simply because they outnumber the rest of us!

The second reason they're unbelievable is that they take goody-goody to its ultimate stretch. And this is no publicist's invention. The Osmonds are Mormons and their faith is a driving force in their career. They look and act clean-cut, they look and act like a huge, loving family because they *are* those things. It's a little sickly to outsiders but it worked for them. You couldn't accuse them of living a rock & roll life, though. And you don't expect

So many Osmonds! Above: (left to right) Merrill, Marie, Alan, Donny, Jay, little Jimmy and Wayne. A versatile, if sugary, act that plunged to sacharine depths with Donny and Marie's TV show (bottom).

any of them to go out with a rock & roll death. God dammit, they don't even take coffee, let alone narcotics!

The four eldest boys—Alan, Wayne, Merrill and Jay—were earning their living in show business at an early age as a cut-down barbershop quartet. The brothers—taking in Donny as he got older—caused a lot of interest through regular appearances on TV—especially *The Andy Williams Show* (he featured them a lot, perhaps because he had come to prominence via a brother act).

As the years progressed their material got poppier and in 1971 they broke through on record with *One Bad Apple* which hit number 1 in the States. After that all Heaven was let loose!

Their slick, polished, highly professional act, their personal versatility—they played a large variety of instruments, sang in numerous styles from close harmony to hardish rock, danced slickly, gave karate demonstrations!—their sheer hard work and their pleasing appearance made them huge crowd-pullers. Donny's boyish good looks and wide smile caught the hearts (and nascent libidos) of millions. They could not miss. And did not.

The truth was they covered every age and market except the rock freak (and they didn't want or need them although *Crazy Horses* was played ashamedly at campus discos alongside dirty rock songs from some freaked-out weirdos). They

appealed to the Mums and Dads with their wholesome togetherness. They appealed to the Grans who went 'aaaah!' at the brash confidence of the utterly sickening Little Jimmy. Teenage boys had masturbatory fantasies over Marie (so pure and yet with such a wanton mouth!). And so on. . . . In theory they could have lasted forever because there seemed to be an Osmond production line. As soon as one got too old he was shunted off to run the fan club and there was a new one ready to take his place.

The Osmonds were brilliantly marketed in bewildering combinations. The basic unit was the Osmond Brothers who made hits like *Down By The Lazy River*, *Let Me In*, *Love Me For A Reason*. From them Donny was spun off into solo fame with huge hits—*Go Away Little Girl*, *Puppy Love*, *Too Young*, *Why*, *Twelfth Of Never*, all of these and more being rehashes of other people's hits from the bland days of the late Fifties and early Sixties.

There were two other solo ventures—the lovely Marie (*Paper Roses*) and Little Jimmy (*Long Haired Lover From Liverpool*)—and a highly-successful duo in Donny and Marie (*I'm Leavin' It Up To You*,

Morning Side Of The Mountain).

No-one could resist such a barrage.

With their talent, personalities and unceasing hard work they should have dominated the world for three fruitful generations. The trouble was they were just *too* polished, just *too* professional, just *too good* for words. And they had a problem finding the right material. They mined the hits of the Fifties and had no answers for the demands of the Seventies.

They settled into showbiz, wealth and good works and Donny and Marie kept the standard flying with a plastic-packaged TV series that, for no good reason this observer could divine, featured ice skating.

The other family concern of the time was also, probably the most talented and musically-valid of all the teeny-bop stars, the Jackson 5.

Berry Gordy at Motown had realised—as had Kirshner and Bolan—that there was a big teen market ready and waiting for sophisticated pop. But his was a black, affluent teen market. However, he didn't have anybody on his books to fill the role. The Four Tops, the Supremes and the Temptations (his biggest acts) were moving towards the Las Vegas cabaret circuit—entertaining middle-aged, middle-class swingers who liked their music smooth and mellow like the claret they drank with the meal they ate while they watched. Stevie Wonder continued to be un-classifiably brilliant. The rest of the stable appealed more or less across the board.

What Gordy needed was a black equivalent to the Osmonds. (Although Gordy couldn't have considered it in those terms be-

The Jacksons; from contesting teeny prizes with Osmonds to reshuffled '70s slickness.

cause his factory was grooming the Jacksons well before the Osmonds crossed into the pop market.)

The story goes that Diana Ross spotted them in their home town of Gary, Indiana and rushed back to tell Gordy of her discovery. It's said that Gordy trained, rehearsed, clothed and schooled Jackie, Tito, Jermaine, Marlon and Michael (in descending order of age) for a whole year—lavishing on them his best writers/producers/choreographers—before unleashing them. If it IS true that he threw the

Lovely but schmaltzy Diana Ross.

full and awesome Motown machine behind them, it paid off.

The first record was *I Want You Back*. It was bespoke, tailor-made for the group. It was pure exploitation and it sold a million, shot to number 1 in the US in '69 and number 2 in Britain in '70. It MAY have been exploitative, but it was a marvellous record. It had something that most of the works of the Jacksons' rivals did not—soul. It was a joyful, essentially musical record, brilliantly delivered by young Michael—then only 12!—who proved both vocally and visually to be the best teeny-bop performer ever.

The tremendous vitality and genuine ability of the Jackson 5 was soon recognised, first by black

Rock bottom, the Bay City Rollers.

teens (who identified strongly with them) and increasingly and unstoppably by young whites. (There was a danger of violent antagonism, because the middle-class blacks who'd so recently got their own—their first-generation idols resented the adoption of the Jacksons by whites. They pointed out—with some justification—that the whites had the Osmonds to follow.)

The records kept coming—*ABC*, *The Love You Save*, *I'll Be There* and eight more Top 20 hits in the States under the banner of the Jackson 5. Meanwhile Michael, a teen idol to match and surpass Donny, Cassidy et al, was following his own path and turning out really excellent solo hits—*Got To Be There*, *Rockin' Robin*, *I Wanna Be Where You Are*, *Ain't No Sunshine*, *Ben*. . . .

As the brothers, particularly Michael, matured two things happened. Their music starting moving away from first-rate pop and towards the mainstream soul of Motown. The second was growing dissension within the family, the tug o' war of individuals who needed to find self-expression and, ultimately, a rift with Motown.

The majority of the boys did not want to re-sign with the label and did a deal with Epic. Motown, however, held copyright in the name 'Jackson 5' and retained it. Jermaine had married the boss's daughter—Hazel Gordy—and was committed to the company. Jermaine was replaced by young brother Randy and the band, now the Jacksons, reappeared after a long fallow period, in 1977 and slammed right back into action with *Show You The Way To Go*.

The Jacksons were undoubtedly the best of the teen stars. There was a plethora of others ranging from the unutterable Bay City Rollers—whose international success could only continue to perplex anyone with a pair of ears in reasonable working order, they were the nadir of pop lacking talent, musicianship or even charm—to the egregious David Soul and, most bizarre of all, large pieces of soft furnishing which went under the name of Wombles.

These were characters from a TV children's series who had a freak hit with their signature tune – *The Wombling Song* written and performed by Mike Batt – and, not passing up a good thing, followed with *Remember You're A Womble*, *Wombling Merry Christmas* and other anthropomorphic anthems. (It says a great deal for the power of television – and much less for public taste – that it can make recording stars out of both David Soul and large furry toys. Of the two the latter displayed rather more musical verve.)

The massive teen market which created – and often destroyed with even greater rapidity – its own heroes also contributed towards one of the most marked trends of the decade – the rise of the international solo superstars.

They came, in general, out of two main strands. The first was the acknowledgement that a single performer, rather than the group which had dominated the Sixties, could be enormously popular again as he had been in Presley's day. And the trend towards camp, outrageous, entertaining performers; a lesson learned from the great movie stars of the Thirties and Forties, a desire for glamour, for stars looking, acting and performing like stars and not like some jerk off the street. Marc Bolan had pioneered both these trends but he had not, despite enormous self-confidence and ambition, been able to see it through to its conclusion. For Bolan had never really conquered America.

That feat was accomplished by his immediate successor, David Bowie. Bowie (né Jones) remains one of the most enigmatic and cryptic figures in the entire history of rock. Visionary or charlatan? Prophet, genius or conman? One moment he's espousing Fascism and the next he's twinkled off in some new, puzzling direction and probably conceived a look and a persona to go with it. Bowie is rock's chameleon: 'My appearance changes from

David Bowie's many personas.

month to month,' he said at the height of his cult. 'I want to change it. I don't want to be stationary. I want to make myself a vehicle, a prop for my songs. I've always been aware of how much the actor must clothe himself for the role he's playing.'

By the Seventies he was playing roles as if trying for an Oscar, but before that his path had been much the same as that trodden by Bolan and Essex. He'd played with various groups with no success and had become disenchanted and looked for other modes of expression, studying mime for a while and getting involved in multi-media projects.

Then in 1969 he made a most individual single – *Space Oddity*. It really was extraordinary, one of those records that says something in a different way. It was the perfect evocation of the strangeness of space travel, a distillation of the astounding facts of the US moon shots and a homage to the fiction of Kubrick's *2001 – A Space Odyssey*.

So remarkable was *Space Oddity* that it seemed to leave Bowie creatively stranded for a while. He went out on the road and bombed – partly because the audience didn't know what to expect and partly because he really didn't have anything else to give. He fell out of sight again for a while and was written off as a one-hit wonder.

In 1970 he returned with an album, *The Man Who Sold The World* which contained seeds of the works to come. Next was *Hunky Dory* and people were starting to talk, not least because of Bowie's carefully cultivated and well-publicised sexual ambivalence. On the cover of *Hunky Dory* he's pictured looking like a cross between Greta Garbo and Katharine Hepburn. He started acknowledging he was gay but was frequently photographed with wife Angie and their son – burdened with the name Zowie. Later he would assert: 'I'm not ashamed of wearing dresses . . .' and then wistfully add ' . . . but unfortunately it's detracted from the fact that I'm also a song-writer'.

Hunky Dory did moderately well in America, virtually nothing in Britain, but nailed Bowie's rock

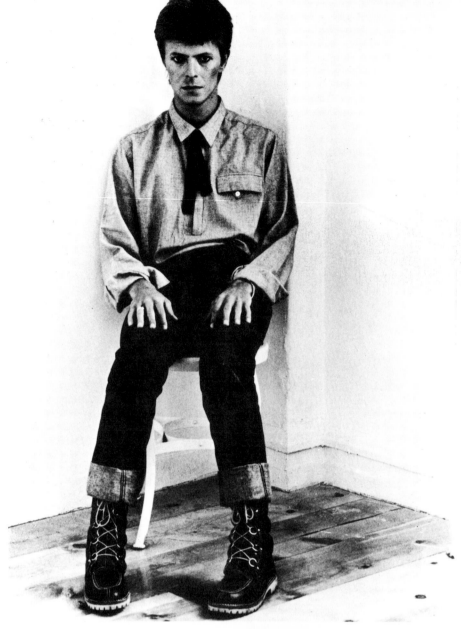

Ch-ch-ch-changes: Bowie in the late-'70s creating images, using his face and body as a canvas.

colours to the mast. He was taking off into some odd directions. He was putting together a lot of elements – themes came from his own inner landscape and a sort of psychic Sci Fi; performance came from the androgynous perversity as portrayed by Liza Minelli in *Cabaret*, welding extreme theatricality to rock. The result was a high camp, occasionally chilling, sometimes ludicrous, often impressive show in which Bowie was more than a rock singer called Bowie, he *became* the persona he portrayed – Ziggy Stardust or Aladdin Sane. He used his own face and body as a canvas, changing the colour and style of his hair with astonishing regularity, painting his skin, clothing his limbs in costumes of increasing extravagance and ambiguity. So extra-ordinary were his shows in their mixture of elements that you might leave the description at Krafft-Ebing meets *Star Trek*!

The Rise And Fall Of Ziggy Stardust And The Spiders From Mars lifted Bowie off and into orbit. Bowie *was* Ziggy and his group—Mick Ronson, Trevor Bolder and Woody Woodmansey—*were* the Spiders. This was more than rock, a progression beyond play-acting, this was Bowie in a parallel existence. He became, as Ziggy in his parable became, the biggest star in the world. There had been stars before. And they had had their fans. But Bowie's fans tried to become Bowie as Bowie had become Ziggy. They wore the same orange hair, the lightning streak of make-up slashing down the face and through the eye. They cultivated the other-worldly stare of the pupils, the alabaster of the cheekbones.

It ran very quickly out of control. Bowie was taken over by it all. Ziggy was not to be thrown aside like stage clothes at the end of the perform-ance, he started getting the upper hand. The legion of Bowie clones that flocked to every gig were closing in. He started getting mor-bid fears of being the first rock star to be assassinated on stage. At the very height of his success in July, 1973 he announced his retirement. He would perform no more in public.

Or at least Ziggy or the 'cracked actor' character of the *Aladdin Sane* album would appear no more. Bowie ducked out yet again, re-dug his roots with some favourite Sixties' songs on *Pin Ups* and then issued the apocalyptic *Diamond Dogs* which took the landscape sketched in *The Man Who Sold The World* and *Ziggy Stardust* to its dismal end.

Bowie decamped to America where he dabbled in some very odd ventures, became something of a one-man Apple for a while, offering help and backing to fringe artists, and had some intense hassles over management and contracts. When these were eventually resolved he came up in 1975 with the *Young Americans* album that revealed an amazing grasp—for a white

foreigner—of soul and which was recorded at the very heart of Seventies soul—the Sigma Studios in Philadelphia.

Next came a part that suited him to perfection—the eponymous hero of Nic Roeg's movie *The Man Who Fell To Earth*. It met with very mixed reviews, but established him further as a personality who would not be bound within the confines of rock. As the Seventies continued he dabbled further in what might be described as 'American' music, had his first American number 1 with a single co-written by John Lennon, *Fame*, and worked with the amazing Iggy Pop, a man who seemed to have all the self-destructive qualities of Ziggy.

Successive albums—*Station To Station*, *Low*—confirmed that Bowie would not be pinned down or categorised. At one point he could have been the biggest solo star since Elvis and one of the most creative, challenging, contrary and teasing ever. He shied off the first course but never fully deserted the second. He retained one of the rarest of all qualities in rock—mystery.

Bowie took some of the elements of Glam Rock—make-up, extreme and sometimes grotesque costuming—and used them to his own creative ends. One of his arch-rivals for the title King of Camp Rock also went in for absurd fancy dress, visual extravaganzas, Busby Berkely-inspired stagecraft, and conspicuous personal adornments but he used them to much more humorous result.

Elton John described himself as a 'pudgy little rock & roller' and even though he reached pinnacles of fame that are difficult, in retro-spect, to comprehend, he never made the mistake of taking him-self too seriously. He realised that there was something essen-tially comic about a shortish, bald-ing, chubby, myopic young man from Pinner, christened Reginald Kenneth Dwight (he changed it by deed-poll to Elton Hercules John) storming the bastions of fame, glamour, success and popularity. So he continued on stage and in the public prints to send himself up

Insane? Perhaps. Bizarre, certainly. Iggy Pop, Bowie's protegé.

something rotten. It was a most endearing trait and undoubtedly helped fuel his popularity even more.

He, like those mentioned before (and Rod Stewart yet to come), paid his dues during the Sixties—together with Long John Baldry in a good group called Bluesology—but his days were to come in the next decade. In 1969 he released an album called *Empty Sky* which was the result of a remarkable partner-ship and an even more remarkable act of faith.

In '67 he had met an aspiring lyricist, Bernie Taupin, and they started working together. Or rather apart as they were physically separated and collaborated via the postal services. Bernie sat in Lincolnshire, wrote his words and mailed them to Elton in London, who put music to them.

Their difficulties were com-pounded by the fact that Elton needed to earn a living and felt trapped in Bluesology, an involve-ment he was viewing with increas-ing depression and frustration. However, help was at hand in the shape of Dick James who had made a considerable fortune by publishing the songs of Lennon and McCartney. He now ran a record label in ad-dition to his publishing empire and was persuaded that Elton and Bernie had potential. They were signed as contract writers on a retainer of £10 per week apiece. Elton was signed as a performer to DJM records. This freed them to make music.

In 1969 a good single with an unusual lyrical and musical construction called *Lady Samantha* ('Lady Samantha rides like a tiger/ Over the hills with no one to guide her' . . . Intriguing!) was released and got a lot of airplay even though it didn't make the charts. *Empty Sky*, an album full of songs by this new writing duo and promising performer, followed and repeated the critical success/commercial failure of *Samantha*.

Next came the excellent album, *Elton John*, containing at least two stand-out tracks: *Border Song*, another great single that caused interest but few sales, and the tenderly romantic *Your Song*. The latter was to be Elton's first big hit.

Britain was lukewarm to John. Inexplicably as he was demonstrably one of the most interesting singer/songwriters to emerge there since Cat Stevens. DJM sent him to the States. He went to Los Angeles, played himself into a frenzy, put across every ounce of showmanship he knew and still managed not to overwhelm the music. The Americans saw instantly that to which the British had been blind and deaf. They made Elton John a star very nearly overnight. And a superstar in short order.

A slew of albums followed after this. It was as if success had released a manic creative energy in John and Taupin. *Elton John* crashed up the US charts and *Your Song* followed into the singles lists. The next album was *Tumbleweed Connection* which was popular in the States because it dealt with Americana. Then came the uncharacteristically dark *Madman Across The Water* which seemed, to the British at least, to confirm their initial doubts and hesitation in embracing John as a superstar. Doubts were dispelled, however, with the lighter, gayer *Honky Chateau*.

In the meantime the single hits were cranking out–*Rocket Man*, *Honky Cat*, *Crocodile Rock*, *Daniel*, *Saturday Night's All Right For Fighting*–and Elton was fast becoming the world's biggest concert draw. He deserved the audiences

he got because he went out–in the best tradition of Hollywood, which he revered–and gave a knock-them-on-their-asses show. His humour, his silly appearance, his knockabout antics, his musical professionalism, his all-too-evident desire to please and entertain, his sheer, contagious and unbridled exuberance were so refreshing. He earned millions but he actually tried to *give* in return when he did a show.

Despite his almost unparalleled popularity (it's doubtful whether anyone has ever been so popular on-stage since Presley) his recordings tended to be patchy. In Britain, at least, his albums came in for stringent critical scrutiny and he was often accused of being musically 'soft', pop-oriented and 'not committed to rock & roll'. (This latter, virtually meaningless, phrase bedevilled the decade. Rock journals would castigate those they thought were not toeing their ideological line by accusing them of 'not being committed' to the music. Paul McCartney–as well as John and Stewart–was particularly singled out by the self-appointed Torquemadas of the rock press for this heresy. It merely betrayed the arrogance and élitism of those who set themselves up as Inquisitors and arbiters. One can only suspect that it springs from the envy that so many rock journalists have for those they chronicle; almost every rock journalist is a performer manqué and one of the least welcome trends of the decade was a brief and thankfully unsuccessful attempt to portray the Journalist As Superstar.)

In October '73 he released a double album that showed both the range and depth of John as a performer and of he and Taupin as writers. *Goodbye Yellow Brick Road* was his best album, maintaining an amazing consistency and quality throughout its 20 tracks, a consistency proved by the fact that four single hits came from it–the aforementioned *Saturday Night*, *Bennie And The Jets* (in the US), the title track and Taupin's sensitive homage to Marilyn Monroe, *Candle In The Wind*.

This was a creative peak and

although John went on to even greater celebrity (if that was possible), his recordings declined in quality and verve. The following album, *Caribou*, was well below scratch, *Captain Fantastic And The Brown Dirt Cowboy* was self-indulgent (it was autobiographical, the Captain being John and the Cowboy being Taupin) but still sold platinum and was reported to be the biggest selling album to that date.

John, however, was tiring of it all. He had done it all and was fast becoming burdened by fame and its demands. His lifestyle was detailed minutely in the press–a great furore following the 'revelation' of his bisexuality–and he felt he was being distanced from life's realities. As the decade progressed he admitted to being more interested in sport than rock, and in 1978 announced his retirement (again!) from performing. He settled into the chairmanship of Watford Football Club which flourished during the 1977/78 season under his patronage.

Despite his 'hyper-fame' John remained–outwardly, at least–the most genial and amiable of rock stars. While others were moody, broody and dabbled in some deep and muddy rock pools, he seemed always to be sunny, cuddly and entirely engaging.

The third of the trio of solo male superstars of the Seventies had probably been trying longest to achieve his fame. From about 1963 onwards Rod Stewart played in a succession of blues-based bands–the Five Dimensions, Long John Baldry's Hoochie Coochie Men, the Soul Agents, Steampacket, Shotgun Express and lastly the Jeff Beck Group (with which he started making a name in the States) with Ron Wood. Interspersed with these were various attempts at a solo career and some singles. He ended up the Sixties with a reputation but little else.

He and Wood left Beck to join what was left of the Small Faces after vocalist Steve Marriott had decamped to Humble Pie and ex-Herd singer Peter Frampton. The Faces started playing and touring and gaining a reputation as an easy-going, good time outfit who gene-

rated a lot of warmth, had fun on stage and came up with the goods musically. Stewart was, of course, pivotal to this and the truth is that even without the Faces his time had come. He had gained considerable performing confidence from his days in America with Jeff Beck, his growly, gravelly voice matched his relaxed, 'don't care' attitude and he was growing daily in stature as a songwriter.

Stewart seems to have recognised the fact of his emergence because from the start of the decade he ran solo and group careers in tandem. It was a strangely schizophrenic arrangement that partially worked– for example, the Faces were a storming carousing, roistering live group (who also exploited soccer-crowd tactics like Slade) but couldn't capture their excitement on record. (Not suprising, perhaps, because you can't bottle lightning!) Stewart, on the other hand, was the master of the recording studio. Therefore, Stewart racked up the hit singles and albums (the Faces did less well in both charts) while the group pulled in the crowds in their

Outrageous in lifestyle, performance and romance, a super-patriot—Rod Stewart.

hundreds of thousands.

The record that made Stewart a star has been described as 'a quintessential rock song', *Maggie May* (taken from his '71 album *Every Picture Tells A Story*). His lazy, booze-sodden, raw-edged voice matched this self-written story of a feckless youth involved with an older, sexually-predatory woman to perfection. A brilliant song and a great performance, both of which were very nearly equalled the following year by *You Wear It Well*.

From now on, even though Stewart denied it, the Faces started to recede into the background. They were still, officially, on an equal footing, with Stewart keeping his solo work separate (and even on a different label) but in public minds it was, inextricably, ROD STEWART and the Faces. Eventually the split came but by then Stewart was soaring in another orbit.

He was unconscionably wealthy and spent his loot conspicuously. He had a long and public affair with Britt

Elton John injected humour and gaiety into performances which packed out every venue including the Los Angeles Bowl (below). It's almost irrelevant that he also made some fine albums, co-written with Bernie Taupin.

Few stars were more successful than Rod Stewart both solo and with the Faces who evolved from the Small Faces and Jeff Beck Group. The second line-up (above right, left to right) was Ian McLagan, Tetsu Yamauchi, Ron Wood, Kenny Jones and Stewart.

Ekland, and the pair comported themselves like characters out of a Harold Robbins novel. They fought and made up; they littered money behind them like a paperchase. In between their spats Rod was seen with a never-ending parade of nubiles. When Rod and Britt finally (finally?) broke up she sued him for $12,000,000—asking for a settlement just as if they'd been married. (It was settled out of court for an undisclosed sum.)

Rod Stewart was disgustingly rich, aggressively fortunate sexually and so famous and untouchable that he could obey rules of his own making. In fact, his weath and attitudes and lifestyle became counter-productive because while he played on his working class Scottish background (both exaggerated—his parents ran their own business and he was born in England) he was alienating those young people in the Seventies who were truly dispossessed—the working class and unemployed. It was in reaction against Stewart (and, to be fair, others) and his flaunted wealth, gained from their scraped together dole money, that spurred the punks of the late decade.

Despite this, one can only be thankful that Rod with his swaggering, naughty-boy, twinkling-eyed, cocky and rather raffish charm *did* flourish in the decade because one could forgive the tedium of his affairs and his bad behaviour and his churlishness when they were set against *Maggie*, *You Wear It Well*, *Georgie*, *Flying*, the albums and some of the cheeriest of shows.

These were the biggest solo stars of the Seventies. There were, of course, others. Alice Cooper took rock theatricality to an absurd degree. He (yes, Alice was a man, christened Vincent Furnier and, from all reports, enthusiastically heterosexual!) marketed bad taste and his band were once so inept as to be reckoned Los Angeles' worst!

It was Stunt Rock—outrageous performances (that included guillotines, simulations of chicken decapitation, acrobatics with a boa constrictor, dismemberment of dolls) wedded to hard, teenage, piledriving music. The best flowering of Cooper's outlandish work were *I'm Eighteen* and the steamrolling *School's Out*—the marriage of

Few stars were more outrageous than Alice Cooper. He brought pantomime to the rock stage, each tour using more elaborate stunts and personas.

these teen themes to Cooper's image resulted in a genre that might best be described as Frankie Avalon Goes Psychotic!
Cooper went completely over the

Global gold: Peter Frampton's album, Frampton Comes Alive, *sold slews of copies around the world. Super-MOR!*

very young and battling to remain sane amid the madness that surrounded him (as the Face Of '68–a press tag that was to hang, albatross-like, round his pretty neck for many an unwelcome year) and his group the Herd.

He hated being a teenybop idol and reckoned he could play heavy, dirty rock. So he joined up with another disaffected teen idol Steve Marriott (on the run from the Small Faces; the group he rejoined in '77 after they had bust with Stewart. Aah irony!) to form Humble Pie. This was moderately successful for a couple of years but he felt he was still being pushed by public expectations into directions he didn't want to go. He quit and formed Frampton's Camel and concentrated his activities on the States.

The new outfit still didn't fully satisfy him so he tried a make-it-or-bust solo effort. This was an album called *Frampton Comes Alive* full of melodic, classy, smooth rock songs, typical of the Middle of the Road (MOR) rock that was to dominate world sales from '76. Who knows how many units (as those cold-eyed men who run the rock industry would term them) this album sold worldwide? Eight million? Ten? Twelve million? The exact figures don't matter. Suffice to say it was enormous and made Frampton and his connections very, very rich.

Did it sell more than the

top but remained underneath the weirdness, the make-up and the drag a rather average sort of human being. As the stage persona staggered on to grosser deeds, the press kept reminding us that the lovely Alice was really in Normal Land–he played golf, ogled the TV and drank beer. Much was made of his Mr America-style beer drinking. It was proof of his good guy normality. He ended the decade trying to fight alcoholism.

If you wanted a really straight guy with a nice smile, neat clothes and a pleasant musical line you had to look no further than Peter Frampton. The truth of the matter is that Peter Frampton always was a nice person. Even way back in '68 when he was

Fleetwood Mac's extraordinary *Rumours*? It's not important except that these and others showed new routes in rock. The children of the Sixties had become the middle-class parents of the Seventies. They still wanted rock music but at a rather genteeler pace than previously. The rock musicians who had grown into their 30s along with the audience gave it to them. An indication of this MOR rock–detested by publications like *New Musical Express*, lauded by *Rolling Stone*–were some British

Re-formed Small Faces. (Left to right) Marriott, Lane, Jones and MacLagan.

posters for Fleetwood Mac's block-busting *Rumours* which depicted an elderly, rubicund vicar, a middle-aged matron, a young Mum and Santa Claus all averring they loved the album! Other big-selling MOR rock artists were Linda Ronstadt and James Taylor; Wings were frequently bracketed in this category as were, of course, the Carpenters. Paul Simon, a huge selling star without his partner of so many years, Art Garfunkel, was also slotted in here.

The MOR rock brigade sold absolutely truckloads of albums; all, it seemed, to the Flower Children of

Sounds of the '70s.
Above: *Fleetwood Mac had mega-sales with* Rumours.
Top right: *David Gates and Bread.*
Centre right: *ex-Lovin' Spoonful's John Sebastian.* Bottom right: *the Carpenters.*

'67 who had become the smooth young executives – with their healthy, glossy, affluent patina – of '77. Other firm favourites and big, big sellers were the Eagles – especially with *Hotel California* – Chicago, Olivia Newton-John, the ever-acclaimed Joni Mitchell, Leo Sayer, Mike Oldfield (whose *Tubular Bells* jangled in every form and media, including advertising

jingles, through the decade) Queen and Emmylou Harris.

The latter lady, like Linda Ronstadt, constituted part of a soft rock/country fusion that found great favour. Other country stars—notably ladies like Tammy Wynette with *Stand By Your Man* and *D-I-V-O-R-C-E* and the inflationary Dolly Parton—benefitted from this renewal of interest in country music. (It had welded into rock, of course, back with Dylan and the Byrds' *Sweetheart Of The Rodeo* album and continued into the decade before being largely replaced by the rather more aggressive, blues-based Southern and Texas boogie of cult bands like the Allman Brothers, Lynyrd Skynyrd—both groups were blighted with tragedy; Duane Allman and Berry Oakley were both killed in almost identical motorbike accidents a year apart and Skynyrd members died in a plane crash—ZZ Top and others.)

The biggest country artist whose appeal was predominantly MOR was the ever-smiling John Denver with his songs of rural whimsy. Black music had its own MOR rock; the brand leader was undoubtedly Diana Ross, who left the Supremes to become one of rock's divas, a black answer to Barbra Streisand, going

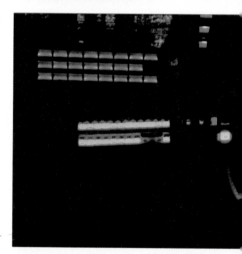

Bee Gees from a '60s group (top left) to '70s disco-fever trio (left and below) retaining Robin, Barry and Maurice Gibb. Harry Nilsson (top right) showed promise of extraordinary songwriting talent but flagged. The Eagles (below right) played soft country rock.

Mike Oldfield's Tubular Bells pervaded. John Denver (above), too good to be true.

Country Queens: Tammy Wynette (above); the inimitable Dolly Parton (below).

Emmylou Harris

Olivia Newton-John

Twiggy

Melanie

Lynsey de Paul

Helen Reddy

Carly Simon

Top left: *jazz-rock fusion, Chicago.*
Bottom left: *supreme showman Freddie Mercury and Queen.*
Above: *Leo Sayer and mentor Adam Faith.*

very Broadway both in material and in style. She starred, to some acclaim, as the tragic Billie Holiday in the movie *Lady Sings The Blues* and then blew all the goodwill accrued

Gladys Knight and the Pips, '70s-style.

from that by indulging herself in *Mahogany*.

Interestingly, as La Ross moved towards mainstream showbiz, Streisand—another whose ego seemed to know no bounds—scuttled crab-like towards rock. She produced, starred in etc., etc., the third movie version of *A Star Is Born*. This time it was the birth of a rock star. The film was almost universally reviled by the critics, a hit with

audiences and a source of great sorrow to country fans who saw one of their brightest sons, Kris Kristofferson (he of the magnificent *Me And Bobby McGee*) dragged down into the mawkish morass. Kristofferson together with Waylon Jennings and Willie Nelson were Nashville 'outlaws' who showed the heart of country music, that the country singer need no longer be a 'Rhinestone Cowboy' or sing

maudlin songs of lachrymose sentimentality. The other two lived up to their raunchy, rock-like, bad boy promise. Kristofferson settled for MOR superstardom.

The other exponents of sophisticated black rock were the hugely-successful Stylistics. They came out of the second great explosion of music that emanated from Philadelphia. This time it was not the result of grooming Italian kids as ersatz rockers, but knocking the edges off black groups, smoothing out their sound in the studio and presenting this new, silky, rather bland product to a seemingly ever-hungry audience. Black music very nearly dominated the charts in the Seventies. Tamla Motown continued unabated in success–Stevie Wonder out-stripped himself with brilliant work; notably his massive *Songs In The Key Of Life* in 1976, a fittingly dazzling crown to a decade that had seen the *Talking Book* and *Inner-visions* albums from a man who continued as one of rock's most singular and consistently startling talents–but for a while the satin 'Philly Sound' held sway.

Philadelphia became a big music centre in the Seventies, revolving around writers/producers/label owners/entrepreneurs like Kenny Gamble and Leon Huff, Hugo and Luigi and Thom Bell. Out of these

Left: *Kris Kristofferson and Barbra Streisand changed their images—he softer, she rockier—for the hugely successful re-make of* A Star Is Born.

talents emerged hit groups—the O'Jays, the Three Degrees, Archie Bell and the Drells, Harold Melvin and the Blue Notes, the Delfonics, Blue Magic. But the greatest of these were the Stylistics.

The voice of Russel Thompkins Junior was liquid gold and the rest of the group were used as a vocal setting for this fluid nugget. The Stylistics represented the very best of Philadelphia's commercial soul with single hits that poured out of the studios—*You Are Everything*, *Betcha By Golly Wow*, *I'm Stone In Love With You*, *Break Up To Make Up*, *Rockin' Roll Baby*, *You Make Me Feel Brand New*, *Let's Put It All Together* and on and on—but it is also significant that their huge-selling *Best Of* album was marketed and sold (aggressively via TV in Britain in one of the first major campaigns to sell currently-popular artists in this fashion) as the perfect accompaniment to the ubiquitous dinner party of the even more ubiquitous young middle-class couple. Social acceptance came, it seemed, with smoked glass dining tables, bottomless coffee pots, a snifter of brandy, chocolate mints and the voice of Russell Thompkins Jnr running through his group's best singles. Black music had come a long way from the ghetto.

While on the subject of black

Philadelphia flourished with soft soul from the Stylistics (far left) and the jumpier O'Jays (far right); Detroit with the Spinners (below) and Wonder (above).

Elkie Brooks in Vinegar Joe

Donna Summer

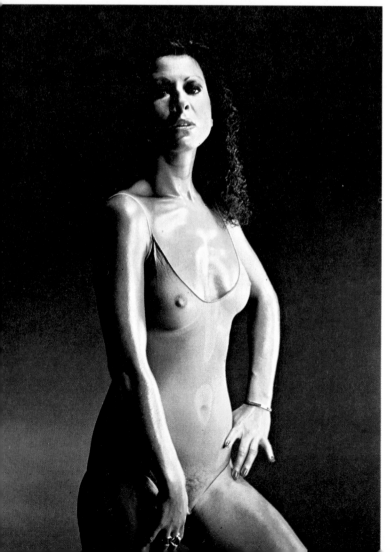

Elkie Brooks

Quatro

Kiki Dee

LaBelle

Natalie Cole

Cher

The Supremes

Above: *Orchestral soul from Harold Melvin and the Blue Notes.*
Right: *Disco queen, the techno-orgasmic Donna Summer.*

music we must not ignore two further trends that set their mark on the decade. The first was perhaps the nadir of music – either black or white. It was, in fact, non-music. It was called Disco, mostly because it was precisely the rubbish played in those hellholes to young people of regrettably limited taste. They demanded nothing more than a bland beat to which they could mindlessly gyrate. Disco was this. It chunked along at precisely the same rhythm (to precisely the same tune, the most jaded among us would say), with precisely the same instrumentation, and precisely the same voices intoning approximately the same words. I said it left its mark on the decade. This is wrong. It slid over the decade like a slug slides across glass, and left the same

Swedish overkill. Bjorn, Agnetha, Anni-fred and Benny. Behind the Abba smiles lies pure plastic gold.

glistening slime. You didn't notice its arrival, you didn't remark on its departure. Disco was *the* music of this dreary decade in that it was nothing at all. It was the bastardised child of a miscegenation between a metronome and a computer. To anyone with the slightest ear it signified the utter paucity of the times.

The Queen of Disco was Donna Summer who simulated orgasms to the pulse of electronics. She breathed heavily and the result was that of a computer on heat. She was the Raunchy Robot – sterile, asexual, unreal. Her music was as blood-stirring and passionate as the internal motions of a quartz crystal watch.

Rolling Stone summed up the significance (or lack of same) of Disco well in its tenth anniversary issue. Writing about the rock of the Seventies – under the sub-head 'The Thrill Is Gone' – Jon Landau said: 'Through the Sixties it was understood that if music did not deal with feeling, it could never really succeed. The name of the major black record style today is Disco; the name of the major style of the Sixties was soul. In the Sixties you could say nothing greater about a record than that it was soulful'.

Sadly, this absence of soul extended into other styles. For example, the biggest pop group of the time was Abba. Everything about Abba smacked of design. Even their name is an acronym of their christian names (*A*gnetha, *B*jorn, *B*enny, *A*nni-fred). They prefabricated modular music, containerised for export.

Take a jiggly pop beat, take two sexy girls and two personable boys, take some simple, preferably monosyllabic words (*English* words of course, even though the writers are Scandinavian, because English is rock's *lingua franca* and acceptable in every market of the world), set up a marketing operation in different territories negotiating with record labels in each country on an individual basis (as opposed to the general policy of signings with one huge multi-national for the whole world) so that you can haggle the best possible deal and sit back in your corporate headquarters to become very, very rich.

Abba did this. The fact that they saw what sold in pop and capitalised on it is not to be decried. Too many artists had been ripped-off by too many sharks over the years, and no one could blame a shrewd singer/ songwriter/producer for wanting to see the best possible return for his efforts. The thing that was offensive was the thin-lipped, bloodless machine-efficiency of the operation. Somehow it was so very *Scandinavian* – clean, cold, passionless, hard-edged, cost effective. There was no warmth, no humour, no room for mistake. It was the ultimate rock bureaucracy, the pop welfare state. Under the Abba umbrella came everything – Abba records, Abba concerts, Abba books, Abba films, Abba T-shirts, officially-approved Abba photographs, Abba statements (that said nothing), Abba smiles (that showed Abba teeth – perfect, of course – and nothing more). The suspicion grew that Abba were androids – a beautiful blonde girl automaton offset by a lovely redhead, one cuddly male drone offset by a rather more svelte variety – designed by a technological genius. (They were the R2D2s and C3POs of rock-Star Bores!) As they appeared on TV to plug their annual albums and thrice annual singles via carefully-directed film clips (quite soon after they achieved success one stopped seeing the members in person), the observer became progressively aware that the stare in those eyes was glassy, that the minimal movements were mechanical, that the smiles were pinned into place and the skins were beginning to take on an unhealthily high surface sheen.

Abba—the waxwork wonders.

Abba went after world domination and achieved it. It was a form of rock imperialism–the hits cranked out following *Waterloo* (which brought them Continental fame in one fell sweep via the Eurovision Song Contest–a TV extravaganza seen in virtually every home–which this tedious and moronic song won in 1974) and spread inexorably all over the 'civilised' world. The hits were pleasant, uninvolving, entirely undemanding and pretty much of a muchness–*S.O.S.* wasn't that different from *Mama Mia* which only differed slightly from *Knowing Me, Knowing You*. Perhaps the most engaging was *Dancing Queen* and certainly the most apt was *Money, Money, Money.*

(I am aware that this view may seem unusually jaundiced. After all, both Abba and Donna Summer *were* incredibly successful and popular–Abba were estimated to have sold fifty million discs worldwide by '78.

As a balance I offer this view by Derek Jewell in the London *Sunday Times*; his opinion is that their music is not 'inconsiderable; it is jolly, accessible, safely sexy, brilliantly constructed for the middle road market. It's just that its dollar harvest seems wildly disproportionate to its musical merit'. Mr Jewell's opinion seems altogether more temperate than mine. Balance is all!)

Somehow Abba and Disco went hand-in-hand and the jaded listener started to wonder if there was any music left in rock that captured the urgency and excitement so evident only a few years before. Thank God, there was. It was black music and it had life and blood and lust and tears and sweat and noise and vitality. It cried and it imprecated and it gave a great shout of joy. It was called reggae and it was very curious indeed. Reggae according to one of its Jamaican exponents living in Britain–Barry Ford of the group Merger, speaking in the London *Guardian*–is 'like the blues–it's the

topical music of the times for telling stories or making statements about current affairs. It can be political, indifferent or tongue-in-cheek'.

Reggae emerged from the rich musical scene of Jamaica. The first rumbles of indigenous Jamaican music had come in the Sixties with odd mini-trends for Blue Beat and Ska and then something called Rock Steady. It leaked out of its native island and was taken up by the West Indian immigrants to Britain who had settled into their own communities– which were in effect ghettos, especially cultural ghettos. Young black kids in Britain were really the bottom of the heap, discriminated against, unemployed, harassed by the police. They needed uniforms, music, images and stars through which they could express their own identity. The music was reggae, the stars were people like Bob Marley and the Wailers and Toots and the Maytals and the image was dreadlocks, tight-fitting wool caps and the philosophy of the Rastafarians.

Number one rastaman, Bob Marley.

There is not the room here, nor do I have the knowledge, to explain the religion of the Rastafarians. Suffice it to stand as a crude explanation that Rastafarians looked to the late Emperor of Ethiopia, Haile Selassie, as a divinity and to Ethiopia (or Abyssinia) as their spiritual and (eventually) actual home. They consider themselves a lost tribe – like the Israelites, the title of a very popular single by Desmond Dekker – who are looking to return to their promised land. Rastamen have their own way of expressing themselves (in a Jamaican patois), their own outlook and their own strong and very sincerely-held spiritual beliefs, one of which involves the frequent use of 'de 'erb' or grass. (This took them outside the law and made them feel even more exclusive.)

Reggae music first emerged from the ghetto underground with a film starring Jimmy Cliff (a singer who had previously hit with the distinctly un-reggae *Wonderful World*, *Beautiful People* and *Wild World*, the latter from Cat Stevens' *Tea For The Tillerman* album) entitled *The Harder They Come* which depicted the tough, violent underworld of Jamaica and its interface with the island's music industry. A few people started taking interest as the film achieved cult status in Britain. Those who were really listening to the music were the young whites, who felt themselves to be just as done down and ill-used and future-less as black youth. These kids had also invented their own uniforms and emerged as Skinheads. The Skinheads adopted reggae. (And later so would their cultural heirs, the punks.)

The first great reggae star – and by 1978 still the only one to become a truly international figure, even superstar – was Bob Marley. He emerged on the thrusting, inno-vative, talent-nurturing Island label (run by a white Jamaican named Chris Blackwell) with an album, *Catch A Fire*. His rise to prominence outside Jamaica (where he was an enormous and controversial star) was initially slow. The truth is that half the time most white men could not understand what he was saying in interviews and in song, nor were their ears accustomed to his reggae rhythms yet. But the rise was to be inexorable, mostly because Marley was primarily a superb and creative musician (some lauded him as 'the black Bob Dylan') and secondly he was an energetic, exhibitionist, overtly sexual performer (the black Mick Jagger?). The image (es-pecially the Ganja-smoking, womanising – his sexual conquests were enviable, impressive and catholic and much-reported in both the rock and muck-raking popular press – and soccer obsession) and the music strode on hand-in-hand, the one supporting the other.

He adopted an anti-authoritarian stance and anti-establishment politics. This led him into problems at home (Jamaican politics tend to be rough-house and rambunctious) and precipitated an attack upon his home in which he and members of his household were injured by flying bullets. This 'bolshiness' was reflected in one of his songs that became a minor classic and a huge hit (for Eric Clapton as it transpired), *I Shot The Sheriff*. Another track achieved similar critical status – the beautiful, sensitive, rather painful *No Woman No Cry*. In 1977/78 he fulfilled every critical and com-mercial promise with a massively

Cat Stevens dug reggae roots.

Marley, the black Mick Jagger?

popular album *Exodus*.

Marley's music – and success – proved to be influential towards the end of the decade. Some of the long-established rock stars were intrigued by the rhythms of reggae and its raw-boned innocence. They decided to check out the island (a holiday paradise for the young and wealthy, incidentally!) and its musicians/music. The Rolling Stones, Cat Stevens, Paul Simon, Paul McCartney and Wings, all went to soak up the reggae sound and/or to record in the studios. They retailed their reggae/rock with varying degrees of success.

Reggae spread west from Jamaica towards America. It was welcome in a market where black music needed a shot of new blood if it wasn't to die amid a succession of smiling, carefully-coiffed and choreographed marionettes, dressed in increasingly unattractive and irrelevant glitter uniforms, who mouthed increasingly foolish words to increasingly predictable and gutless rhythms.

People like Stevie Wonder would never fall into the stereotype that was commercial black music. He would never NEED to have reggae (although he would, of course embrace and transform it by dint of his own genius). But the rest? Well, most of the black artists of the Seventies had forgotten the cry of agony and frustration and despair that was the blues. Had forgotten that the blues was the cradle of all black and most white popular music. They had gone so far down an increasingly easy street that they'd lost what the blues and, thank God, reggae had – immediacy, urgency, fire, passion, sex.

Reggae and Marley (and his contemporaries) gave all that back to popular music both black and white. Inevitably people clambered onto the bandwagon (it was particularly sad to see ageing superstars trying to 'go reggae' and largely failing) but the boisterous music was proving remarkably resistant to dilution and contamination. Perhaps a lot of its appeal lay in its curious argot and innate, rather good-tempered, humour. A big British '78 single hit was a virtually incomprehensible song by two young Jamaican girls, Althia and Donna, called *Uptown Top Ranking*. It was infectious reggae-pop with an absolutely compulsive beat, quite nonsensical and irresistible. (The title meant, as far as translation is possible, the best, the greatest, the swankiest.) Even after singing and performing their song for six months Donna maintained the record's massive success lay in 'The rhythm. Every time we hear it we still jump'. That's true, generally, of reggae. There's another truth expressed by the young lady's father/manager who said that the words were the source of the

Below: *consistent hit makers Hot Chocolate.*
Right: *the juggernaut rocks on; Led Zeppelin wiping out perfectly innocent fans. Plant and Page on the offensive.*

record's success: 'They feed theirself right into the proper place with the people'. And THAT is true of reggae–like all great popular music it feeds itself into the proper place with the people.

With reggae black music still had some adrenalin left in its blood-stream. One might ask if the same was true of white rock. The biggest group of the early to mid-decade was, without the slightest doubt, Led Zeppelin. Between them Robert Plant, Jimmy Page, John Paul Jones and John Bonham released some-thing that might be described as Rock Of Attrition–the loudest, heaviest ever heard. Led Zep was a musical juggernaut, an armageddon machine powered by the crash-ingest rhythm drive ever un-leased on an innocent public. Seeing Led Zeppelin for the first time may be compared to going into battle against Hannibal and coming face-to-face with armoured elephants–you don't know whether to flee for your life or stand and watch this incredible sight and thus risk being ground under foot.

Led Zeppelin was the only truly successful supergroup. It made up for in sales, popularity, money-spinning and sheer physical devastation what all the others had promised but failed to deliver.

This rock apocalypse rose from the ashes of the Yardbirds. Jimmy Page was yet another virtuoso guitarist to have served with the group although his major work before that time had been as a legendary sessionman. Another legend in this lucrative but gen-erally anonymous field was John Paul Jones who pioneered new ground in bass playing and brought it a respectability it had never previously enjoyed. Vocalist Plant and drummer Bonham were not as well-known but enjoyed good reputations.

The foursome started life as the New Yardbirds to undertake commitments left by the old Yard-birds on their disintegration. They gigged under that name for a while, became Led Zep but were not

achieving much acclaim in Britain. They, like others before and since, looked towards America and spotted a gap in the market. The gap was the need for a heavy-metal, guitar-dominated, power-drill bass-and-drum outfit with a lot of energy and personality. It was indicated by the success of Rod Stewart and Jeff Beck in the Jeff Beck Group, but Beck was unable to maximise his advantage and when the group nose-dived, Led Zep were very ready and very heavy.

They ripped, bludgeoned, charged–what's the word? rhino'ed?–their way through two albums, *Led Zeppelin* and *Led Zeppelin II*, that defined their style (and,unfortunately, inspired a lot of imitative groups who could not emulate their skill and thus inflicted a great deal of pain on perfectly decent folk) and established them as THE practitioners, the onlie be-getters of heavy rock.

Somewhere into the early years of the decade Led Zep became some-thing more than a rock group and something less than a major world power. They earned more money than some African nations per annum. They attracted more people to their concerts than anyone could count. It was entirely ridiculous and excessive and slightly disgusting. They were a rock band; they were, admittedly, extremely good. But they became a Force. They became in quick time superstars, hyper-stars, megastars. They were beyond royalty, nearer demi-gods. And all they did was play instruments!

Heroes old and new: ex-Drifter Ben E. King meets the Average White Band.

Mixed in with their flesh-rending music was a silly pseudo-philosophy; the sort of untutored, unformed, unthought-out quasi-mysticism that had been such a pretentious blight in the latter years of the Sixties. The music, however, crashed on. There were two further albums named after the group and distinguished by numerals–*III* and *IV*–which contributed to the lore. Then in 1975 came *Physical Graffiti* which was simply silly. It was a rock album that sold, reputedly, 500 copies an hour at its height!

The group had to go into films, of course. And so they made one all about themselves and their fantasies and whatever else they wanted in it because they were so big that no one dared gainsay them. It was called *The Song Remains The Same*, everybody hated it and the album sold platinum or whatever the most valuable precious metal on earth might be!

Led Zeppelin achieved fame, popularity, sales, wealth and global acceptance that eclipsed those even of the Beatles. And what ultimately

Roxy Music began in 1970 and in their last line-up consisted of Bryan Ferry (keyboards), Eddie Jobson (keyboards), Andy Mackay (sax, oboe), Phil Manzanera (guitar) and Paul Thompson (drums); Brian Eno was also once a member. Initially their high-camp, avante-garde image won Roxy a cult following in the UK and Europe but by 1976 personality clashes and the solo ambitions of Ferry had effectively ended the band.

Genesis (left and above) very nearly equalled Alice Cooper for theatricality particularly under Peter Gabriel.

guardian/nanny/heavy Peter Grant. They were losing their lustre and fast becoming objects of contempt. And who's to wonder? They were not gods. When boiled down to reality, Led Zep are four musicians who have contributed a great deal to a vinyl shortage, made some music that might last to be reasonably well-regarded in their middle age and the memory, for some, of a couple of hours of excitement in a vast auditorium when the ears were assailed to the point of pain.

Lep Zeppelin helped to bring about two things in Seventies rock. They broke ground for a whole barrage of heavy metal groups (some of whom mixed in dubious spirituality) and they set up a re-action against the exaggerated and, largely, undeserved stature these groups were accorded.

In the wake of Led Zeppelin came other bands like Yes, Emerson, Lake and Palmer, Deep Purple, Status Quo and Thin Lizzie who incorporated the all-pervasive ripping, zinging, growling, chunking, grating electric guitar riff. Some were lighter, some were heavier, some aspired to symphonic forms, some kept strictly to kicking ass and giving the audience a good time. All took themselves fairly seriously, all became exceeding wealthy, all commanded devoted followings. Some overstretched themselves, most overestimated themselves. Few acknowledged that they knew what rock & roll, original rock & roll, the spirit of rock & roll was all about. There was nothing in common between these rock princes and

did it profit them or us? By the end of the Seventies the very excess of it all was starting to turn stomachs. Those who had built Led Zep into super-

heroes were turning against them. The stories started appearing about the arrogant behaviour of the group members and their manager/

Two '60s hits and a series of flops preceded Status Quo's boogie blitzkrieg.

The black arts meet mystical mumbo-jumbo. Yes (above) and Black Sabbath (right) combined rock and 'religion'.

their subjects. They had allowed an unbridgeable gulf to open up between themselves and their audience. They could not see the writing on the wall. They were so obsessed by their own narcissism, so surrounded by panderers and flatters, so insulated by the trappings of fame that they did not realise their reign was coming to an end. They could not hear the serfs hurling curses against their privilege and position.

The solo superstars and the Led-Zep-style supergroups made

deprived, unemployed kids with no future, sick to their stomachs. Rock & roll had started as the echo of street noise. As a raunchy, gutsy, sweaty, $2\frac{1}{2}$ minutes of power and energy. THAT had been rock & roll. THAT had been the mainspring of the Beatles and the Stones. THAT had been the thrust behind Motown. All that had gone by the last quarter of the Seventies except, perhaps, in reggae which was now the music of the underprivileged.

Most of the music purveyed to the masses said nothing. It was not, as Peter Townshend had been so many years before, 'talkin' 'bout my generation'. It wasn't talking about anything that had relevance to a 14-

year-old in London, Manchester, New York or Los Angeles. A 14-year-old who hates school, can't get on with his parents, won't have a job to go to or money to spend. A kid who cannot be part of the affluent world he sees thrust at him via the media.

There were no points of contact between kids like this and Elton John or Yes or Stewart or Led Zeppelin. Their worlds did not coincide at all. No street kid in the depressed Seventies could relate to them or their music. To him rock & roll wasn't about 60-piece orchestras, quadrophonic sound, 24-track tape machines and all the other technological gimmicks of the recording studio. To him rock & roll wasn't intellectual, did not express any spiritual truths, had nothing to do with 12-minute guitar solos, chartered jets, sterling silver coke spoons or chauffer/bodyguard-driven limousines.

Rock had left the street kids behind in their high-rise tower block flats, in their sterile school-rooms with their beaten uninterested teachers, in their dead-end jobs, in their dole queues. There was no sound of *their* cities in the rock of the Seventies. It neither reflected their lives and anger nor did it give them a chance to forget both. A young man named John Lydon—who was as angry as any and angrier than most—expressed it well: 'Rock & roll is supposed to be FUN . . . You're supposed to enjoy it. It's not supposed to be about critics or about spending a hundred fucking years learning a million

Both Bad Company (top left) and 10cc (far left) were UK bands who went over big in the States, the latter with a welcome dash of humour. Poppier Rubettes conquered Europe.

Mick Jagger on tour with the Rolling Stones. The line-up on the Tour of the Americas in 1975 was (left to right) Ron Wood, Billy Preston, Ollie Brown, Mick Jagger, Charlie Watts, Keith Richard and Bill Wyman.

Thin Lizzy's Phil Lynott.

beat-up), a basic, puny even, amplification system, a great deal of energy and an audience.

There was no worry about finding the latter. The audience was made up of the thousands of kids who littered the decaying centres of the great urban sprawls of the Western world. There were punks, in fact or in the making, in Dusseldorf and Dijon, in Rome and Stockholm, in Birmingham and Orange, New Jersey. All you needed to do was assemble them in one place—be it CBGBs in New York or the Roxy in London—set up your second-hand gear, and play your songs. Oh yes, you needed a bit of bottle, a touch of chutzpah to do it. Unless you're Johnny Rotten, of course. He'd never done anything like it before in his life, didn't know he could sing, didn't play an instrument but wasn't fazed. 'I never understand why people are scared to go on stage, 'cause it don't take anything,' he told New York's *Punk* magazine. 'You don't have to be drunk or out of your head. Just walk up there.'

In a way, this is exactly what the punks did. No one was offering them opportunities or venues or re-hearsal rooms or contracts or media exposure so they took them. Some rehearsed and played literally wherever they could—the tunnels connecting London's underground system seemed to be popular for a while. They found pubs, small clubs,

chords on the guitar. It's the spirit. It's what you *say* that's important'.

That should be engraved on every rock musician's heart— 'You're supposed to enjoy it . . . It's the spirit. It's what you *say* that's important'. And above every portal to every recording studio and every concert hall stage door should be emblazoned the legend: ABANDON HYPE ALL YE WHO ENTER HERE!

John Lydon was a good person to act as spokesman for what became known as the punks. He became far more notorious under the *nom de guerre* Johnny Rotten.

Rotten and the punks of his generation absolutely rejected the whole supposition upon which Seventies rock was built. Paul Weller—vocalist/guitarist with the Jam—summed up part of the philosophy of the so-called New Wave of rock performers: 'The scene is about being accessible to the people who come to see you . . . Getting away from all that 1,500 audience crap'.

Just as skiffle had, all those years before, shown that music could be made by anyone on virtually any-thing, so now the punks—in furious reaction against the huge banks of equipment costing many thousands of pounds, the 12-strong road crews, the million-pound investment

in studio time and recording technology—set up their alternative world of rock. Rock that reflected their own lives because, as Chelsea singer Gene October insisted, 'rock comes from a dirty old playground in the slums'.

They realised that you don't have to have thousands of pounds-worth of gear to start a rock band. You don't have to have a recording contract with an upfront advance of a quarter of a million pounds against future royalties, nor the backing of a multi-national recording corpora-tion. You don't even have to be a great musician. All you need are the essential instruments (no matter how

Steve Harley (standing) and Cockney Rebel played good, driving rock.

Top left: *Post-Led Zep heavy metal came from Uriah Heep.*
Above: *Lou Reed earned the title 'Godfather of Punk'.*
Left: *Eddie and the Hot Rods (left to right): Barrie Masters, Dave Higgs, Steve Nicol, Paul Gray. Excess succeeds as Kiss proved by going far too far.*

anywhere they could set up their gear. They wrote their own songs even though they had no musical background. They kept everything short, abrupt and razor sharp. Not for them extended guitar solos—their whole programmes, including full repertoire, lasted no longer than the individual songs of some of the heavy metallers! The Sex Pistols' Steve Jones laid it on the line for *New York Rocker*: 'I have guitar solos. There's two reasons for that—I can't play solos, and I hate them anyway'. Not articulate but he makes the point!

In London and New York there was an undercurrent of feeling, a need to sweep away the bullshit and claptrap of modern rock and get back to basics. While the hysterical media pounced, howling, onto pin-impaled lobes and nostrils; leather fetishist fashion; spitting, pogoing, spikey hair cuts; violence and the extreme excrescences of the 'movement'; the true intent of performers like the Sex Pistols, Buzzcocks, Damned in Britain and Heartbreakers, Ramones and Television in the States went un-noticed.

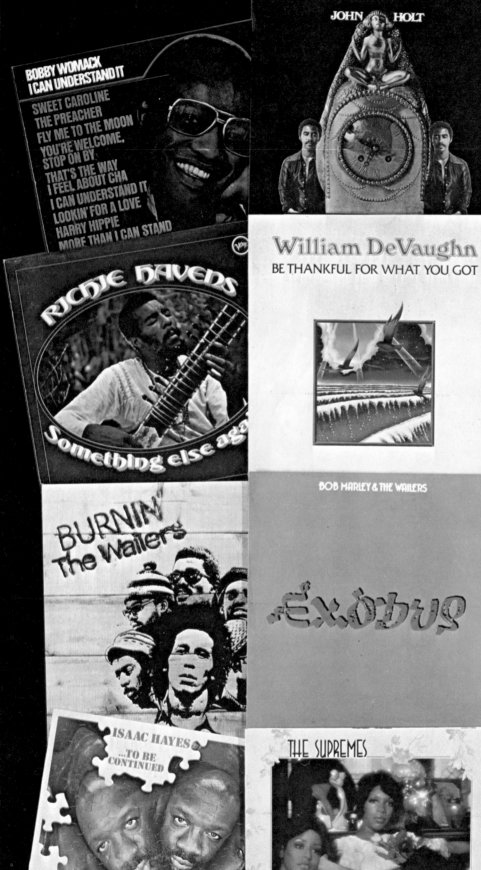

the typical escalator to rock's pinnacles. They had beaten their own path, garnered their own following, and by dint of sheer hard work, a policy of non-compromise and the gradual realisation by blind and/or deaf critics of their worth, had forced their way to success and recognition.

On their heels came the true punks. Spearheaded, of course, by the Sex Pistols. They were to the Seventies what the Rolling Stones had been to the Sixties. They thrived on outrage, on public disapproval and the simulated shock of the media. They courted unpopularity, went out of their way to offend and cultivated a most repellent image. In one year they went from utter obscurity to a world fame backed up by only one album and four singles. They smashed into prominence by swearing on TV and then set about building on that infamy.

In a matter of months the Sex Pistols had signed with three record companies in the UK, broken with two and received over £100,000 in settlements! Their first single, for EMI, *Anarchy In The UK* had crashed into the Top 30 purely on word-of-mouth. Shortly after its release they appeared on a news magazine TV show in London, got into a slanging match with the presenter (after he had provoked it) and swore saltily. EMI dropped them.

A & M signed and dropped them with indecent haste. Virgin signed them and put out *God Save The Queen* as a single. This was bound to distress many as it was the name of the British national anthem and was released at the peak of nationalistic and monarchical fervour for Queen Elizabeth's Silver Jubilee celebrations.

The Pistols lurched on. Johnny Rotten became the most hated young man in Britain. They were banned from just about every possible venue in the land and yet sold hundreds of thousands of singles—even though hardly anyone had ever seen them perform, had

Top: *The lugubrious Patti Smith, poetess and punk philosopher.*
Left: *The Damned featuring Dave Vanian (left) and Rat Scabies (right).*
Above: *John Sparks of Dr. Feelgood.*

The straws had been in the wind for some time. Performers like the New York Dolls, Iggy Pop, Lou Reed, Patti Smith and Bruce Springsteen in the States had been clearing the way for what was to come. They had been setting up outrageous and/or radical alternatives to mainstream rock for some years. All had achieved a degree of notoriety and carved a niche in the hearts of a small but growing minority.

The mid-Seventies in Britain had seen the rise to popularity of furious rocking bands like Dr Feelgood, the Kursaal Flyers and Eddie and the Hot Rods. All of these had ignored

The punks: the Sex Pistols (top left) forced themselves onto the public but Johnny Rotten (top right) was a true star. AC/DC (bottom left) and the Tubes weren't true punks but went over the top.

The Stranglers

A punk princess

The Sex Pistols

The Damned

Chelsea punks

Blondie

The Runaways

The Tubes

barely heard their music (most of their records were banned from the broadcasting media) and had difficulty buying the discs, as many of the largest retailers refused to handle them!

Everyone hated the Six Pistols and, it seems, they hated each other. But there was something about their music and about J. Rotten. Their music had genuine anger and fire and Rotten had genuine magnetism. As he spat out *God Save The Queen* or its follow-up *Pretty Vacant* there was so much refreshing energy and charge, so much tension and volcanic dynamism that you could not fail to be impressed, even excited, perhaps refreshed, by it.

This feeling assailed the viewer/listener when presented with the work of the Pistols' contemporaries—to watch the Buzzcocks, the Clash, the Damned, the Jam, the Stranglers was to re-experience the excitement and frisson of watching the Stones, the Who, the Pretty Things or Them in the Sixties. Likewise, to listen to the New Wave bands from America (and most specifically New York) like Blondie, Mink DeVille, the Ramones, Jonathan Richmond (who brought a marvellous and very welcome sense of humour back to rock) or Television was to feel again that rock DID have something new, alert, alive and thrilling to offer.

The punks, for all their manic depression and ugliness and rather self-conscious attempts to horrify and shock, did at least have life. They had something to say if only like the Ramones it was two minutes of frantic noise—sex packed into compressed sound. The tired blood of rock was getting a transfusion. The patient was responding. Rock would continue despite the deprivations of the past ten years. Hail, hail rock & roll!

Within a few weeks of each other in 1977, Elvis Presley and Bing Crosby died.

I never saw Elvis Presley. He never performed in Britain.

I was at the last concert Bing Crosby ever gave.

Both were saddening deaths. Although separated by over 30 years in age and from entirely different musical worlds, both were important to rock. Presley for all the reasons we've explored. Crosby because he was the first singing star to gain mass global popularity. Crosby laid down a carpet in the Thirties and Forties which Presley scuffed up again in the Fifties.

Their deaths brought an era to an end. Gone so close to each other were the one who began it and the one enduring rock figure whose very life bound together rock's history. Crosby had started it all. Presley had established rock and, a quarter of a century later, was still a towering, popular, respected, successful figure in popular music. With these two deaths the first volume of rock's story came to a close.

This has been a version of the story of rock music. Rock & roll was never invented to be written about. It was invented to listen to, to dance by, to love with. Go to the music. Listen to it, from *Heartbreak Hotel* to whatever's in the charts as you read. Listen to all that music and to Don McLean's *American Pie* because THAT is the *real* history of rock & roll.

217

Bibliography

The following is a list of books used for reference in the writing of this work. Each book is mentioned under the chapter where it was first consulted whether or not it was referred to in connection with material in other chapters. Many newspapers and magazines have also been consulted and those from which I've quoted are mentioned in the text. Of course, I have constantly referred to the *New Musical Express* (whose charts I have used throughout), *Melody Maker* and *Rolling Stone*.

Chapter One

After The Ball Ian Whitcomb; Allen Lane 1973 · *All You Need Is Love* Tony Palmer; Weidenfeld and Nicholson 1977 · *A WopBopaLoo-BopALopBamBoom* Nik Cohn; Paladin 1970 · *The Book Of Golden Discs* Comp by Joseph Murrells; Barrie and Jenkins 1974 · *Buddy Holly* Dave Laing; Studio Vista 1971 · *Buddy Holly: His Life And Music* John J Goldrosen; Charisma 1975 · *Celluloid Rock* Philip Jenkinson and Alan Warner; Lorrimer 1974 · *Concert Guide* Dr Gerhart von Westerman; Sphere 1968 · *Elvis* Jerry Hopkins; Abacus 1974 · *Elvis* Dick Tatham; Chartwell 1976 · *Encyclopedia of Pop, Rock And Soul* Irwin Stambler; St Martin's Press 1974 · *Encyclopedia Of Rock: Vol 1: The Age Of Rock And Roll* Ed by Phil Hardy and Dave Laing; Panther 1976 · *The Illustrated New Musical Express Encyclopedia Of Rock* Comp by Nick Logan and Bob Woffinden; Hamlyn 1976 · *Lillian Roxon's Rock Encyclopedia* Lillian Roxon; Grosset and Dunlap 1971 · *NME Book Of Rock 2* Ed by Nick Logan and Bob Woffinden; Star Book 1977 · *Paul McCartney In His Own Words* Paul Gambaccini; Omnibus Press 1976 · *The Poetry of Rock* Richard Goldstein; Bantam 1969 · *Rock File Vol 1* Ed by Charlie Gillett; NEL 1972 · *Rock File Vol 4* Ed by Charlie Gillett and Simon Frith; Panther 1976 · *Rock 'n' Roll* Chris May; Socion · *The Sound Of The City* Charlie Gillett; Sphere 1971 · *The Story Of Pop* Ed by Jeremy Pascall; Phoebus 1976 · *The Story Of Rock* Carl Belz; Harper Colophon 1969 · *Those Oldies But Goodies: A Guide To 50s Record Collecting* Steve Propes; Collier Macmillan 1973 · *20 Years Of British Record Charts 1955-75* Ed by Tony Jasper; Queen Anne Press 1975

Chapter Two

The Coasters Bill Millar; Star Book 1975 · *The Drifters* Bill Millar; Studio Vista 1971 · *Encyclopedia Of Rock: Vol 2: From Liverpool to San Francisco* Ed by Phil Hardy and Dave Laing; Panther 1976 · *Making Tracks: The History Of Atlantic Records* Charlie Gillett; Panther 1975 · *Owning Up* George Melly; Weidenfeld and Nicholson 1972 · *Rock File Vol 3* Ed by Charlie Gillett and Simon Frith; Panther 1975 · *The Sound Of Philadelphia* Tony Cummings; Methuen 1975

Chapter Three

All Together Now Harry Castleman and Walter J Podrazik · *The Beatles Get Back* Jonathan Cott and David Dalton; Apple 1969 · *The Beatles – The Authorised Biography* Hunter Davies; Mayflower 1969 · *A Cellarful Of Noise* Brian Epstein; Four Square 1965 · *Encyclopedia Of Rock: Vol 3: The Sounds Of The Seventies* Ed by Phil Hardy and Dave Laing; Panther 1976 · *The Longest Cocktail Party* Richard Di Lello; Charisma 1973 · *"Love Me Do" The Beatles' Progress* Michael Braun; Penguin 1964 · *Motown* David Morse; Studio Vista 1971 · *The Rolling Stones* Ed by David Dalton; Star Book 1975 · *The Rolling Stones* Jeremy Pascall; Hamlyn 1977 · *Rolling Stones File* Ed by Tim Hewat; Panther Record 1967 · *The Sixties* Ed by Anthony D'Abreau; Sociopack 1973 · *The Soul Book* Ed by Ian Hoare; Methuen 1975 · *The True Story Of The Beatles* Billy Shepherd; Beat Books 1964

Chapter Four

Album Cover Album Ed by Hipgnosis and Roger Dean; Dragon's World 1977 · *As Time Goes By* Derek Taylor; Abacus 1974 · *Bamn – Outlaw Manifestos And Ephemera 1965-70* Ed by Peter Stanstill and David Zane Mairowitz; Penguin 1971 · *The Beach Boys* John Tobler; Hamlyn 1978 · *The Beatles* Comp by Jeremy Pascall and Rob Burt; Octopus 1975 · *Bob Dylan* Anthony Scaduto; Abacus 1972 · *Cassandra At His Finest And Funniest* Comp by Paul Boyle; a Daily Mirror Book published by Paul Hamlyn 1967 · *Civilisation* Kenneth Clark; BBC and John Murray 1969 · *Drugs: Medical, Psychological And Social Facts* Peter Laurie; Pelican 1969 · *Encyclopedia Of Folk, Country, And Western Music* Irwin Stambler and Grelun Landon; St Martin's Press 1969 · *The Grateful Dead* Hank Harrison; Star Book 1973 · *The Pendulum Years: Britain And The Sixties* Bernard Levin; Pan 1972 · *The Rolling Stone Rock 'n' Roll Reader* Ed by Ben Fong-Torres; Bantam 1974 · *Writings And Drawings* Bob Dylan; Panther 1974

Chapter Five

Elton John Dick Tatham and Tony Jasper; Octopus 1976 · *The Osmonds – The Official Story Of The Osmond Family* Paul H Dunn; W H Allen 1975 · *Paul McCartney And Wings* Jeremy Pascall; Chartwell, Hamlyn 1977 · *Punk Rock* John Tobler; Phoebus 1977 · *The Stars And Superstars Of Black Music* Comp by Jeremy Pascall and Rob Burt; Phoebus 1977

Acknowledgments

The publishers would like to thank the following record companies for providing photographs and/or record sleeves for use in the book: A & M, Arista, Atlantic, Avco, Buddah, Capitol, Casablanca, CBS, Charisma, Chrysalis, Decca, DJM, Elektra/Asylum, EMI, Ensign, Island, Jet, Magnet, MCA, Mercury, Polydor, Purple Records, RCA, Riva, RSO, Sire, State, Tamla Motown, Vertigo and Warner Bros.

The record sleeves were photographed for the Hamlyn Group by Michael Plomer.

Thanks are also due to the following who supplied material from their collections: Dennis Barker, Mary Evans, Anne Finlay, Derek Hall, Leigh Jones, Marian McVey, Ian Muggeridge, Janice Pennell and Sound 2000, Feltham, Middlesex, England.

Black and white photographs

Camera Press, London 41, 56B, 132R, 139T, 150TL, 178BR; Keystone Press Agency, London 13T, 67T, 78, 119; London Features International 26, 28B, 37, 45TL, 49, 51, 52T, 55BC, 57, 60, 61T+B, 77, 79T,C+B, 81, 82B, 86T, 87, 90T, 94T, CL,CR+B, 95TL, 98T+C, 99B, 105T+B, 108-109, 109, 112, 115BL, 118, 122B, 124B, 128T+B, 131T, 136TR, 138, 139B, 142TR, 143CL, CR+B, 145BL, 152R, 153, 160TR, 166BL, 167B, 168TR, 169TL, 170T+B, 171T, 178T, 180TL,BL+BR, 182B, 183TR+CR, 188TL, 189TC, 190BL, 194TL, 197, 200BR, 201B, 206T, 206-207B, 207BR, 209TR, 212BL, 213TL+TR, 213BR, 217; Kenneth Pitt, London 171B; Popperfoto, London 113T, 115T, 122T; David Redfern Photography, London 212CR; Ron Reid 150B, 151; Rex Features, London 42, 62-63, 67B, 76, 95BL, 140CR, 150TR; Syndication International, London 13B, 17, 18T+B, 19, 22, 36, 43T, 45B, 46, 56TL, TR+C, 84B, 98BL+BR, 110, 114L, 129T, 136BL, 140T, 149B, 150TC, 191T.

Colour photographs

Camera Press, London 178 inset; London Features International* 4-5, 6-7, 8-9, 10-11, 14, 24B, 25R, 34-35, 43B, 45TR, 47T+B, 54T, 66, 74, 75T+B, 80B, 86B, 88BL, 88-89B, 89TL, TR+BR, 91T+B, 92B, 95TR, 97TL+C, 99T, 100-101, 114R, 115BR, 123T+B, 124T, 126, 129, 130, 133, 136TL+TC, 136CR+BR, 137TL, TR+B, 141T, 142TL, 143TR, 146T, 146-47T+B, 148B, 149TL, 151 inset, 157BR, 161R, 162T+BL, 163T, 166T+BR, 167TL+TR, 168CR, 169TR, 172T, BL+BR, 178BL, 179BR, 181TR+B, 182-83, 186TL, 186-87B, 190BR, 193TL, 195TL+BR, 198, 200BL, 201T, 202T, CR, BL+BR, 203, 205TL, 207TR, 214TL, CR+BL, 215TR+B, back endpapers; David Redfern, London 92T; Rex Features, London 16L+R, 20TL, TR, CL, BL+BR, 21, 38TL, TR+BL, 39, 53T, 55TL, 58-59, 68T, insets L+R+B, 69T+B, 70, 82T, 83B, 84T, 88TL+TR 90B, 96, 97TR, 102, 116, 125, 132L, 134T, 140BL, 144, 146BL, 149TR, 156, 158TL, TC+TR, 158-59, 160TL, 169B, 188TR, 192T, 194TR, 195TR, 196B, 214TR+BR, 215TL.

*LFI photographs are by Waring Abbott, Adrian Boot, Henry Diltz, Brad Elterman, Sam Emerson, Jill Furmanowsky, Neil Jones, Barry Levine, Janet Macoska, Neal Preston, Michael Putland, David Redfern, Peter Sanders, Claude VanHeye, Chris Walter, Barry Wentzell.

B: Bottom   BL: Bottom Left   BR: Bottom Right   C: Centre
CL: Centre Left   CR: Centre Right   L: Left   R: Right   T: Top
TC: Top Centre   TL: Top Left   TR: Top Right.

Index

Page numbers in *italics* refer to illustrations.

Abba 197, *197*, 198, *198*
Abbey Road 117
ABC 170
AC/DC 213
Adventures Of Ozzie And Harriet, The 54
After The Ball 14
Ain't No Sunshine 170
Ain't That A Shame 24
Alabama Song 115
Aladdin Sane 175
Alamo, The 44
Albatross 140
Aldon Music 51
Alexander, Arthur 63
All Day And All Of The Night 99
All I Have To Do Is Dream 80
All You Need Is Love 123
Allison, Jerry 30
Allman Brothers 186
Allsup, Tommy 30
Almost Grown 25
Along Came Jones 49
Altamont 152
Althia and Donna 200
Amen Corner 143, 147
America 160
American Bandstand 38, 39, 54, 55
American Graffiti 167
American Pie 30
Among My Souvenirs 46
Anarchy In The UK 212
And When I Die 142
Anderson, Ian 140, *140*
Andy Williams Show 168
Animals 96, 97, *97*, 122, 123, 135
Anka, Paul 54, *55*
Anna 63
Another Side Of Bob Dylan 134
Apache 61
Apollo 50
Apple 116, 130, 131, 156
April Love 24
Archie Bell and the Drells 193
Archies 145
Arnold Layne 141
Association *122*, 123, 166
At The Club 51
At The Zoo 160
Atlantic 50, 87
Avalon, Frankie *38*, 39, 46, 166
Average White Band *201*
Axton, Estelle 87

Baby I Love You 52
Baby It's You 63
Baby Love 84
Bacharach, Burt 104
Bad Company 205
Bad To Me 66
Baez, Joan 148, *149*
Baker, Ginger 94, 128, 129
Baldry, Long John 94, *94*, 175, 176
Balin, Marty 152
Ball, Kenny 44, 46
Ballad Of Hollis Brown 134
Ballard, Hank 56
Ballroom Blitz 162
Band *134-35*, 138, *138*
Bang A Gong 161
Barber, Chris 43, 44
Barclay James Harvest 142, *143*
Barry, Jeff 52, 144, 145
Bart, Lionel 41
Batt, Mike 171
Bay City Rollers 166, 170, *170*
Beach Boys 26, 81, 82, 102, 103, *103*, 104, *105*, *108*
Beatles *58-59*, 60, *60*, 61, *61*, 62, 63, 64, 65, 66, 67, *67*, *68-69*, 70, 71, 74, 75, 76, 77, 78, *78*, 81, 82, 84, 93, 103, 104, *109*, 111, 114, 116, 117, *118*, 122, 130, 132, 133, 134, 138, 144, 156, 157, *158-59*
Beatles For Sale 63
Beatles' Hits, The 66
Beatles No. 1 66
Be-Bop-A-Lula 40
Beck, Jeff 95, 125, 177

Bee Gees 143, *186*
Being For The Benefit Of Mr Kite 117
Bell, Thom 193
Belmonts 34
Ben 170
Bennie And The Jets 176
Benton, Brook *50*
Berns, Bert 51
Bernstein, Sid 77
Berry, Chuck *10-11*, 14, 23, 25, 26, *26*, 27, 29, 30, 63, 75
Berry, Richard 48
Betcha By Golly Wow 193
Big Bopper 30
Big Brother and the Holding Company 115, 123, 156
Bilk, Acker 44, 46, 63
Billboard 30, 48, 77
Bird Dog 80
Black, Bill 19
Black, Cilla 66, *70*
Black Sabbath *205*
Blackboard Jungle 15
Blackwell, Chris 199
Blake, Peter 116
Blind Faith 129, *129*
Blockbuster 162
Blonde On Blonde 135
Blondie *215*, 217
Blood, Sweat and Tears 142, *142*, 148
Blood, Sweat And Tears 142
Bloomfield, Mike 135
Blowing In The Wind 133
Blue Flames 94
Blue Magic 193
Blue Moon Of Kentucky 19
Blue Suede Shoes 18, 28
Blueberry Hill 24
Bluejean Bop 40
Blues Incorporated 94, 95, 96
Bluesology 175
Bob Dylan 135
Bobby's Girl 65
Bolan, Marc 161, *161*, 163, 169, 171, 174
Bolder, Trevor 175
Bond, Graham 94, *94*
Bonham, John 201
Bonzo Dog Band 134
Bookends 160
Booker T and the MGs 87, *91*
Boomtown Rats *216*
Boone, Pat 23, *23*, 24, 25
Border Song 176
Bowie, David *171*, *172-73*, 173, *174*, *174*, 175
Boxer, The 160
Boyce, Tommy 144
Boys 63
Brando, Marlon 15
Bread *183*
Brecht, Bertold 115
Bridge Over Troubled Water 156, 157, 160
Brill Building 51, 52, 54, 144
Bringing It All Back Home 134
Bristol Stomp 55
Brooks, Elkie *194*
Broonzy, Big Bill 19
Brotherhood Of Man 145, *145*
Brown, Jackson *160*
Brown, James 87, 90, 91, *92*
Brown, Joe 65
Bruce, Jack 94, 128, *128*
Brunswick 30
Buddah 145
Buffalo Springfield 122, 123, 130
Burdon, Eric 96, 97
Burke, Solomon 87, *90*
Butterfield, Paul 148
Buzzcocks 209, 217
Bye Bye Love 80
Byrds 123, 130, *134*, 135, 138, 157, 186
Byrnes, Ed *38*

Calendar Girl 54
California Girls 81, 104
Candle In The Wind 176
Canned Heat 123, *123*, 148
Can't Buy Me Love 78

Capehart, Jerry 29
Capitol 77, 78
Captain Beefheart *111*
Captain Fantastic And The Brown Dirt Cowboy 176
Caribou 176
Carnal Knowledge 160
Carol 26
Carpenters 183, *183*
Carr, Roy 52
Carton, Johnny 22, 29, *29*
Cash, Johnny 22, 29, *29*
Cassandra *111*
Cassidy, David 166, *166*
Catch A Fire 199
Catch My Soul 40
Catch-22 160
Cathy's Clown 80
Cecilia 160
Cellarful Of Noise, A 77
Chains 63
Chancellor Records 39
Chandler, Chas 97
Channel, Bruce 65
Chantilly Lace 30
Chapman, Roger *129*
Charlatans 113
Charles, Ray *92*, 93
Charlie Brown 49
Checker, Chubby 56, 57, *57*, 78
Chelsea 208
Cher *195*
Cherish 166
Chess, Leonard 27
Chess Records 27
Chewy Chewy 145
Chicago 183, *190*
Chicken Shack 140
Children Of The Revolution 161
Chirpy Chirpy Cheep Cheep 145
Chords 27
Circus Boy 144
Clapton, Eric 95, 96, 99, 117, 125, 128, 129, 130, 199
Clark, Dick 38, 39, 54
Clark, Petula 57
Clash 217
Cleave, Maureen 77
Cliff, Jimmy 199
C'mon Everybody 29
Coasters 48, *48*, 49, 52
Cochran, Eddie 29, *29*, 30, 40
Cocker, Joe 148, *148*
Cockney Rebel *208*
Co-Co 162
Cole, Nat King 12, 23
Cole, Natalie *195*
Collins, Judy 131, *133*
Colyer, Ken 43
Come And See About Me 84
Come On 74, 75
Come On Over To My Place 51
Comets *13*, 14, 15, 16
Como, Perry 39
Conley, Arthur 87
Cook, Little Joe 56
Cookies 63
Cooper, Alice *180*, 181, *181*
Coral 30
Corrina, Corrina 133
Could It Be Forever? 166
Coz I Luv You 162
Crazy Horses 168
Crazy Man Crazy 15, 28
Cream 96, *126-27*, 128, *128*, 129
Creedence Clearwater Revival 148, *148*
Crickets 30, *31*, 34
Crocodile Rock 176
Cropper, Steve 87
Crosby, Bing 217
Crosby, David 129, 153
Crosby, Stills and Nash 130
Crosby, Stills, Nash and Young *130*, 148
Crowns 50
Crows 27
Crudup, Arthur 'Big Boy' 19
Crumb, Robert 114
Crystals 52
Cum On Feel The Noize 162
Cumberland Gap 44
Cummings, Tony 39, 56
Curtis, Sonny 30

Da Doo Ron Ron 52
Daily Mirror 71, 111
Daily News 78
Daily Telegraph 71
Dakotas 98
Daltrey, Roger 98
Damned 209, *212*, 214, 217
Dancing Queen 198
Daniel 176
Darin, Bobby 14, 51, 52, *52*
Dave Clark Five 79, *79*, 96
Dave Dee, Dozy, Beaky, Mick and Tich 143, *143*
Davies, Hunter 65
Davies, Ray 98, 99, *99*
Dawn 145, *145*
Day, Doris 12
Day In The Life, A 114, 117
Days Of Future Passed 141
Dead End Street 99
Dean, James 15
DeAngelis, Peter 39
Decca 23, 29
Dedicated Follower Of Fashion 99
Dee, Kiki *195*
Dee, Tommy 29
Deep Down Inside 87
Deep Purple 142, *142*, 204
Deja Vu 148
Dekker, Desmond 199
Delfonics 193
Denny, Martin 63
Denver, John 186
Derounian, Steven 38
Desolation Row 135
Devil In Her Heart 63
Diamond Dogs 175
Diamond, Neil 144, *145*
Diana 54
Dictators *216*
Dimension 51
Dion 54, *55*
Do You Love Me? 83
Do You Wanna Touch Me? 163
Do You Want To Know A Secret? 163
Dock Of The Bay 90, 143
Does Your Chewing Gum Lose Its Flavour On The Bedpost Overnight? 44
Dolenz, Mickey 144, 145
Domino, Fats 23, 24, *24*, 27, 53, 56
Donays 63
Donegan, Lonnie 43, 44, *45*
Donna 30
Donovan 131, *131*
Don't Knock The Rock 16
Don't Knock The Twist 57
Don't Think Twice 133
Doors 115, *115*, 116
Doors Of Perception, The 110
Doors, The 115
Dovells 55
Down By The Lazy River 168
Dozier, Lamont 83
Dr Feelgood 212, *212*
Dr Robert 108
Dreja, Chris 95
Drifters 49, *49*, 50, 51, *51*, 52
Driscoll, Julie *139*
Dunbar, Aynsley 96
Dunn, Donald 'Duck' 87
Dury, Ian 149
Dylan, Bob *100-101*, 117, 132, *132*, 133, 134, 135, 138, *138*, 139, 186

Eager, Vince 42
Eagles 183, *186-87*, *187*
Early In The Morning 30
Earth Angel 27
Ebony Eyes 80
Eddie and the Hot Rods *209*, 212
Edison Lighthouse 145
Ekland, Britt 180
El Condor Pasa 160
Eleanor Rigby 108
Electric Light Orchestra *201*
Elliott, Jack 131
Elton John 176
Elvis 40
Emerson, Keith 142

Emerson, Lake and Palmer 141, 142, 204
Empty Sky 175, 176
EMI 212
Encyclopaedia Of Pop, Rock And Soul 29
End, The 116
Entwistle, John 98
Epic 170
Epstein, Brian 62, 66, *70*, 77, 78, 128, 130
Essex 15
Essex, David 166, 167, *167*, 174
Everlasting Love 145
Everly Brothers 80, *80*, 157
Every Picture Tells A Story 177
Everybody's Trying To Be My Baby 63
Everyday 30
Everyday People 143
Exodus 200

Fabian 14, 39, *39*, 166
Faces 176, 177, *180*
Faith, Adam 42, 43, *43*, *191*
Fame, Georgie 42, 95
Family 129
Family Dog 112, 113
Fat Man, The 24
Fillmore Auditorium 113
Finger-tips 84
Five Dimensions 176
Flack, Roberta 87
Fleet, Hughie 96
Fleetwood Mac 96, 125, 140, *140*, *182-83*, 183
Fleetwood, Mick 96
Flowerpot Men 116
Floyd, Eddie 87
Flying 180
Fool, The 130
For No-One 108
For What It's Worth 130
For Your Love 95
Ford, Barry 198
Fortunes 96
Four Tops 27, *82*, 84, 169
Fourmost 66
Frampton Comes Alive 182
Frampton, Peter 176, 182, *182*
Frampton's Camel 182
Francis, Connie 46, 47, 47, 51
Franklin, Aretha 87, 90, 92, *92*, 93
Fraser, Robert 118
Fratto, Russ 27
Freddie and the Dreamers 96
Freed, Alan 12, 13, 14, 15, 16, 27, 39
Freewheelin' Bob Dylan 133
Freight Train 44
From Me To You 66, 77
Fun, Fun, Fun 81
Funny, Funny 162
Fury, Billy 42, 44

Gamble, Kenny 192
Garcia, Jerry 152, *152*
Garfunkel, Art 123, 156, 160, *160*, 183
Gaye, Marvin 84, *85*, 143
Gee 27
Genesis *204*
Georgie 180
Gerry and the Pacemakers 66, *66*, 79
Gillett, Charlie 13, 23, 24, 27, 47, 48, 50
Gilmore, Voyle 78
Girl Of The North Country 133
Give Peace A Chance 139
Gleason, Ralph 27, 113
Glitter, Gary 163, *163*
Gnome, The 142
Go Away Little Girl 65, 168
Go Now! 141
God Only Knows 104
Godspell 167
Goffin, Gerry 51, 52, 144
Goldstein, Richard 104
Goldwyn, Sam 22
Gonna Make You A Star 167
Good, Jack 40
Good Vibrations 82, 105, 108, 112
Goodbye Yellow Brick Road 176

Gordy Junior, Berry 82, 83, 169
Got To Be There 170
Got To Get You Into My Life 109
Gouldon, Graham 95
Graduate, The 95
Graham, Bill 113
Grand Coulee Dam 132
Grand Ole Opry 19
Grateful Dead 113, 148, 152
Gravy (For My Mashed Potatoes) 55
Great Balls Of Fire 28
Great Pretender, The 27
Grech, Rick 129
Greco, Juliette 44
Green Leaves Of Summer, The 44
Green Onions 90
Green, Peter 96, 125
Greenwich, Ellie 52
Groovy Kind Of Love 144
Guardian 198
Gudbuy T' Jane 162
Guthrie, Arlo 131, 148
Guthrie, Woody 131, 132, 133, 134

Hair 167
Haley, Bill *13*, 14, *14*, 15, 16, 17, 22, 23, 27, 60
Happy Birthday Sweet 16 54
Hard Day's Night, A 64, 130, 144
Hard Rain's A-Gonna Fall, A 133
Harder They Come, The 199
Harold Melvin and the Blue Notes 193
Harris, Emmylou 186, *188*
Harris, Rolf 65
Harrison, George 63, 108, 111, 117, *157*, *158-59*
Hartley, Keef 96, 148
Havens, Richie 148
Hawks 138
Haworth, Jann 116
Hayes, Isaac 90
Hazy Shades Of Winter 160
Heartbeat 30
Heartbreak Hotel 23
Heartbreakers 209
Heatwave 84
Heckstall-Smith, Dick 94, *94*
Hell Raiser 162
Hell, Richard 216
Hello Little Girl 66
Hello Mary Lou 54
Help! 130, 144
Hendrix, Jimi 97, 123, 125, *125*, 130, 131, 148, 156, *157*, 161
Herd 182
Here Comes That Feeling 47
Here Today 104
Herman's Hermits 77, 79, *79*, 95, 96
He's A Rebel 52
Hey Baby 65
Hey! Schoolgirl 157
High Society 44
Highway 61 Revisited 135
Hit The Road Jack 93
Hoare, Ian 85, 87
Hoffman, Dustin 160
Hofman, Albert 109
Holder, Noddy 162
Holiday, Billie 191
Holland, Eddie 83
Hollies 79, *79*, 95, 96, 130
Holly, Buddy 29, 30, *31*, 76, 80
Hollywood Palace 78
Homeward Bound 160
Honey Don't 63
Honeycombs 96
Honky Cat 176
Honky Chateau 176
Hot Chocolate 200
Hot Love 161
Hotel California 183
Hound Dog 48
House Of The Rising Sun, The 96, 135
How Can I Be Sure? 166
How Do You Do It? 66
Howlin' Wolf 22
Huff, Leon 192
Humble Pie 176, 182
Humperdinck, Engelbert 143
Hunky Dory 174
Hunter, Meredith 152, 153
Huxley, Aldous 110
Hyde Park 149

I Am A Rock 160
I Can't Explain 98
I Can't Stop Loving You 93
I Didn't Know I Loved You 163
I Get Around 81, 82
I Got You 92
I Heard It Through The Grapevine 143
I Love You Love Me Love 163
I Only Have Eyes For You 160
I Saw Her Standing There 67
I Shall Be Free 133
I Shot The Sheriff 199
I Think I Love You 166
I Wanna Be Where You Are 170
I Wanna Be Your Man 65, 66, 71, 75
I Want To Hold Your Hand 65, 66, 77, 78, 102
I Want You 135
I Want You Back 169
I'd Rather Go Blind 140
Idol With The Golden Head 48
Ifield, Frank 65
I'll Be There 170
I'll Get By 46
I'll Keep You Satisfied 66
I'm A Believer 144
I'm A Man 39
I'm A Moody Guy 163
I'm Eighteen 181
I'm In Love 66
I'm Leavin' It Up To You 168
I'm Stone In Love With You 193
I'm Walkin' 24, 53
In My Life 103
In Search of The Lost Chord 141
In The Court Of The Crimson King 141
Incredible String Band 130, 148
Ink Spots 19, 27
Innervisions 192
International Times 139
Isley Brothers 63, *64*
It Might As Well Rain Until September 51
It Only Took A Minute 65
It's All Over Now 77
It's All Right 133
It's Late 54

Jackson, Al 87
Jackson, Lee 94
Jacksons 87, 166, 168, 169, *169*, 170
Jagger, Mick 71, 75, 76, 77, 94, 118, 119, *119*, 122, *122*, 149, *149*, 152, *153*, *206-207*
Jailhouse Rock 37, 48
Jam 217
Jambalaya 46
James, Dick 175
Jardine, Al 81
Jealous Mind 163
Jeepster 161
Jeff Beck Group 176, 201
Jefferson Airplane 113, 114, 123
Jefferson Airplane Takes Off 114
Jennings, Waylon 30, 191
Jesus Christ, Superstar 167
Jethro Tull 140, *140*, 141
Jewell, Derek 198
Jimi Hendrix Experience *124*
John, Elton 175, 176, *178-79*, 205
John Wesley Harding 138
Johnny Duncan and the Bluegrass Boys 44
Jones, Brian 75, *75*, 94, 122, 148, 149
Jones, David 144, 145
Jones, John Paul 94, 201
Jones, Shirley 166
Jones, Steve 209
Jones, Tom 143, *143*
Joplin, Janis 46, 148, 156, *156*
Just Like A Woman 135

Kasenatz, Jerry 145
Katz, Jeff 145
Keep The Customer Satisfied 160
Keisker, Marion 19
Keller, Jack 51
Kerouac, Jack 44
Kesey, Ken 110, 114
King And I, The 44

King, B. B. 22
King, Ben E. 49, 50, 52, 85, *201*
King, Carole 51, 52, 54, *55*, 144, 157
King Creole 37, 48
King Crimson 141
Kinks 98, 99, *99*
Kirshner, Don 51, 52, 144, 145, 169
Kiss 209
Klein, Allen 156
Knight, Gladys 83, *191*
Knowing Me, Knowing You 198
Kodachrome 160
Kooper, Al 135
Korner, Alexis 94, *94*, 96
Kramer Billy J. 66, *67*, 77
Kristofferson, Kris 191, 192, *192*
Kursaal Flyers 212

Lady Samantha 176
Lady Sings The Blues 191
Laine, Denny 141
Laine, Frankie 12, 38, 39
Laing, R. D. 110, 111
Lamplight 167
Landau, John 197
Last Time, The 77
Last Train To Clarksville 144
Last Train To San Fernando 44
Laurie, Peter 111
Leary, Timothy 110, 111, 131
Led Zeppelin 96, *154-55*, *200*, 201, 204, 205
Lee, Brenda 46, 47, *47*
Leiber, Jerry 48, 49, 50, 51, 52, 63
Lennon, John 44, 51, 63, 64, 65, 66, 71, 74, 102, 104, 108, 111, 117, 156, *157*, 175
Let Me In 167
Let's Do The Twist 56
Let's Go To San Francisco 116
Let's Jump The Broomstick 47
Let's Put It All Together 193
Let's Spend The Night Together 118
Let's Twist Again 56
Levin, Bernard 133, 134
Lewis, Jerry Lee 22, 23, 28, *28*, 29, 30, 61
Light My Fire 115
Like A Rolling Stone 135
Lillie Lou 39
Lipstick On Your Collar 46
Listen To Me 30
Little Bit Me, A 144
Little Deuce Coupe 81
Little Eva 51, *52*
Little Help From My Friends 9, 10
Little Queenie 26
Little Red Rooster 77
Little Richard 16, 23, 24, 25, *25*, 28, 30, 132
Little Willy 162
Living In The Past 141
Lllloco-Motion 51
Locke, Albert 71
Loco-Motion, The 51
Lonely Boy 54
Lonely Teenager 54
Lonesome Death Of Hattie Carroll, The 134
Long Haired Lover From Liverpool 167
Long Tall Sally 16, 24, 99
Look Back In Anger 44
Look Wot You Dun 162
Louisiana Hayride 19
Love Affair 143, *143*, 145
Love Is Strange 80
Love Letters In The Sand 24
Love Me 48
Love Me Do 64, 65, 66
Love Me For A Reason 167
Love Me Tender 37
Love, Mike 81
Love Of The Loved 67
Love You Save, The 170
Love You To 108
Lovely Rita 117
Loves Me Like A Rock 160
Lovin' Spoonful 112
Loving You 37
Low 175
Lucy In The Sky With Diamonds 117
Lynch, Kenny 65, 67, 70

Lynott, Phil 208
Lynyrd Skynyrd 186

McCartney, Linda 14
McCartney, Paul 51, 63, 66, 71, 102, 104, 108, 114, 130, 141, 156, *157*, *158-59*, 175, 176, 200
McDevitt, Chas 44
McDonald, Country Joe 148
McGuinn, Roger 123
McGuinness, Tom 96
McKenzie, Scott 112, *112*, 116
McKnight, Jimmy 15
McLean, Don 30
McPhatter, Clyde 49
McVie, John 96
Madman Across The Water 176
Maggie May 177
Maggie's Farm 134
Magical Mystery Tour 130
Mahogany 191
Making Tracks 50
Mama Mia 198
Mama Weer All Crazee Now 162
Mamas and the Papas 123, *123*
Mambo Rock 16
Man Of The World 140
Man Who Fell To Earth, The 175
Man Who Sold The World, The 174, 175
Manfred Mann 94, 95, 96
Mann, Barry 61
March Of The Siamese Children 44
Marley, Bob 198, 199, *199*, 200, *200*
Marmalade 143
Marriott, Steve 176, 182
Martin, Dean 39, 78
Martin, George 65, 66, *67*
Marvellettes 63, *82*, 83
Mashed Potato Time 55
Masters Of War 133
Matthews Southern Comfort 148
Maughan, Susan 65
Mayall, John 96, *96*, 140
Maybe Baby 30
Maybe Tomorrow 42
Maybelline 25, 27
Me And Bobby McGee 191
Me And Julio Down By The Schoolyard 160
Melanie, 148, *189*
Mellow Yellow 116
Melly, George 43, 44
Melody Maker 104, 125
Melvin, Harold 196
Merger 198
Merry Twistmas 57
Metal Guru 161
Mick Mulligan Band 45
Mickey's Monkey 84
Middle Of The Road 145
Midnight In Moscow 44, 46
Midnight Rambler 152
Millar, Bill 117
Misery 67
Mitchell, Guy 38, 41
Mitchell, Joni 129, *138*, 148, 183
Mogg, William Rees 119
Money 63
Money, Money, Money 198
Monkees 144, *144*, 145, 166
Monroe, Gerry 160
Monterey 112, 122
Moody Blues 141, *141*
Moon, Keith 98
Moondog Ball 14
Moondog's Rock And Roll Party 13
Moore, Johnny 49
Moore, Scotty 19
Morning Side Of The Mountain 169
Morrison, Jim 115, *115*, 116
Mother And Child Reunion 160
Motorpsycho Nightmare 134
Mound City Blue Blowers 43
Mountain 148
Move 51, *97*
Move It 42
Mr Tambourine Man 134, 135, 157

Mrs Robinson 160
Mrs Roosevelt 132
Muddy Waters 94
Murray, Mitch 66
Music Man, The 63
My Coo Coo Ca Choo 163
My Generation 98
My Happiness 19
My Old Man's A Dustman 44
My People Were Fair 161
My Prayer 27
Myers, James 15

Na Na Hey Hey 145
Nash, Graham 130, 131
Nashville Skyline 138
Nashville Teens 96
Natural Woman 92, 93
Nelson, Rick(y) 39, 40, 53, 54, *54*, 166
Nelson, Willie 191
Nesmith, Mike 144
Nevins, Al 52
New Musical Express 52, 143, 145, 161, 182
New York Dolls 212
New York Rocker 209
New York Times 134
Newsweek 77, 116
Newton-John, Olivia 183, *188*
Nice 142, *142*
Nicholls, Mike 160
Night Of Fear 51
Nilsson, Harry *186*
No 104
No One Can Make My Sunshine Smile 80
No Woman No Cry 199
Norwegian Wood 103, 104, 108
Not A Second Time 103
Not Fade Away 30, 76
Nutrocker 142

October, Gene 208
Odetta 131
Oh Boy 30, 76
Oh, Carol 54
Oh, Neil 54
Oh Well 140
Ohio Express 145
Ohio Players 87
O'Jays *193*
Old Castle, The 142
Oldfield, Mike 183, 186, *186-87*
Oldham, Andrew 74, 75
Oliver! 41
On Broadway 51
On The Threshold Of A Dream 141
One Bad Apple 167
Only A Pawn In Their Game 134
Only You 27
Orbison, Roy 22, 23, 70, 80, 81, *81*
Orlando, Tony *145*
Orlons 55
Osmonds 166, 167, *168*, 169, 170
Outsider, The 44
Owning Up 43, 44
Oxford Town 133

Page, Jimmy 95, 96, 125, 201
Palmer, Tony 123
Papa's Got A Brand New Bag 92
Paper Roses 167
Paramount Jazz Band 44
Parker, Colonel Tom 22, *22*, 23
Parker, Graham *216*
Parker, Junior 22
Parnes, Larry 42
Parton, Dolly 186, *187*
Partridge Family, The 166
Paul Butterfield Blues Band 135
Paul, Lynsey de *189*
Paxton, Tom 131
Peel, John 140
Peggy Sue 30
Pendulum Years, The 133
Penguins 27
Perkins, Carl 18, 22, 28, 29, *29*, 63
Pet Sounds 82, 104, 105, 108, 116
Petite Fleur 44
Petty, Norman 30
Phillips, Sam 18, 19, 22, 23
Physical Graffiti 201
Pickett, Wilson 87, *87*, 90
Pictures At An Exhibition 142
Pin Ups 175

Pink Floyd 131, 140, 141, 143, *146-47*
Piper At The Gates Of Dawn 141
Plant, Robert *110*, 201
Platters 83
Please Mr Postman 63, 83
Please Please Me 63, 66, 77
Poetry Of Rock, The 104
Poison Ivy 49
Politics Of Experience, The 110
Poor Little Fool 54
Pop, Iggy 175, *175*, 212
Poppa Joe 162
Positively 4th Street 135
Power, Duffy 42, 67
Presley, Elvis 17, *17*, 18, *18*, 19, *20-21*, 22, 23, 24, 26, 27, 28, 29, 30, *36*, 37, *37*, 39, 41, 44, 48, 60, 78, 80, 132, 217, *217*
Pretty Things 217
Pretty Vacant 217
Price, Alan 97
Price Of Love 80
Pride, Dickie 42
Prisoner Of Love 91
Procul Harum 112, *113*
Punk 208
Punky's Dilemma 160
Puppy Love 54, 167

Quarrymen 44
Quatro, Suzi *195*
Queen 186, *190*
Quickly, Tommy 67, *70*

Rafelson, Bob 144
Raining In My Heart 30
Rainy Day Woman 135
Ramones 209, 217
Rave On 30
Ray, Johnny 23, 38
Razzle Dazzle 16
RCA 23
Rebel Without A Cause 15
Red Dress 163
Redding, Otis 87, 90, *91*, 123, 143
Reddy, Helen 181
Remember You're A Womble 171
Respect 92
Revolver 108, 112
Richard, Cliff *41*, 42, 61, *61*
Richard, Keith 77, 78, 118, 119, 149
Richmond, Jonathan 217
Ride A White Swan 161
Righteous Brothers 52
Riot In Cell Block 11 48
Riot In Cell Block Number Nine 48
Rise And Fall Of Ziggy Stardust, The 175
River Deep, Mountain High 53
Robins 48, 50
Robinson, John 122
Robinson, Smokey 63, 82, 84
Rock & Roll 163
Rock & Roll Music 25, 63
Rock Around The Clock 15, 16
Rock File Vol 3 51
Rock Island Line 44
Rock Me Baby 166
Rock 'n' Roll Woman 130
Rock On 167
Rock With The Cave Men 41
Rocket Man 176
Rockin' Roll Baby 193
Rockin' Through The Rye 16
Rockin' Robin 170
Roeg, Nic 175
Roll On Columbia 132
Roll Over Beethoven 63
Rolling Stone 18, 23, 105, 113, 114, 182, 197, *206-207*
Rolling Stones 66, 71, 74, *74*, *75*, 76, 77, *77*, 78, 93, 94, 99, 117, 119, 135, *136-37*, 148, 149, *149*, 152, 153, 200, 217
Rondo A La Turque 142
Ronettes 52, *53*
Ronson, Mick 175
Ronstadt Linda, 183, 186, *188*
Ross, Diana 84, 169, *169*, 186, 191

Rotten, Johnny 75, 205, 208, 212, *213*, 217
Roxon, Lillian 15
Roxy Music *202-203*
Rubber Soul 103, 104
Rubettes *205*
Rubin, Jerry 112, *114*
Ruby Tuesday 118
Ruffin, David 83
Ruffin, Jimmy 83
Rufus and Carla 87
Rumour 216
Rumours 182, 183
Runaround Sue 54
Runaways *215*
Rydell, Bobby *38*, 39

Saddlemen 15
Sager, Carole Bayer 144
Samantha 44
Samwell-Smith, Paul 95
San Francisco 112, 116
Santana, Carlos 148, 152, *152*
Satie, Erik 142
Satisfaction 77
Saturday Night At The Movies 51
Saturday Night's All Right For Fighting 176
Saucerful Of Secrets, A 141
Save The Last Dance For Me 51
Savoy Brown 140
Say It Loud 92
Sayer, Leo 42, 183, *191*
Scaduto, Anthony 135
Schneider, Bert 144
School Days 14, 25
School's Out 181
Searchers 75, *76*, 77, 79
Searchin' 48
Sebastian, John 148, *183*
Sedaka, Neil 51, 54, *55*, 144
See Emily Play 141
See You Later Alligator 16
Seeger, Pete *131*
Self Portrait 138
Send Me The Pillow That You Dream On 163
Sergeant Pepper's Lonely Hearts Club Band 114, 116, 117, 130, 141
Sex Pistols 209, 212, *213*, *214*, 217
Sha Na Na 148
Shadows *42*, 61, *61*
Shaft 90
Shake, Rattle And Roll 15
Shankar, Ravi 148
Shapiro, Helen 67, 70
Sharp, Dee Dee 55
Sh-Boom 27
She Belongs To Me 134
She Loves You 65, 66, 71, 77, 78
She Said She Said 109
She's Leaving Home 117
Shelton, Robert 134
Shirelles 63, *63*
Sholes, Steve 23
Shop Around 82
Shotgun Express 176
Sigma Studios 175
Simon, Carly *189*
Simon, Paul 123, 156, 157, 160, *160*, 183, 200
Simon Says 145
Sinatra, Frank 12, 14, 39, 56
Singing The Blues 41
Sittin' In The Balcony 29
6.5 Special 40, 43
Skweeze Me Pleeze Me 162
Slade 97, 117, 162, *162*
Sledge, Percy 87, *90*
Slick, Grace 114, *114*
Sly and the Family Stone *142*, 143, 148
Small Faces 98, *98*, 176, 182, *182*
Smith, Patti 212, *212*
Smoke Gets In Your Eyes 27
Soft Machine 140
Solid Gold Easy Action 161
Some Kind Of Wonderful 51
Somebody To Love 114
Song Of The Earth 103
Song Remains The Same, The 201
Songs In The Key Of Life 192
S.O.S. 198
Soul Agents 176
Soul Book, The 85
Soul, David 170, 171, *171*
Soul Limbo 90

Sound Of Fury, The 42
Sound Of Philadelphia, The 39, 56
Sound Of The City, The 13, 23, 47
Sounds Of Silence, The 157, 160
Space Oddity 174
Spanish Harlem 52
Speak To Me Pretty 47
Spector, Phil 52, *53*, 104
Speedy Gonzales 24
Spencer Davis Group 125
Spinning Wheel 142
Springsteen, Bruce 212
Stambler, Irwin 29
Star is Born, A 191
Stardust 167
Stardust, Alvin 163, *163*, *166*
Starr, Ringo 63, *158-59*
Station To Station 175
Status Quo 204, *204*
Stax 63, 82
Steam 145
Steele, Tommy *40*, 41, 42, 44
Stevens, Cat 176, 199, 200, *200*
Stewart, Jim 87
Stewart, Rod 175, 176, 177, *177*, 180, *180*, 182, 201, 205
Stills, Stephen 130
Stoller, Mike 48, 49, 50, 51, 52, 63
Stood Up 54
Stranger On The Shore 44, 46
Stranglers *214*, 217
Streisand, Barbra 186, 191, *192*
Strong, Barrett 67, 82
Stupid Cupid 51
Stylistics 27, 192, *192*, 193
Subterranean Homesick Blues 134, 139
Sugar, Sugar 145
Summer, Donna *194*, *196*, 197, 198
Summertime Blues 29
Sun Records 18, 22, 23
Sunday Night At The London Palladium 70, 71, 117
Sunday Times 198
Sunny Afternoon 99
Supremes 84, *86*, 169, 186, *195*
Surfer Girl 81
Surfin' Safari 82
Surfin' USA 26, 81
Surrealistic Pillow 114
Sutcliffe, Stuart 62
Sweet 162, *162*
Sweet Dream 141
Sweet Little Sixteen 26, 81
Sweet Nothin's 46
Sweetheart Of The Rodeo 138, 186
Sweets For My Sweet 51
Sympathy For The Devil 152

Take Me Back 'Ome 162
Take Me To The Mardi Gras 160
Take These Chains From My Heart 92
Talking Book 192
Tamla Motown 63, 82, 83, 84, 85, 87, 169, 170, 192
Taste Of Honey, A 63
Taupin, Bernie 175
Taylor, James 183
Taylor, Mick 96, 149
Tea For The Tillerman 199
Teddy Bears 52
Teen Age Idol 54
Teenage Rampage 162
Teenager's Romance, A 53
Telegram Sam 161
Television 209, *216*
Tell Me Why 163
Temptations 83, 84, *86*, 169
10cc 95, *205*
Ten Years After 148, *148*
Texas Playboys 15
Thank Your Lucky Stars 74
That'll Be The Day 30
That'll Be The Day (Film) 167
That's All Right (Mama) 19, 23
That's Love 42
That's When Your Heartaches Begin 19
Them 217
Then He Kissed Me 52
There Goes My Baby 50
There Goes Rhymin' Simon 160

Thin Lizzie 204
Think It Over 30
This Boy 102
Thompkins Junior, Russell 193
Three Degrees 193
Three Stars 29, 30
Tie A Yellow Ribbon 145
Tiger 39
Till There Was You 63, 71
Time 77
Time Is On My Side 79
Time Is Tight 90
Times, The 102, 119, 122, 133
Times They Are A-Changin', The 134
Tip Of My Tongue 67
To Know Him Is To Love Him 52
To Our Children's Children's Children 141
Tommy 90
Tomorrow Never Knows 108, 109
Too Young 167
Toots and the Maytals 198
Top Of The Pops 144, 161
Tork, Peter 144
Townshend, Pete 98, 99, 125
Traffic 97, 125, 129
Travellin' Man 54
Troggs 96
Trois Gymnopédies 142
Tubes *215*
Tubular Bells 183
Tumbleweed Connection 176
Turn Me Loose 39
Turner, Ike 22
Turner, Joe 15
Turner, Tina 52
Tutti Frutti 16, 24, 92
Twelfth Of Never 167
Twiggy *189*
Twist And Shout 63, 66, 71
Twist Around The Clock 57
Twist, The 56
Twixt Twelve And Twenty 23
Two Lovers 84
2001—A Space Odyssey 174
T(yrannosaurus) Rex 140, 161

Ummagumma 141
Under The Boardwalk 51
·Unit 4 + 2 96
Up On The Roof 51, 65
Uptown 52
Uptown Top Ranking 200
Uriah Heep *209*

Valens, Richie 30
Van Vliet, Don 111
Vandellas 84
Vee, Bobby 30, 53, *54*, 79
Vincent, Gene *34-35*, 40, 61
Vipers 44
Virgin 212
Voidoids 216

Wah-Watusi 55
Wake Up Little Susie 80
Walk Right Back 80
Walker, Junior 83
Walking In The Rain 166
Wanderer, The 54
Warlocks 112, 114
Warwick, Dionne 93, *93*
Waterloo 198
Waters, Muddy 26, 27
Watts, Charlie 94
Way Over There 83
Wear My Ring 40
Wednesday Morning 3 A.M. 157
Wee Wee Hours 27
Weill, Cynthia 51
Weill, Kurt 115
Wells, Mary 83, *83*, 84
Wexler, Jerry 50, 87, 93
What'd I Say 93
Whelan, Bernadette 166
When I Grow Up To Be A Man 81
When I'm Sixty-Four 117
When My Little Girl Is Smiling 51
Where Did Our Love Go? 84
Whiskey, Nancy 44
Whitcomb, Ian 14
White Plains 145
White Rabbit 114
Whiter Shade Of Pale, A 112
Whitfield, Norman 85
Who 98, 99, 119, 123, 125, 148
Who's Sorry Now? 46
Whole Lotta Shakin' Goin' On 28

Why 167
Wig Wam Joe 162
Wild One, The 15
Wild Thing 125
Wild World 199
Wilde, Marty 42, *43*
Will You Still Love Me Tomorrow? 52
Williams, Danny 70
Williams, Hank 65
Williams, Richard 104
Wilson, Brian 81, 82, 98, 103, 104, 105, *105*, 116
Wilson, Carl 81
Wilson, Dennis 81
Wilson, Murray 104
Wings 141, *157*, 183, 200
WINS 14
Winter, Johnny 148
Winwood, Stevie 125, 129
With God On Our Side 134
With The Beatles 63, 66, 75
Within You Without You 117
WJW 13
Wombles 170
Wombling Merry Christmas 171
Wombling Song 171
Wonder, Stevie 84, 169, 192, *193*, 200
Wonderful World 199
Wood, Ron 176
Woodmansey, Woody 175
Woodstock 148
Words of Love 30, 63
World In Action 119
Wouldn't It Be Nice 81
Wyman, Bill 75
Wynette, Tammy 186, *187*
Wynter, Mark 65, *65*

Yakety Yak 48
Yardbirds 95, *95*, 96, 125, 201
Yasgur, Max 148
Ya-Ya Twist 57
Yellow Submarine 108
Yes 204, 205, *205*
Yesterday 71
You Are Everything 193
You Make Me Feel Brand New 193
You Really Got A Hold On Me 63
You Really Got Me 99
You You You 163
You Wear It Well 177, 180
Young Americans 175
Young Blood 48
Young, Neil 130
Young Rascals 166
Your Song 176
You've Made Me So Very Happy 142
Yummy Yummy Yummy 145

Zombies 96
Z Z Top 186

Reading Festival